How do bad girls get away with it? How did Madonna, subject of public outcry for her controversial performances and her book *Sex*, become a superstar of pop culture and a role model for teenage girls? Why now, as star of *Evita* and a new mother, is she becoming a mainstream hero?

Karlene Faith says that Madonna signifies the times we live in. We are, in a sense, all responsible for who Madonna is. As fans, moral critics, media journalists, or university scholars, we mediate what she means to our society. And Madonna, as a shrewd career woman, has known how to exploit our attentions with her multiple talents. Her representation of sexual practices and values has not taken place in a political or social vacuum. She has counted on our readiness to witness the smashing of cultural taboos. Feminist reactions to Madonna have been divided. In her early career Madonna was a teenage role model, applauded as a liberated sex crusader. Later, she raised eyebrows by portraying cynical sex with multiple partners across identity boundaries and by capitalizing on sadomasochistic imagery.

Madonna, Bawdy & Soul is a celebration and critical analysis of Madonna from a feminist perspective. It will, like Madonna, provoke controversy among fans, critics, and scholars. The book includes a comprehensive listing of songs, videos, tours, films, stage roles, and Internet sites.

KARLENE FAITH is a pop culture fan and associate professor of criminology at Simon Fraser University. Her previous books include *Unruly Women: The Politics of Confinement and Resistance*, which won the VanCity Book Prize in 1994.

KARLENE FAITH

Madonna, Bawdy & Soul

Appendix:
Selected Works of Madonna
by Frances Wasserlein

UNIVERSITY OF TORONTO PRESS
Toronto Buffalo London

© University of Toronto Press Incorporated 1997
Toronto Buffalo London
Printed in Canada

ISBN 0-8020-4208-2 (cloth)
ISBN 0-8020-8063-4 (paper)

Printed on acid-free paper

Canadian Cataloguing in Publication Data

Faith, Karlene
  Madonna, bawdy & soul

  Includes bibliographical references and index.
  ISBN 0-8020-4208-2 (bound)   ISBN 0-8020-8063-4 (pbk.)

  1. Madonna, 1958–   .   2. Sexuality in popular culture.
  3. Rock musicians – United States – Biography.
  4. Motion picture actors and actresses – United States –
  Biography.   I. Title.   II. Title: Madonna, bawdy and soul.

  ML420.M1387F34 1997   782.42166'092   C97-930985-9

University of Toronto Press acknowledges the financial assistance to
its publishing program of the Canada Council and the Ontario Arts
Council.

In memory of Vickie LaVaun

Any royalties from this publication will be shared with community groups in Vancouver, British Columbia, and New Orleans, Louisiana, who are giving care to women living with AIDS.

Contents

Preface

At Simon Fraser University, in the School of Criminology, I have twice offered a course titled 'Bad Girls in the Movies' (cross-listed with Women's Studies), which is, in part, how I got interested in Madonna the performer. As presented by the media, in her early career Madonna represented the quintessential example of a really bad girl who could get away with it. As this book attests, I have a lot to say about Madonna and the reasons she didn't get punished when she was at her naughtiest, at least not by the law – although some nations tentatively refused to let her enter, and then gave her a very hard time when she made it over their borders.

As I learned in my first decade-plus of sporadically paying attention to Madonna, many other people also have a lot to say about her. Since 1985, when she caught my attention, I've successfully invoked her name as an ice-breaker with students, and with strangers on buses, trains, and planes; at parties; or in line at the grocery store, where for over a decade her picture has been staring back at us from the tabloids on the rack by the check-out counter (though never accompanied by any gossip of consequence). Each of these countless conversations has sharpened my perspectives and validated the seriousness with which I take her work.

This book covers Madonna's career in the 1980s and into the 1990s, to the point of her supreme achievements in 1996 – motherhood and the movie *Evita*, in which she starred in the dream role she sought for seven years. The text ends with Madonna at this crossroads, enjoying her baby and the glory of winning the 1996

Golden Globe award for Best Actress in a Comedy or Musical. Certainly, from how things look today, she could have a brilliant career in film or stage musicals, for which her recording, video, and theatrical-concert work have trained her well. She may well become a director, as she has said she would like to do. Whatever she chooses, by the time this book is in print she will have done something new, something headline-grabbing. For now, in early 1997, at age thirty-eight, Madonna has made a smooth transition, charmingly (and still irreverently) entering maturity as an individual and as an artist.

Although Madonna has gotten away with being bad, and has reaped both massive material rewards and wide-open opportunities for artistic expression, she also pays a big price. Not the least of it is constant, aggressive, globally telecast intrusions into whatever passes for her personal life by tabloid paparazzi as well as respectable journalists who feed public appetites for celebrity gossip. As referenced throughout this text, a number of academics have examined certain dimensions or selected pieces of her work, as I have done, in the quest for a better understanding of our varied societies, or because we can't get our fascination with a compelling cultural figure out of our heads unless we write about her. She is tracked and scrutinized by her die-hard fans, and she is routinely and shamelessly dissected and judged by people who do not always share her values, and who may not appreciate or pay attention to popular culture in general, but who have taken moralistic positions against her. Now, early in 1997, Madonna is respected and appreciated by those who a year ago disdained her. Julie Salamon, who interviewed Madonna in her seventeenth week of pregnancy for *Vogue*, describes her as 'a portrait of matronly elegance, with barely a trace of the bawdy girl who had become, by dint of her inventive outrageousness, the most famous woman in the world' (1996: 302).

I am interested in Madonna as an artist, and particularly in the effects of her work on others. Her biographers and most of her interviewers and critics have been men who, to varying degrees, have objectified her even more than she objectifies herself. My favourite interviews have been those she's done with other celebrity women: Carrie Fisher in *Rolling Stone* in June 1991, and on television in January 1997 with Oprah Winfrey, a woman as powerful and rich as herself, and with her pal Rosie O'Donnell. I hope I have humanized Madonna even while holding her in awe. Relatively few of those who have written about her have brought a feminist perspective to bear on her work, although her gutsy performance begs the question of her relationship to women's liberation movements. Thus, one of the aims of this book has been to join my fascination with Madonna, and the political and cultural contexts which bred and sustain her, with a feminist analysis. I say 'a' feminist analysis advisedly, because I don't presume to speak for any other feminist, or to represent women's movements in any of their diverse and often conflicting strands and social locations. I do, however, speak to issues generated from within various feminist communities.

I must also clarify what I mean by 'popular/pop culture.' I use this term simply to refer to that on which the most cultural-consumer money is spent – concerts, records, tapes, CDs, videos, film – often, initially, in response to multimillion-dollar marketing campaigns; but, for an artist to be 'popular,' such exposure must coexist with a strong grassroots audience connection with the work.

Since beginning her career, Madonna has evidenced impeccable timing and commercial prescience in gauging her audience's readiness to witness the smashing of yet another cultural taboo. Her transgressions of boundaries have sometimes resulted in shifts in her fans' demographics. I'm interested in the reasons for her fans' devotions, as well as the reasons for vociferous resistances against her widespread influence. In the first decade of her career, Madonna invited attention by presenting herself as radically controversial. I expect she will continue to be controversial, even while appealing to more 'mature' audiences. And although I sometimes in the pages ahead, on principle, sit on the side of her self-appointed judges, I hugely respect her talent.

Madonna's representational focus on sexual practices and values through the early 1990s is a primary theme of this book because, in her first decade-plus as a superstar, her work has been primarily about sex. Sex, however, does not occur in a political or social vacuum; thus, considerable portions of the introductory discussion ahead are concerned with contextualizing some of the questions aroused by her work.

I made a decision to not present Madonna's song lyrics, because, when seen flat on the page in the absence of the music, they often seem trite, and sometimes silly – even when, as is most evident through her video performances, they are not. The very nature of music itself transcends the written word. One can't replicate music in the mind through language except in so far as language refers the mind back to music. One can't verbally describe what one musically remembers. Norman O. Brown once said that the only proper response to poetry is poetry, and the same is especially true of music, dance, or any other non-verbalizable, visceral, sensory experience. Some expressions can't be spoken. As Isadora Duncan famously said, 'If I could say it, I wouldn't have to dance it.' No narrative description can look like dance or sound like music.

This is, then, a very partial account of one woman's early career as a major pop-star phenomenon who sings, dances, and acts, among other career activities. It presents Madonna as viewed from the outside, primarily from the perspective of just one observer. Holding the attention of critics and fans alike, Madonna signifies the times we live in, as mediated by audiences, technology, and media journalists, and as analysed by university scholars. I wander among them, crossing boundaries.

Karlene Faith
Vancouver, BC
January 1997

Acknowledgments

My paternal great-grandfather, Joseph, was a French-Canadian fiddler. Early in this century, my great-grandmother, Lula, traded a team of horses for a piano. In 1911, Lula and her second husband, Abraham, with her teen-aged daughter Aquina in tow, carried the treasured Kimball upright in their covered wagon north from South Dakota to the south country of Saskatchewan. There my future grandma, Aquina, rode horseback from one homestead to another, using a cardboard, fold-out keyboard and her own perfect pitch to teach kids how to hear and read music. In time she taught many of her own twelve children to play various instruments, starting with my father. She also taught my mother, who as a child lived down the road and traded baby-sitting for piano lessons from her future mother-in-law. Eventually Aquina became a mentor to the musically-inclined among her dozens of grandchildren. For the love of Joseph, Lula, Abe, and Aquina, and their abiding spirits, I give everlasting thanks.

I give loving thanks to my grown kids, Craig, Kim, Todd, and Woody, nieces Liza and Terra, and goddaughter, Merunka, for tuning me in to their favourite music when they were young, and to my daughters-in-law, Nicole, Jacque, and Eve, and my grandchildren, Abraham Danièl, Zöe Alexandra, and Keegan Adicus, for being so full of zest for life.

Lasting thanks to Norman O. Brown, for instigating illuminating sex talk among University of California History of Consciousness students, so many years ago.

Special thanks to Pamela Sleeth, and to Barbara Kuhne, Della McCreary, and Dawn Currie, for giving me encouragement at the beginning of these musings.

Loving thanks to inspiring artists, friends, and former neighbours Carolyn Bell and Dorothy Dittrich for their insightful, generous readings; solid suggestions for improvements; elegant meals; stimulating conversations; beautiful music; and helpful encouragements. They've followed it right through with me, and their aesthetic influences and positive attitudes found their way to many of these pages.

Thank you, Cheryl (Tapwé), for help with the title.

Others to whom I'm grateful for myriad kindnesses and helpful assistance with the development of the manuscript include Scott Anderson, Brian Burtch, Tret Fure, Ann Hackler, Gayle Horii, Réa Jansen, Judy Lynne, June Millington, Cath Moody, John Moody, Jenica Rayne, Kristen Roth, Michael Rotkin, Sharon Rynders, Kephra Senett, Debbie Sentance, Liz Straker, and Cris Williamson.

I'm particularly grateful to Executive Editor Virgil Duff of the University of Toronto Press for his respectful regard for the work from the beginning, his acute publishing awareness and strategic reassurances, and his patient shepherding of the manuscript through to print. Thanks to Beverley Beetham Endersby for her excellent copy-editing and especially for her irrepressible wit and delightful sense of humour. Thanks to Jill Foran, Rosmarie Gadzovski, Barbara Porter, Margaret Williams, and the rest of the talented University of Toronto Press team for giving care to this work. And thanks to the anonymous reviewers who helped me clarify my reasons for wanting to write in the ways I do about the ways I read Madonna.

Most special gratitude in this project goes to Frances Wasserlein, friend, teacher, writer, and community and arts activist/advocate. She has supported my and many others' work by showing genuine interest and responding with constructive, useful, critical feedback. In this case, her research skills and her grasp of the workings of the Internet, and her generosity with her time, produced listings of Madonna's prodigious body of work from 1983 to 1996, as provided in the useful, clearly organized appendix. This turned out to be a much bigger project than we'd anticipated. Thank you, Frances, for seeing it through so gracefully.

Finally, I thank Madonna for keeping me interested in her creative intelligence and chutzpah for over a decade. She's not the only commercial artist to captivate my interest, by a long shot, but she's the only one on whom I took extensive notes. Her music enters my life unexpectedly some days and nights, thanks to young occupants of highrise apartments across the lane, in Vancouver's West End, who play their tapes or CDs at high volume. As I write, someone is playing some driving, throbbing Brazilian rhythms reminiscent of the urban beats which propelled Madonna when she was writing disco tunes as a baby New Yorker, now approaching two decades ago. In January 1997, I see her Evita image on billboards as the city bus passes through the Granville Street cinema row. Whenever I watch television I see the commercial for the just-released movie *Evita*, with Madonna singing 'Don't Cry For Me, Argentina' with a passion befitting the song, the artist, and the subject. She is at present, every day, in every newspaper, on the radio, TV, magazine covers, and in movie theatres, across the globe. As Frances shows, she is everywhere on the Internet. The world is shrinking and, whether or not we pay attention to her, in early 1997 Madonna is close and getting closer to all of us.

KF
Vancouver
January 1997

MADONNA, BAWDY & SOUL

1

Setting the Stage

Through reflections on the first decade-plus of Madonna as a contemporary, enduring pop sensation, I engage in mostly plain talk about some of the ways that popular entertainments can both serve and exploit us. As an elder, paying critical attention to popular trends (in Canada and the United States) gives me a more complicated and respectful perspective on youth, who are the motor force and trend-setters of contemporary Western pop music. I hope my views of Madonna as a complex cultural force will be of academic interest to undergraduates in interdisciplinary studies. But it is more to Madonna's thinking fans (often closeted), or unabashed fans of pop culture generally, that I address myself.

Among commercial performers, Madonna has held my interest because, through words, motion, music, images, and symbols, she's been in a position to tell the world what to think and how to act out – and globally millions of young people have paid attention. She uses media technology with finesse, to both mimic and mock the platitudes and clichéd messages of the commercial culture of which she has been the intermittent reigning queen. Through her young adulthood, her stage, film, and video work has been compelling for reasons I identify in the chapters to follow. She represents a threat, a wild woman who disrupts the norms of feminine propriety without abandoning smart, sure, sexy female entitlement.

It is risky to write about another person from a distance, and especially an artist who may be more skilled than most at compartmentalizing her public performance and her private opinions and experience. Even her most benign meanings can be distorted through the decontextualization of quotes from print or television interviews, or the failure to note nuanced inflections or innuendos in her speech or body language that indicate her tongue is in her cheek. I tried to be careful. I have avoided offering 'facts' that didn't come from credible sources, and, when in doubt, I threw it out. Still, I regret any unwitting errors of fact that might remain in my account of Madonna, her career, her global effects, and what it all might mean.

First, I'll say what this book is *not* about. To be fair to Madonna, it is not necessarily about her. It is about how I and others see her – in her work and in the public eye. My perceptions of her sometimes differ widely from those of others, and are certainly very different from how she would see herself. I do not believe there is some ultimate, concealed, mysterious Truth to Madonna. Rather, I've gathered, contemplated, and analysed countless contradictory pieces of truths conjured up and mediated by her fans and detractors, in all our identity diversities, and by her contradictory presentations or inventions of Self through performance.

When I capitalize a word, such as 'Truth' and 'Self' in the previous paragraph, and other potentially loaded words to come, I am adding ironic weight to what is commonly meant by it. 'Truth,' for example, has been reified by religion, science and even philosophers, who should know better, as a pure, identifiable condition or state of being; a factual reality; a description of how things really are; a goal to which we aspire as a species or culture; a search to which we must dedicate ourselves. But, in the human world, there is little verifiable truth to which all people can agree or ultimately adhere. When I use the word 'Truth,' the subtext is: Whose truth? according to whom? when and where? defined or exercised for what purpose and for whose benefit? I'm sceptical about cavalier, inflated uses of the word 'truth' because I've seen so much painful harm caused by the authoritarianism which a belief in Truth so often produces.

Lest the 'bawdy' in the title should suggest otherwise, this book is not at all about prostitution as occupational sex. I am saying that, in the first decade of her career, Madonna's work is about over-coming inhibitions about Sex and the Body, capitalized to empha-size the parody and bawdy excess of her performance. Because she has made so much money with sexualized imagery, she has fre-quently been charged by her detractors with 'prostituting' herself. I speak of the great mythical Whores, of whom Madonna is one, whose charisma, independence, taste for unrestrained pleasure and beauty, and keen business sense result in autonomy and power over men that is uncommon among women. I also speak figura-tively of prostitutes and whores in terms of the political economy in which Madonna is situated. However, Madonna has considerably more autonomy than other working people, and therefore less need to 'prostitute' herself, which implies compromise. By defini-tion, most people in capitalist societies are obliged for survival to sell, rent, or trade their marketable assets (physical, social, or men-tal) for the best wage or salary. Whether or not they take satisfac-tion from or believe in the work they do, or are consciously or unconsciously alienated from it, if they've ever been unemployed they know they're fortunate to have a job at all, and that usually settles the matter.

In some respects, sexual whoring for survival, and grand Whor-ing as a creative woman's triumph, are not so far apart, but the dis-tinction is significant. Madonna has been an inspiration to young women to be sexy, but also to develop independence and to avoid the hazards of the street. Unlike a sex worker who is at the mercy of johns, pimps, and the police, a Whore holds men of power in her thrall. From the start of her career, Madonna demonstrated both in life and in performance the mammoth distinction between a woman who is constructed as a success-story Whore who refuses victimization, and a girl who runs away from home as a sexually abused victim and who is revictimized on the street as a girl who prostitutes her sex because there are no perceived alternatives.

In much commentary on popular culture, the artist is subsumed by the theory and abstracted out of the fundamental flesh of the entertainment equation. Part of my purpose here is to explore the-oretical questions evoked by a Madonna-centred view of popular culture, but my focus is on Madonna herself. Although I insert relevant personal details when I can reasonably trust the sources, this is not at all a biography or exposé of Madonna's personal life. I chronicle career events of significance and discuss the social contexts from which Madonna developed her career. I also analyse the steady stream of contradictory images of Madonna as projected relentlessly by print media, television, and film; as created by herself on stages, in studios, and (when she was younger) on the streets and in clubs; and especially as these images are implicated in the contradictory ways in which Madonna affects lives.

I'm not here to persuade anyone that Madonna, and pop culture at large, deserve serious attention. I think it's obvious they do, and in that sense I'm writing to the already converted. Nor do I use her as an exemplar for my theories; rather, I hope to demonstrate that Madonna herself shifts the paradigms, even when she seems to be reinforcing them. I'm also not here to suggest that, on the subject of popular culture, academic opinions are worth more than others; the very idea is oxymoronic. Critical academic voices, however, from the safety of ivory towers, often offer perspectives not available through popular media. Beginning in the 1980s, a flurry of literature produced by fans, popular essayists, scholars, and journalists has bridged academic and popular cultures in some illuminating ways. Their work is multi- and interdisciplinary, frequently characterized as postmodernist, and commonly grouped under the rubric 'Cultural Studies.' This new tradition started formally in England with Stuart Hall and others at the Birmingham Centre for Cultural Studies in the late 1960s. The field is still growing as an (anti-disciplinary) academic category claimed by scholars from every discipline, who collectively have employed marxist, populist, deconstructionist, psychoanalytic, standpoint, radical-pluralist, feminist, diasporic, and other methods of inquiry (cf. Hall, 1996; Grossberg, Nelson, and Treichler, 1992).

As Henry Giroux writes, echoing others, 'postmodernism breaks down the distinction between high and low culture and makes the everyday an object of serious study' (1993: 55. Cf. Bourdieu, 1984; Kaplan, 1987; Collins, 1989). Postmodern times have issued 'a refusal of modernism's relentless hostility to mass culture and its reproduction [of élitism]' (Giroux, 1993: 120–1). Approaches to cultural studies based on theories of cultural pluralism, identity politics, colonization, or the politics of difference engender questions concerned with political economy and systemic power relations as they affect every thread of the cultural fabric. I've given this literature selective attention, as referenced throughout the text, setting contexts and interweaving theoretical perspectives with descriptions and interpretations of Madonna's artistic performance.

I devote chapter 4 to comparing Madonna with one of the key figures in twentieth-century intellectual history, Michel Foucault. Side by side, they illustrate contrasting contexts through which similar knowledges are circulated. I became interested in both Foucault and Madonna in the mid-1980s, and observed peculiar synchronicities in their mutual unfolding as postmodern icons who occupied very different cultural spaces. Traditionally, academic and popular cultures represented appositional communities as a result of systemic exclusions from universities on the basis of sex, religion, ethnicity, class, and racism. Stereotypically, the working class was relegated to the spheres of body and soul (as in action, physical labour, rhythm and expressive emotion), leaving the soulless, effeminate, physically atrophied, detached white (male) professional intellectuals huddled up in the universities, wearing rumpled, elbow-patched tweed jackets, puffing on pipes, and living the life of the mind. Old stereotypes, however, do not hold in these tradition-smashing, postmodern times (Collins, 1989). Structural class oppressions and systemic racism continue to exclude many people from universities, but parallel tracks in Foucault's and Madonna's careers led to and signified new cultural intersections, where bodies, minds, and souls converge across boundaries of class, colour, and sex.

Much of this first contextualizing chapter is not about Madonna explicitly but rather about how it is possible, historically, for her to be here now as she is. Subsequent chapters are about Madonna as someone who gave young people a running musical, lyrical, and theatrical account of sex, race, class, age, and religion. I join the debate on whether Madonna has responsibility as a role model. I review a career in which Madonna has been consistent in her creativity, incredibly productive in her output, and highly disciplined in her training. Although criticized by some for arrogance, and even cruelty, as a young performer, she also earned respect and admiration from co-workers for her overall professionalism.

In her early career, Madonna was scandalous (to some) in her performance and she often irritated the critics. With the 1996 birth of her daughter and the release of the film *Evita* (as discussed in the Postscript), Madonna is enjoying more across-the-board respect than at any time in her career. She is no longer the darling of (pre) teeny-boppers or gay boys so much as an internationally acknowledged multitalented grand diva from the old school, on her own terms. After years of insults, in the mid-1990s she's as much appreciated by 'discriminating' patrons of the arts as she is by grassroots fans of popular culture, especially youth, but of every age, who appreciate her gutsiness and have been her fans from the start. The critics, identified in the pages ahead, still find ways to insult her (like calling her a 'she-wolf from down Argentine way'), but some are coming around, given the glory shed on her by audiences from all quarters. This book, then, is a story of what came before her enormous success with *Evita* and the birth of her daughter, each event a significant turn in Madonna's road towards *grande dame* status in the history of entertainment.

SITUATING MADONNA

As a young artist, Madonna was consistently, boldly resistant to good-girl scripts, and she has been richly rewarded across the globe for her gender transgressions. She has also been vilified, which she has turned to her advantage. Some of the criticisms against her have been meaningless. For example, one common, derisive charge against Madonna is that she is a chameleon who constantly reinvents herself, but perpetual reinvention of Self would accurately describe the activity of any mindful artist who is engaged in a steady creative process. Metaphorically, a powerful second-wave feminist image, introduced by poet Pat Parker, among others, as one whose time had come, was that of a woman giving birth to herself – women's renaissance. Almost two decades later, Drucilla Cornell introduced the concept of 'natality,' based on 'the demand to ever renew oneself in the very effort to maintain an "I" over time.' In this perpetual process, 'the self is continuously "birthed" again through time and its encounters with others' (1993: 41). This is very unlike the ancient religious rebirthing that is a prerequisite to Christian salvation, wherein someone who is born again surrenders herself to God, is fixed in faith, saved for all time, and, although sometimes succumbing to temptation, can always with sufficient remorse be forgiven for lapses and confessed sins. By contrast, for the person in Western culture who is perpetually reinventing herself, the process is purposefully dynamic, always unfolding, never satisfied, never certain, full of risk, combative of guilt and regret, and, although often spiritually informed, in the terms of organized religion deemed secular by definition.

Madonna's characters in her early career (in song, and on stage, video, and film) were commonly perceived as more provocative, evocative, sexy, humorous, or offensive than those of other artists. She made a stronger impression than most. If we didn't like the Madonna images that got into our heads uninvited, she was easy to trash as a bimbette whore who perverted the libidos of vulnerable young people. That doesn't tell the story as I see it. I do, however, use the 'Whore' word to describe what I see as Madonna's great triumph. She remakes the rules. She challenges establishment etiquettes, and conquers antagonists with her charms. For the same reason that 'whore' is the worst insult, 'Whore,' when said with a certain respect, is the best compliment. The 'whore' epithet can be transformed through reclamation of the word, as a lot of 'working girls' are doing in these times. Some of the more interesting of the new-wave Whores are those who had been in the sex business but who began performing their trade in earnest and in parody as public theatre (cf. Bell, 1994; Sprinkle, 1991). Such women are indeed kin to Madonna. The Whore is the ultimate uppity woman, her own woman, a proud woman who trusts her own value and who dissolves the Whore/Madonna dichotomy. The great Whore is the very opposite of the woman who sleeps her way to the top; rather, this she who is the Whore (or, indeed, it could be a he) is the one with whom men (or women) would be honoured to sleep, whether or not a job was at stake.

I have been in awe of Madonna's surprises and staying power.
She's in sync with the speed and irreverence of the postmodern
age; yet, while still very young, she was wearing the mantle of a traditional diva. She in no way resembles the cute, naïve, white-girl
stereotype of popular radio singers of my youth on the prairies;
nor, in her totality as a performer, does she resemble any of her
contemporaries. When she is at her best, she infuses mainstream
commercial culture with daring reconfigurations of familiar life
ingredients, symbolic referents for resistance, choice, and forbidden pleasures.

In the mid-1990s, women have periodically occupied up to 40
per cent of the slots on U.S. and Canadian music charts, including
the culturally and musically diverse Mariah Carey, TLC, Whitney
Houston, Tracy Chapman, Enya from Ireland, Bjork from Iceland,
and Canadians Jann Arden and Shania Twain, as well as the omnipresent Janet Jackson and Madonna. Also high on the charts has
been the intense, monster success story Alanis Morissette, signed
in 1995 to Madonna's artist-driven label, Maverick, and managed
by Freddy DeMann, Madonna's manager (and formerly Michael
Jackson's manager). Morissette and k.d. lang (both Canadians),
Annie Lennox and P.J. Harvey (from the United Kingdom), Joan
Osborne (New York blues rocker, asking 'What if God was one of
us?'), and other commercially successful women of the 1990s, represent a clear break with cultural restrictions against white women
expressing sacrilege or embodied sexual desire, including the
anger of it, through music.

In this tradition-smashing decade of the nasty nineties, we have
seen the intelligent Courtney Love popularize the 'Kinderwhore'
look, indy labels geared to girls in the 'post-punk' underground,
and Riot Grrrls, such as 7 Year Bitch, who have taken 'feminism'
to its sexualized limits and, in the raw, are who Madonna could
have been in the eighties, had she lacked well-financed studio production, mainstream tracking, and commercial promotion. In
this cultural climate, Madonna's, and her imitators', uses of four-
letter words, once a gutsy feature of her style, already seem redundant, old-fashioned, unimaginative. The white-girls-can-talk-dirty
trend has run its course as entertainment. Fortunately, there's a

lot more to Madonna than time-worn words that have lost their punch.

Since the 1950s, coincident with the popularization of the Fender Stratocaster electric guitar (in the shape of a curvy woman's body), young men have been the primary producers and consumers of popular music. Typically, from the 1950s through the 1980s, only 10 per cent of featured singers (and many fewer instrumentalists) getting radio play, or making the U.S. or Canadian charts, were women, with only minor fluctuations until the 1990s' upward trend (or blip, as only the future will tell). Until recently, few commercially successful women musicians were inclined, permitted, trained, or confident enough to compete vocally or, especially, instrumentally with the aggressive, raunchy, wall-of-sound that characterizes so much live-wire rock'n'roll, especially since metal stormed in.

There have been major exceptions to the gender gap over the years, extraordinary women, all unique in the music world at large, and different from one another: the inimitable Janis Joplin; the twentieth-century popular-music goddess Tina Turner; the likewise cross-culturally esteemed blues rocker Bonnie Raitt; the first and best early women's rock band, Fanny, and their progeny; and later rockers such as street-smart Deborah Harry of Blondie, Terry Garthwaite, Ellen McIlwaine, Chrissie Hynde, Christine McVie, Joan Jett, Carole Pope, Pat Benatar, Alannah Myles, Melissa Etheridge, and the Indigo Girls, all of whom, with other exceptional artists, have demonstrated that rock'n'roll is not a genital matter. Yet, although styles vary radically, whatever other qualities a woman brings to a commercial music career in the 1990s, she has to be sexy to young hetero-malestream audiences, even if she comes out as lesbian, dyke, bi- or queer.

When women do achieve success as songwriters, singers, players, and performers, they're likely as not to be ignored in the archives. The CBC reported that the Rock and Roll Hall of Fame in Cleveland compiled a list of the 500 most influential rock songs to 1990 and only 59 were by women, the proverbial (just over) 10 per cent. The work of megahit singer–songwriters such as Carly Simon and Janis Ian is passed over, as are, incredibly, the songs of Linda Ronstadt, Laura Nyro, Ann and Nancy Wilson (of Heart), and most others.

Pop-music fans in Canada into the 1990s, who may be more cross-generational and cross-genre than their U.S. counterparts because of Canada's nationalistic support of domestic talent, show pride in international blockbusters like Céline Dion, Shania Twain, and Alanis Morissette, but sentiment leans towards gentle vocalists epitomized by country-pop icons Anne Murray, from the Maritimes, and Sylvia Tyson, from the Prairies. Canadians have been charged by the success of home-growns such as the ethereal Sarah McLachlan and Margo Timmins, and jazz interpreter Holly Cole. Especially popular at the grassroots level are performers whose material reflects social consciousness and sense of place, such as Rita MacNeil, the McGarrigle sisters, Nancy White, Ferron, Heather Bishop, Lucie Blue Tremblay, the Rankin Family, Connie Kaldor, Loreena McKennitt, Jane Siberry, Susan Aglukark, and the always-welcome-back-home emigrants Buffy Sainte-Marie and Joni Mitchell. For more risqué or raunchy entertainment, Canadians have generally looked to the United States, and Madonna has been a popular staple in Canada as everywhere.

RADIO DAYS

By way of easing into the very 'american' slash-and-burn world of Madonna in the 1980s and '90s, I find myself returning to the pre-Elvis 1950s to get some perspective on how or whether we got here from there. The next several pages are about me, should any reader want to know where I'm coming from. My life is irrelevant to Madonna's story, but selected autobiographical details may help explain why I interpret her as I do.

I've been an avid follower of pop culture since I was a kid in pre-TV, pre-stereo, small-town Saskachewan. I spent long hours listening to the radio, dreaming of far-away places, and fantasizing that one day I would be a drummer in an all-girl dance band. Our large family lived for a time down south, in Montana, where I *did* become an ensemble drummer, but as the only girl in the band, which was okay. When I entered high school as a preadolescent, the two older boys who most attracted me were Paul Meissner, a talented saxophonist, and Kim Potter, who was the first person I'd ever seen playing trap drums. These boys, and the gospel singers I heard in a neighbourhood evangelical church, introduced me firsthand to sounds and rhythms that tapped right into my soul and changing body. About this time I moved in with my friend Suzie, who lived with her older sister, Debbie, and brother-in-law, Ike, who had been transferred from the east with an oil company. When they introduced me to modern jazz, I liked it so much they felt like instant family, and the music got my head working.

Among my lucky breaks as a young teenager in Montana was being hired to sort, label, and file records (78s and 45s) at KXGN, a then-1400 kilowatt AM radio station in Glendive (pop. 12,000, *circa* 1952). There, at age fourteen, I discovered dusty treasure bins of discarded promotional singles which had never been on our station's playlists – blues, R&B, jazz, and gospel ('race records,' as they were once called), and recordings of both 'Negro' and 'White' (segregated) all-girl orchestras.

Thanks to an imported deejay who liked the '40s Big Bands so popular in the east, on our otherwise mostly country station in Glendive we also heard swing/pop/jazz singers like Jo Stafford, Peggy Lee, Dinah Shore, Rosemary Clooney, and other mostly blonde white girls (though it was rumoured, as a juicy scandal, that Dinah Shore had 'mixed blood'). They were aptly called 'canaries' – apt because their voices were sweet as songbirds' and because canaries are the birds sent into the tunnels ahead of the miners, to determine the toxicity of the air.

I accepted any babysitting job if the family had a short-wave radio, because you needed one to hear the most recent recordings of jazz pianists such as Mary Lou Williams, or the voice of Ella Fitzgerald or any of the other classic blues or gospel-trained jazz singers. I heard compelling music broadcast live from far-away places like Chicago, New York, New Orleans, and San Francisco, whose clubs I read about, in *Billboard* and *Down Beat*, and would call on the phone with questions about upcoming performances just to hear the music in the background. The only good jukebox in Glendive was at Sam's, a sleazy club at the edge of town. We'd go there to boogie, but we'd get kicked out for being under age and/ or our parents would find out, which was worse. (To solve the problem, in our junior year a group of us organized a youth-centre committee, and, with support from merchants, the use of a boarded-up building donated by the Catholic church, and work marathons, teenagers had a place to go where we could dance to our own music. We called it the 'Shanty.')

After a long time cataloguing records at KXGN, I wrote some (bad) commercials and graduated to air, co-hosting (with my pal Gary Nelson) a 'news, views, music' show for 'teenagers,' a new word and concept coined by hero Alan Freed, a Cleveland, Ohio, disc jockey who also popularized the term 'rock'n'roll' when he hosted the rowdy 1954 Moon Dog Rock'n'Roll Party, to introduce white teens to soulful music with a beat, specifically black R&B. These were the days when the charts were dominated by wholesome (white) people with truly beautiful voices – Eddie Fisher, Rosemary Clooney, and Perry Como. We also had the De Castro Sisters singing 'Teach Me Tonight,' making clear with euphemism that girls know about sex. The 'race records' had major distribution as independents, but you didn't hear black R&B on mainstream radio in our part of the country, or in most other places, until Freed began a crusade.

Freed rebelliously programmed Rhythm & Blues and other popular black artists instead of playing white covers of black music by the likes of Pat Boone. Freed loved the music and rhythm, pure and simple, but his commitment to putting black music front and centre on the airwaves, and his appreciation for bawdy humour, got him in big political trouble with the Ku Klux Klan, the Catholic Church, and eventually the FBI under J. Edgar Hoover, who predictably thought that rock'n'roll, like interracial sex (and one would lead to the other), was a tool of the Communist conspiracy. There were other unruly deejays fighting station managers over playlists, such as Hound Dog Lorenz, of Buffalo and Niagara Falls, the first disc jockey to broadcast rock'n'roll into Canada, in the mid-1950s (Smith, 1989: 6–7). These times produced Elvis Presley, whose soulful covers of black music and body moves took off from what Freed was trying to do – namely, get white kids in the groove.

The commercial promotion behind him also underscored the racist dynamics of the music industry.

As an apprentice radio programmer in our friendly little badlands town on the Yellowstone River, I began learning firsthand about exclusion – how so many fewer female than male voices were on vinyl or on the airwaves, and how dominant, regional music 'tastes' affected station formatting. The station manager was a liberal who defied 1950s age and gender codes when he gave me a job. His programming decisions, however, were virtually dictated by local advertising clients, who were mostly small merchants. They could accept the swing of Benny Goodman, Mel Tormé, and even Duke Ellington, beside the country of Hank Williams and Hank Snow, but the marketplace was closed to the jazz of Sarah Vaughn or Carmen McCrae, or the R&B of Ruth Brown. (When the renowned Marion Anderson came to Glendive to perform a concert in the early 1950s, the most significant live-music event in the town's history, it took an aggressive citizens' protest committee to persuade the Closed-to-Coloured-and-Indians local railside hotel to rent her a room.) KXGN provided me with an elementary education in the social significance of music, tuning me in to the charged complexities of political life that swirl the tides of popular culture.

As a postscript to my high-school radio days, in 1975 still doing radio as a hobby, I taught a course titled 'Women and Music' at the University of California, in Santa Cruz, where a hundred or so young women and some young men gathered weekly to revel in new sounds (Faith et al., 1975). As their class project, a subgroup of about fifteen students organized four separate radio-production collectives, each of which for three months broadcast a weekly hour of 'women's music' from our campus FM station. Each group, according to their affinity for a particular musical genre, collectively produced, researched, programmed, and hosted shows featuring blues and soul, rock, country, and eclectic 'blatantly feminist' music written and performed by women. Along with the music, they gave listeners information about the artists, the songs, and the history of the genre. Occasionally they managed to interview one of their featured artists. A number of the young women and several young men also studied, took the exams, and became bona fide radio engineers. Others developed regular women's-music programs for local community stations and continued to program music by women for years after finishing university. The enthusiasm with which these students embraced this project in 1975 told me that they craved hearing and sharing the music women make, in all their varieties, as much as I had in the early 1950s.

In 1984 I went to my Glendive, Montana, thirtieth-year high-school reunion and felt all the ruptures of place, time, and identity, simultaneously with feeling that nothing at all had changed since I'd last seen my friends. The radio station had relocated from our small building on the outskirts of town to the off-Main downtown neighbourhood of my early adolescence, in a modern building with triple the staff. KXGN now signified the new Hot or Power Radio, with deejays following urban charts from New York to L.A., including the women recording artists of the day. Pre-programmed playlists were now distributed as part of the commercialization of communications media. With the blessing and curse of technology, and although the town's population had dropped to about 9,000 with the end of the oil boom, Glendive had entered the global music village. KXGN has added FM, and has for many years been a television as well as a radio station. It holds the important distinction of serving the smallest market area of any station in the entire United States, with the fewest people within reach of the station's advertising. Yet, KXGN is a thriving, sophisticated communications operation which performs a vital unifying function in the community.

When I walked into the classy new reception room, I remembered how, over three decades earlier, I once got in big trouble at KXGN. Our manager doubled as newscaster, and six o'clock news time was sacrosanct. I helped him pull items from the teletype, and although he told me what to look for (name recognition, continuing stories, relevance for Glendive), I felt the power of being able to decide, from the entire pool of knowledge and reports of events that poured in all day, what is important to relate and what people are willing or wanting to hear. Anyone who was at the station during news time dutifully listened while our kind boss, alone at the microphone in the glass-walled studio, with his earphones, brought us up-to-date on the war in Korea, challenges to the new Eisenhower administration, the Rosenberg trial, and the price of wheat. No one ever called him between six and seven, because they were listening to him on the radio, as was everyone in town. Except the station's biggest client – he called frequently during news time, and on each occasion I would explain that my boss was on the air. One day after a week of this, I very rudely barked at the guy that, if he'd turn on his damn radio, he'd know the manager couldn't come to the phone right then. For my big mouth the station was threatened with losing the account, and I learned some more lessons about how the adult world operates. (I should have learned a few years earlier, at age twelve, when I'd been fired from a hamburger joint after the owner overheard me advising two customers against ordering hot-fudge sundaes because, as I explained to them, I'd found cockroaches in the chocolate syrup that morning.)

Many of my generation's used-to-be bad girls have loved Madonna's gutsy (whether planned or impetuous) forthrightness, and felt in some remote way akin to her spirit. Even as a very young woman, she never let herself be dissuaded by critics, instead using them to her advantage. She would, no doubt, prefer that critics adore her as much as her fans do, and she reassuringly shows her vulnerabilities from time to time. But she receives global adulation and attention beyond what can be easily fathomed, to compensate for hurtful insensitivities from ill-informed critics or other snipers. She has a great laugh. She dares to exploit people by shocking them, while knowing that her representations will not alienate or confuse the multitudes of fans who understand her meanings. She seems to want to wake up sleeping, taboo-ridden minds, souls, and bodies and, at the same time, to race away with her soulmates to a bawdy world without taboos or critics. Although she appears to need to shock glibly and irreverently, to keep it interesting, she does, at the same time, ponder the serious meanings behind the big questions, especially about sexuality, a realm in which bad girls and gay boys invariably dwell.

All of us, to various degrees affected by our respective buffer zones, are products of the often treacherous waters of our social environment, and Madonna herself did not just wash up onto the shores of 1980s pop-culture world stages from a political vacuum. Her work, like that of the rockers of the 1960s and 1970s, has been a persistent, 'bawdy' reaction against values and fears that were entrenched in the 1950s, and which reclaimed hegemony through the turbulent, punitive political economy of the 1980s – spurred by Reagan and Thatcher. Some of that grim history, as it affected popular culture, is reviewed here as a way of contextualizing Madonna's impact on world stages for well over a decade, and almost certainly far into the future.

BEFORE MADONNA: A SELECTIVE UNITED-STATESIAN HISTORY

The insularity of hegemonic U.S. culture in the 1950s was framed by postwar aggressive conservatism. The terms were set by a wide gamut of authorities and bureaucrats, with the ideological ramifications well explained by sociologist Max Weber in the nineteenth century. These hierarchical bureaucracies (in which the most authoritarian bullies are often on the front lines; that is, 'just doing my job') were embedded in government, the military, religion, social welfare, family law, crime control and punishment, medicine, psychiatry, and education. These varied discourses, in practice, imposed substantive limits (though with professional disagreements among them) on what could be known by whom. This was the age of popularized Freud, and of the John Birch Society, a far-right organization which made Arizona senator Barry Goldwater's advocacy of non-interventionist foreign policy sound progressive.

In the 1950s, the popular media and entertainment industries only rarely posed a challenge to the patriotic, nuclear family–centred status quo. Some people conformed to this conservative prescription in a spirit of nationalistic agreement that there was a need for caution and protections (extending in the late 1950s to backyard bomb shelters in the new suburbs). Others felt trapped in the times against their will. All were denied important knowledges and/or, if they were resourceful in their research, denied the means of free expression. They were coerced into silence from a politically constructed postwar fear of instability and difference, a hatred of those who are structurally subjugated as both cause and result of irrational but purposeful socially constructed fear.

One could caricature the 1950s as the 'Three Monkeys' decade – hear no, see no, speak no evil, with 'evil' defined and regulated by (European-heritage male) professionals. The evil secrets had primarily to do with sex and communism, shadowed by omnipresent racist paranoias. Authoritarian voices speaking from government chambers, courtrooms, pulpits, welfare offices and those of medical practitioners and psychologists, school boards, and every other site of social control, mediated official knowledges to establish the moral proprieties of the times. As a challenge to prudery, the first issue of *Playboy* magazine came out in December 1953, and, although it was ostensibly about white boys and sex, it was in fact a magazine about white wannabe playboys' sex/power fantasies about women, few of which had anything to do with women themselves. Most pointedly, the airbrushed photo-centrefolds of nude women bore little resemblance to women's bodies in the real world. (To state the obvious, when a woman is on her back, her breasts do not normally protrude firmly upward.)

In universities in the 1950s, professors who exercised academic freedom were silenced when their counter-ideologies conflicted with conventional ('commonsense') wisdom. Very few of my high-school girlfriends were financially able, academically motivated, and sufficiently resistant to gender roles to proceed directly to higher education. I finished high school early, worked for a year as a government stenographer in Saskatchewan, got engaged twice, got hepatitis, began university studies with correspondence courses from the University of Chicago, studied music for six months in college back in Montana, and after all that, like several close friends, I got pregnant and was married by age eighteen. (Four children and thirteen years later, I graduated.)

One of my exceptional university-bound friends came home to stay after just one despairing semester, having been silenced by her psychology instructor's 'disgusting,' uncritical lecture on Freud's notion of 'penis envy.' What people didn't know of the dark side couldn't hurt them, especially the young and females of any age; what was known wasn't to be spoken. The authoritative voices speaking for the dominant culture didn't reveal what ordinary people, especially women, knew from their own experience but also weren't telling. Silences drove the innocent mad and protected the guilty. Like the scolds of old (Faith, 1993: 29–30), who, in early England, were sometimes made to wear the brank, or scold's bridle (a metal apparatus which fit over the head and into the mouth, preventing speech), women who did speak were punished. Mouthy women in the Western world have been on the defensive since time immemorial. Madonna has been a fabulous, inspiring example of a woman who won't be silenced.

Convergences of dramatic social processes and political events in the 1950s manifested and exacerbated conservatism and paranoia in the United States: these included the ongoing witch-hunts of the House Un-American Activities Committee against (accused) 'communists' and their 'sympathizers'; dramatic challenges to the institutionalization of Jim Crow segregation, and racist retaliations; and a concerted effort to get Rosie riveted securely in her Betty Crocker kitchen and Dr Spock nursery. At the same time as social forces converged in the project of redomesticating white women, in 1955 the 'radical' intelligentsia wildly praised the reissue of Philip Wylie's 1942 novel, *A Generation of Vipers*. In this work, Wylie elegantly articulated the gross misogyny behind the idealization of the Wife and Mother, the social need to transform the natural female monster, in Lombrosian terms (1899), into some model of desexed, defanged, passive, compliant, quiet perfection who can readily accept authority and not get in the way, of which the Madonna, the mother of Jesus, is the Western prototype. Wylie himself personified misogyny in the culture at large; he ranted against mothers, and issued contempt for what he called 'momism' – the glorification of the she-vipers in the kitchens and bedrooms who are out not only to suffocate their children, but also to castrate and destroy men with their sharp tongues and sharp-toothed vaginal traps. 'Respectable' women were put on the defensive for playing the only role open to them.

Meanwhile, in the 1950s, Mother's Day cards came into their

own as a major commercial industry, propagating a sentiment exemplary of Wylie's thesis. This internationally traditional holiday became official in the United States on 8 May 1914, when Congress jointly approved a bill declaring the second Sunday of every May as Mother's Day, signed by President Woodrow Wilson. The bill honours mothers as 'the greatest source of the country's strength and inspiration' and refers to 'the home' as 'the fountain head of the State.' Because women do so much for 'moral uplift and religion,' they directly benefit 'government and humanity' (Rice and Schauffler, 1927: 4–11). The holiday was not always observed, but fervour for it was renewed in the 1950s in the context of a shifting economy and the need to get women back in the home. Commercial glorification of stay-at-home motherhood produced a moral imperative to give mom a card, and even a gift, but the deeper effect was ideological. Given the nature of the job, and the responsibility put on mothers for their children's success in life, mothers *have* needed reassurance.

Contradictions mounted in the 1950s. There was rapid growth of both the prison and mental-illness industries, with institutions populated disproportionately by black men and white women, respectively. Women who were physically abused by their husbands went to mental hospitals voluntarily, for safety, or more often were committed by others to get cured of their 'irrational' marital discontent. On the new medium of television, Pauline Fredericks, a special reporter for NBC, hosted a TV documentary called *The Trapped Housewife*, a graphic account of how entrapment in suburban homes was driving women crazy. The innocuous, banal innocence of the most popular music of the time masked the dis-ease of a frighteningly chauvinistic period in U.S. history: Debbie Reynolds singing 'Abba Dabba Honeymoon' and Patti Page singing 'How Much Is That Doggie in the Window?' are voices from an eerie time when white girls could be cute, and that was about it.

With hindsight, one can also view the United States in the 1950s as a place crackling with undercurrents of rebellion. The most overt radicalism of the quiet decade was epitomized, not by opposition to U.S. 'involvement' against the 'communists' in Korea, but by support for historic civil-rights movements – represented most memorably by Martin Luther King, Jr, and later, as urban African-heritage energies mounted and coalesced, by Malcom X and other important leaders and martyrs. Simultaneously, among politicized Jews, radical women, socialist-minded industrial workers, and various ethnic and other political minority groups, activists were quietly (re-)organizing. Many of those who went underground as a result of the communist witch-hunt were discreetly mobilizing, and grassroots organizations were quietly developing strategies for peace with justice, human rights, workers' rights, women's rights, free speech, and opposition to capitalism, capital punishment, racism, apartheid, colonialism, and imperialism.

Music is always in the background and often in the foreground of dissident movements, and radicals of every stripe learn one another's musical traditions. Folk troubadours still traverse continents as repositories of knowledge about local struggles, and help link and sustain resistant cultures. In the 1980s and 1990s, superstars have done this on a grand scale in connection with famine, AIDS, farmers and farm workers, hunger, and political prisoners. In the 1950s, with 'Goodnight Irene,' the Weavers proved, as Paul Robeson had done, that radical cultural workers could break into the popular charts. The Weavers, however, like Robeson and the commercially popular black-power singer Eartha Kitt, and others, were harassed for their 'communist' leanings: as 'radicals' they threatened the social order by advocating world peace, racial equality, safety for workers and food for children.

The 1950s was also the Beat Generation decade that spawned protest poetry written by the free-thinking 'beatniks' – nicknamed by Herb Cain of the *San Francisco Chronicle*, following Jack Kerouac's coining of the 'beat generation' and the Soviet 'Sputnik' of spaceship exploration. Beat was inspired by jazz slang: to be 'beat' was to be exhausted and rejected. Fundamentally, beatniks constituted an intellectual movement of resistance to the superficially conformist thinking that gripped and overtly characterized the dominant WASP culture of the decade. These latter-day bohemian communities in the late 1950s and into the 1960s, and the mythologies and freedom aspirations attached to them, attracted dissident teenagers. These pockets of protest were filled with mostly male, artsy intellectuals, but beatniks also appealed to sensitive young women (including restless, teenaged housewives).

The beatniks and their wannabes clad themselves in tight black clothing, including leather jackets, when they could afford them, and French berets. They read the likes of William S. Burroughs, J.D. Salinger, Richard Wright, James Baldwin, and Langston Hughes. They ignored the late-night TV variety entertainment of Jack Paar (the mentor of Johnny Carson, who preceded Jay Leno), and Steve Allen, and grooved instead to the music of Miles Davis, Charlie Christian, John Coltrane, and Dave Brubeck, and to the recorded satire and polemics of Mort Sahl and Dick Gregory. They wrote passionate poetry with a political edge, and pondered the meaning of the universe. They espoused free love, confessed to or defended atheism, and parroted the hip vernacular of ghetto poets.

Exercising the healing properties of truth-telling, the beatniks outed the hypocrisies. Jazz, a gift of African Americans, was the backdrop against which beat poetry was read in urban coffee-houses that proliferated to accommodate (and sometimes profit from) the beatnik movement. It was a significant cultural alliance with political signifiers. Through vagabond writers, notably the prototype Jack Kerouac with his *On the Road*, and beat poets like Allen Ginsberg, Lawrence Ferlinghetti, Robin Blaser, Denise Lever-tov, Diane de Prima, Robert Duncan, and Gary Snyder, and with inspiration drawn from Zen Buddhism, French existentialism, and Walt Whitman, among other sources, the movement sprouted strong, dissident, and highly censored free speech literary net-works which flowered into the mid-1960s, and which have been periodically revived in new incarnations.

Back in the high schools in the late 1950s, people who were pop-ular because of their athletic prowess, clean-cut cuteness, or good personality thought the 'hipsters' were 'drips,' at a time when overt braininess was a disadvantage in popularity contests. To the hip-sters, the 'squares' were those with minds like a closed box, those who unthinkingly/unblinkingly echoed common moral judg-ments; stifled their own imaginations; and repressed their secrets, shames, and desires. Among others, Doris Day, Sandra Dee, and Pat Boone (each of whom had a personal scandal to conceal: 'interracial affair'; eating disorder and prescription abuse; marital betrayal in the perfect marriage, respectively), dispensed saccharine sentiments to a squared nation. An aspiring (white) middle class in the emerging tract-housing suburbs was willing to pretend that honesty and marital fidelity were common virtues and that all was well.

Resistance to the rigidity of the 1950s materialized dramatically in the politically turbulent events of the 1960s, when colonized nations, political minorities across the world stage, and, in the United States, farm workers, women, blacks, Natives, homemakers, welfare-rights activists, gays, lesbians, draft resisters, people with physical disabilities, and many other special interests were aggressively claiming identity and political solidarity with their group, and often in coalition.

Madonna was a wee child when the Beatles showed up on *The Ed Sullivan Show* in 1964, and the next year, when Bob Dylan gave new meaning to popular folk music when he picked up an electric guitar at Newport. Major changes in commercially viable popular music were facilitated by new technologies. The growth of corporate, globalized mass media had the effect of homogenizing popular culture across regions, the significance of which was anticipated by Canada's media guru, Marshall McLuhan. Berry Gordy took the world by storm with his Motown ('Motor Town') label, with artists out of Detroit, including wildly popular teenage-girl groups such as the Shangri-Las, Shirelles, and Supremes.

As increasing numbers of aspiring singers and musicians came forward to be recorded, so did the numbers increase manifold of those who failed to build a career, with often-tragic consequences. For example, when I was living in Los Angeles in 1975–6, working for Olivia Records, I was struck by the paradox of two simultaneous events: Florence Ballard, one of the original Supremes, died at home, still young, but broken in spirit and body; the tiny news item about her death, in a Sunday edition of the *Los Angeles Times*, pointed out that she and her children had been dependent on welfare for years. In the same issue of the paper, juxtaposed against

this bleak image, in a terrible, ironic coincidence, was a special feature series of glossy images of an always triumphant Diana Ross,
the lead, Gordy-favoured Supreme. She was the flamboyant subject
of full-page colour photos on every page of a thick insert, modelling fashions and jewels worth millions of dollars while earning
millions from album sales and stage shows.

In contrast with, but also often inspired by Motown, white, male
music consumers consolidated enthusiasms for variations on
rock'n'roll. With the internationalization and institutionalization
of these bottom-heavy new sounds, pop music was changed forever.
U.S. hegemony in the burgeoning multinational entertainment
industry in the 1960s, combined with the global impact of electric
instrumentation and rock'n'roll, brought Western influences to
teen music culture throughout the world.

Elders everywhere in all times attempt to protect youth from
influences which betray their own values. Just as blues, bebop, and
boogie woogie had been condemned by WASPs as devil's music, so
did parents fear the influence of rock'n'roll. And so do nations
inundated with U.S. culture fear the 'americanization' of their
youth. Canadian federal communications officials, since the 1960s,
have held perennial debates concerning the extent to which a particular share of airtime must be dedicated to Canadian content.
(In the mid-1990s the regulations hold that at least 60 per cent of
television content, and 30 per cent of radio content, must be produced by Canadians.)

With the catalysts of the 'Cuban crisis'; the assassinations of President John F. Kennedy and Martin Luther King, Jr; mass, sustained
protests against racist segregation; and the anti-war movement, a
broad, fragmented spectrum of U.S. political issues, which had
been articulated by dissidents for decades, cohered after a fashion
and burst into public consciousness in ways never anticipated. It
was a massive resistance to cynicism. The call for social and political change was inclusive, and the cultural revolution laughed at
itself, with anarchist characters like Wavy Gravy, the serious-think-
ing, fun-loving artist clown; Paul Krassner, the sardonic, no-holds-
barred satirist and editor of *The Realist*; Ken Kesey and his Merry
Pranksters, who acted out hallucinogenic fantasies; and Dick Gre-

gory, who became a national success with his biting political commentary.

The first issue of *Rolling Stone* magazine was published in 1967, the same year the Monterey Pop Festival, especially the performance of Jimi Hendrix, blew minds; the New York Woodstock festival created a new Nation; and the California counter-culture flourished, with communes, hitchhikers spreading the good word, and the energies of migrant urban 'hippies' – another term coined by Herb Cain from his ringside seat to the happenings of San Francisco's Haight-Ashbury district. In my adopted home town of Santa Cruz, we took our kids out of school and joined the Summerhill-inspired 'free school' movement. In the Bay Area, psychedelic-rock bands, notably Jefferson Airplane (later Starship) and the Grateful Dead, were the rage, and young people celebrated a life enhanced by LSD and marijuana. And then it unravelled.

Accelerated, raging mass opposition to U.S. aggressions in Vietnam in the late 1960s and early 1970s resulted in middle-class war resisters joining more conventional 'offenders' in prisons and jails (alongside middle-class youth convicted of marijuana possession); prisoners' rights groups and support for political prisoners sprang up all over the land. In California, the murders orchestrated by Charles Manson made suspect anyone driving a Volkswagen bus, the preferred vehicle of hippies. The counter-culture movement was grossly contaminated when the Hells Angels killed a rowdy fan at a Rolling Stones concert at the Altamont racetrack. U.S.-presidency hopeful Robert Kennedy, like his brother before him, was assassinated, in a Los Angeles hotel. Richard Nixon finally got to be president and was re-elected, only to be forced to resign under threat of impeachment after the Watergate scandal.

In the late 1960s and early 1970s, new (second wave) feminist thinking was exercised (and exorcised) in consciousness-raising groups, and the country was swarming with renegade women. Gay liberation was breaking out, and lesbians were self-identifying. Black Panthers across the nation, led by Huey Newton, from Oakland, were jailed or informally executed by law enforcement, one after the other. Angela Davis (finally acquitted), Ericka Huggins, and other African-American activist women were incarcerated for generally transparent political reasons. The Red Power movement, reclaiming the rights of First Nations peoples, was also seeking freedom for political prisoners. La Raza Unida organized within Mexican-American communities and changed the face of Texas politics. The anti-war and draft-resistance movements resulted in progressive coalitions and organized challenges to state powers and business-as-usual. At their trial following the riots at the Democratic convention, Bobby Seale of the Chicago Eight was chained and gagged, and all the defendants were degraded by Judge Julius Hoffman and treated generally as unpatriotic swine.

Former Panther Eldridge Cleaver, after an exchange of gunfire with police, took off for Castro's Cuba. As a fugitive, he later gave precarious refuge in Algeria to escaped convict and LSD mind-expansion guru, former Harvard professor Timothy Leary, who was a gentle soul. Recaptured and sent to San Quentin, Leary was imprisoned in a cell next to Charles Manson – who had fed regular doses of LSD to his followers as part of his cult brainwashing *modus operandi* before setting them up to kill people. As a pair they represented the best and worst possible uses and effects of hallucinogens.

The punk movement came and went in the mid-1970s (and later returned with a vengeance), with independent women represented by the androgynous New Yorker poet/protest rocker Patti Smith. Disillusionment reigned in the counter-culture, and cynicism took hold in the left. Feminist women stayed aloof from negative prognoses and proceeded to make the 1970s their decade – although not everyone noticed at the time.

Multinational corporations, based primarily in the United States and later in Japan, financed electronic-media conglomerates which, in the 1990s, still have control over the production and distribution of film, television, recording, radio, and new electronic communications. These conglomerates now own huge concert stadiums in major cities in many nations. They effectively control which artists will be promoted, according to predicted market trends. By selecting particular sounds to promote from among diverse talent, they create the trends they predict. Bruce Springsteen and Rickie Lee Jones were both hyped by the 1970s media long before most people had heard their music or formed an opinion.

As it turned out, in both cases their talent warranted the attention, but, as in Jones's case, sheer talent, even with mega-promotion, is seldom enough to sustain fame and fortune. Ultimately, the fans (that is, the fanatics) make their choices when they put down their money.

RESITUATING MADONNA

Promotion worked swift magic in building Madonna's career in the 1980s. In the 1990s, up to $3 million is expended on advertising each time she produces a new album. She has had the fiscal benefits of working with Time Warner Inc., the financial giant of the industry who also financed her own Maverick label in 1992. By 1996, with the success of Alanis Morissette and other artists, Maverick had long since recovered the original $10-million investment and was making big profits, due in part to the vigilance of co-CEO Freddy DeMann and talent scout Guy Oseary. Resistance is the steady companion of power, but Madonna folds that principle back on itself in her creative act. Whatever character she plays, she personifies resistance to repression; at the same time, her career capitalizes on others' desires.

In her first decade of fame, Madonna showed herself to be an ally in spirit, if not in substance, of cultural rebels who preceded her. She has directly benefited from the free-speech actions of 1950s and '60s cultural rebels such as Lenny Bruce and the activists who were jailed during the Berkeley movement against speech censorship. Her performative interracialism follows the courageous path of anti-racists who, when they were the wrong colour in real life, were often lynched. She has projected fleeting, though not always convincing, kinship with feminists and gays, capitalizing on their risks to personal safety and at the same time loosening biases against same-sex love. And to the unhip observer, she epitomized early punks in the know, perpetually changing or taking off their costumes. Riding on the coat-tails of other people's resistance movements, in her public life Madonna has served as a mediating lens for cultural vanguards, and no one is throwing her in jail, lynching her, applying the epithet 'feminist' or 'lesbian' to her, or

moving to the other side of the street when she approaches.
Instead, her staged attitudes have made her a wealthy woman.

Madonna is now, in the late 1990s, one of the most powerful
people in the world, as gauged by income, independence, posses-
sions, mobility, influence over others, and the astounding energy
at her disposal – her own energy, that which she commands, that
which she generates, and that which is showered upon her. She has
been blessed with, or has cultivated, multi-artistic talents and also,
apparently, the habits of focus, big dreams, belief in herself, imagination, extreme discipline, hard work, impatient perseverance
artistically, and a patient taste for business – all attributes which are
necessary (but not sufficient) to self-made success in a highly individualistic, materially invested culture.

Named for her mother, Madonna Louise Ciccone was her Italian
Catholic parents' first daughter, born in 1958. The name Veronica
was added as her baptism name. She was a loved child, but her
mother died when Madonna was only five, and emotionally she
had to fend for herself. Early on, she recognized her own apti-
tudes, set goals, found good teachers, and worked hard. Before
turning twenty, she had the gumption to take a bus to New York
City, where show-business careers are made. One of her early gigs
was as a drummer with a New York band that called itself the
Breakfast Club (Lewis, 1990: 102), and she modelled, danced, and
had a job as a hat-check girl; she worked on her voice and sang
disco back-ups during a brief sojourn in Paris. She had the charm
to make friends easily, the nerve to lean on others when she
needed them, and, in five years of sometimes intense poverty, she
didn't lose her focus (Andersen, 1991). But the same, and a lot
more, in terms of paying dues, could be said for thousands of
other unwavering, well-trained, gutsy, gifted talents who never get
their big break in the music industry but go on pleasing audiences
on smaller circuits.

Like the 1920s flapper Clara Bow, the original Hollywood 'It'
girl, Madonna got very lucky, but in the end she does have It – the
sexy, amorphous, charismatic It that resonates with and comes to
symbolize the spirit of a culturally specific time and place in
human history. In the United States in the twentieth century,

Bessie Smith had It, and Billie Holiday. James Dean, Elvis Presley, and Marilyn Monroe had It. Jim Morrison had It, and Jimi Hendrix had It, and so did Janis Joplin. And John Lennon. With their premature deaths, they became everlasting icons for their generation. Madonna has It, but, given her disciplined health regimen, her charmed luck, and her grounded fortitude, she's not likely any time soon to lose control over herself, her life, her career.

CULTURE, COMMERCE, AND INDEPENDENT WOMEN

Every day, through every medium, Madonna's sounds and images, amidst those of other superstars, are being transmitted from the United States to distant lands across the globe. A performer's commercial popularity in the United States is commonly a prerequisite to gaining a major international audience, or (for 'foreigners') even a substantial audience share in one's own country, a problem that has plagued Canadian performers, among others, competing for the markets. Exceptional trail-blazers aside, there are inherent artistic limitations to commercial music globally, given the lowest-common-denominator values of the U.S. mass market. But because doors have opened via proliferating technologies in recent decades, no matter where we live, people with access to technology in 1997 have a much wider range of choices in the kinds of music we listen to on radio, jukeboxes, turntables, or tape/CD systems, or see performed on TV, video, or computers.

We now have many variations on 'world music,' and blends of Afro-Cuban and other cross-fertilizing, indigenous rhythms have entered pop music globally. This trend originated with independent labels, which generally target a specific market. Notable among the independents is the 'women's music' network, catalysed in the early 1970s with concerts, festivals, albums, and distribution networks featuring music of every genre. In the mid-1970s, this activity, dominated by the Olivia and Redwood record companies, became a significant musical force which linked feminist and lesbian communities throughout the United States.

The women's network has drawn Michigan festival audiences of 10,000 and more for abundantly talented women who recorded for and/or were distributed by women's labels. Much of the nascent women's-music industry was based in California in the late 1970s, but artists travelled the continent and, in some cases, the globe. Early headliners included Meg Christian, the witty and soulful musical member of the Olivia founding collective, who unflinchingly presented lesbian-explicit artistry; Cris Williamson, enduring superstar of the independent market, with one of the all-time best-selling albums on an independent label, a uniquely inspiring and engaging entertainer who gave the idea of a women's recording company to the Olivia women in 1972; and Holly Near, of her own Redwood Records, a powerful songwriter and vocalist who supported new artists across cultures and who has been a strong force internationally for human rights. In 1976, Margie Adam, charismatic pianist, lyricist, and composer who recorded on her own Pleiades label, joined Christian, Williamson, and Near for a six-city sell-out California tour that confirmed the viability of 'women's' music (Faith, 1976).

Other performers based in California during the mid-1970s, recording for women's labels, included Teresa Trull, a versatile, musical wonder from North Carolina via New York; Linda Tillery, an R&B crossover artist whose amazing voice preceded Janis Joplin with Big Brother and the Holding Company in San Francisco in the 1960s; Mary Watkins, brilliant composer, arranger, and jazz/classical/gospel keyboardist from Colorado, via New York; June Millington, from the Philippines, a rock pioneer with her sister Jean in the all-girl band Fanny, who, as singer–songwriter, electric-guitarist, teacher, engineer, and album producer, gave singular support to women entering the music business, and later, with Ann Hackler, formed the Institute for the Musical Arts; Rhiannon, powerful solo singer, international teacher, and theatrical performer who served as vocalist with the popular women's jazz quintet Alive!; and Tret Fure, a postmodern renaissance woman whose skills with recording technology complement her dazzling songwriting and performing artistry. Various other independent women, through the 1970s and into the 1980s, built strong followings in the U.S. women's circuit and beyond – including celebrity Canadian singers–songwriters–musicians like Ferron, from the

West Coast, Heather Bishop from the Prairies, and Lucie Blue Tremblay from Quebec. What all these extraordinary musical artists have in common is that, despite strong followings and successful grass-roots careers spanning decades, and, notwithstanding periodic, fleeting recognition from the mainstream press, they lack the mass-media exposure without which monster sales are virtually impossible.

Madonna's extraordinary success both underscores and sidesteps issues of gender exclusion from the industry. One cannot say she sold out; she appears to be doing exactly what she wants to do, on her own terms. Given women's traditional powerlessness in the music industry, as elsewhere in the worlds of commerce, her very existence as a powerhouse has been terrifying to her critics for the same reasons that she is uplifting to her fans. For some feminist fans, however, she has sometimes posed problems, and she evoked longing for the perfect, politically conscious and articulate woman to represent us on world stages. Women are taught to fear other women who take their power and who use their self-cultivated freedoms to express themselves without self-censorship. Madonna acts out the world as she finds it, and sometimes this can make some of us uncomfortable. Nevertheless, she hooks us and positively or negatively energizes us. What she's managed to do in a mean, greedy man's world is simply astonishing.

YOUNG MADONNA IS ABOUT SEX

In contrast to women whose music careers are grounded outside the mainstream entertainment industry, when Madonna broke into the pop scene in 1983, the people of Glendive, Montana, and people in small towns and in every major city on every continent, knew about her almost instantly. It had very little to do with her talent; rather, her sudden fame was the outcome of a marketing commitment by male music executives. I heard Madonna on the radio when her first album came out, but, like many people, I didn't pay close attention to her music until seeing her with Rosanna Arquette in Susan Seidelman's 1985 film, *Desperately Seeking Susan.*

In this book I praise Madonna for leaping boundaries, but I also

criticize aspects of her performative treatment of sex in the first
decade-plus of her career. My grousing may expose me as a sexual
conservative, although lesbian-identified (which would have been
an oxymoronic statement not so many years ago). Like music, the
experience of either good or bad sex can't be communicated
through talk about it or theatrical representation, but we try. In my
experience, sex at its best is a private exchange between two eager
adults who already know each other intimately, whether or not
they've had sex before; who have an equal voice and a balanced
relationship; and who undress together to give mutual, soulful,
uninhibited, sometimes hilarious, unconditional, ecstatic, passionate physical love, which sometimes feels so good it hurts, all made
possible by quiet emotional trust and mutual respect. Thoughts,
feelings, and desires for the other person are transmitted through
to the body that inspires the lust. Through mutual, direct stimulus,
sensuous attraction, erotic ritual, and orgasmic fusion and release,
opening and entering all the sensual and sexual zones of each
other's bodies/spirits/personalities/minds, they abandon themselves to the universe, and experience Oneness for a while.

It's quite a gift, to my mind, whether accomplished sexually,
spiritually, artistically, intellectually, or even politically, to be able
to arouse someone else's passion and evoke a sense of being one
with the universe – work more traditionally done through religion.
I agree with the gay Irish priest-activist Bernard Lynch, who states:
'A spirituality without sexuality is as truncated as a sexuality without spirituality' (1995: 216). A similar observation is expressed by
author Beth Brant, a Mohawk woman, who titles her essay 'Physical Prayers': 'As a creative human being who is also Native and
Two-Spirit, I will not make distinctions between sexuality and spirituality. To separate them would mean to place these two words in
competition with each other, to rate them in acquiesence to white-
European thought, to deny the power of sex/spirit in my life, my
work' (1994: 55).

The joy of sex infused with the spirit doesn't negate the potential value of celibacy, nor does it necessitate perpetual sexual activity; but it does require celebrating the fact of sexual pleasure and
spiritual quest as related in human experience. Just as we can, at

any time, with the stimulus of an image, memory, or suggestion of it, internally celebrate the power of ocean waves without perpetually living on the shores, so can we, at any time, affirm for ourselves or with others the beauty of good sex.

My idea of good sex is pedestrian compared with Madonna's adventuresome approaches, as gasped at in the pages ahead. Given everyone's uneven lifetime access to fulfilling sexual commitment with the right partner(s), I expect she would agree that it's a good idea to have a back-up plan for how to channel one's energies and desires for deep pleasure. Yet, sex and religion, historically linked and mutually eroticized, remain the most commonly exalted means to ecstasy, and Madonna's work reflects on this tradition. As discussed by Margareta Bertilsson, if Nietzsche is right, '"when God is dead", the religion of erotic love will be the one and only means of salvation in the modern world' (1991: 303).

Madonna said as a young woman that she wasn't privately obsessed with sex. This makes sense, given her wide-ranging interests in the arts; the demands on her time, her strenuous, daily physical work-out; and her constant exercise of business power. With her audience she laughed at sex, played with it, was virtually naked, but not intimate or giving; she used sex performance as a shield, a barrier which sustained her power. She treated sex as public theatre, which breaks through the privacy factor into dangerous, collective-voyeurism territory. Her powerful sexual representations on stage appear to have had more to do with her parodic power-plays with masses of anonymous fans than with sex as consummate communication, generosity, and ecstasy. Rarely do her video representations of sex-related activity offer an explicit representation of love, and she is seldom sentimental. And yet, from this cynical posture in an age of romance-novel addiction, she attained a wider following among young women than any female entertainer before her.

Like many others, to the point of cliché, through numerous of her incarnations I have read Madonna as a refreshingly proud Whore in the Mae West tradition, where it's all make-believe. They both popularized cheerful sex and aggressive femaleness. On the stage they liberated themselves from working-class conditions but kept their stereotype working-class personas, exemplified in the direct, brassy put-down. Conspicuously, they acted as free, independent agents. Beyond that, and much more to their credit, they both exposed the foolishness of secrecy about sex by exaggerating and mocking sexual encounters. In the process, especially in Madonna's case, her artistic talent surpassed the parodies she performed. She flaunted her goods with panache, as only a triumphant Whore could do.

Most of us are grateful for any opportunity to sell whatever skills we possess for which the market will pay. As Tania Modleski puts it, 'in reading as in writing one is [one's self] always already a whore' (1991: 42). By virtue of her self-cultivated public celebrity, Madonna invites observers, but she has no control over how she will be read or written. Marilyn Monroe, who, like Madonna, invited the attention of the press but was often disappointed in the results, let it be known that she didn't appreciate being judged by them: 'I don't think I've ever met a writer I'd like as my judge. They observe people, but often they don't feel them ... But I think you've got to love people, all kinds of people, to be able to have an opinion about them that's worth anything ... We can try to be better, and part of trying is not to condemn other people' (quoted in McCann, 1991: 325).

Loving all kinds of people is a reasonable prerequisite to forming (much less expressing) opinions about any of them. I do love all kinds of people, certainly including Madonna, but, given my own values and the workings of my own mind, I'm critical of some of her work. By virtue of exploiting Madonna's celebrity by writing about the way I read her, I, too, am prostituting myself. I'm in awe of her enormous power to anticipate and catalyse cultural trends. I appreciate her wizardry enough to have spent considerable time researching, viewing, listening to, thinking and writing about her work, seeking understanding of her as an icon for our times. Because she has positioned herself in the public eye, and brings focus to important social issues, she *de facto* gives us licence to look at her and, by extension, to think, talk, and write about her. The impulse to pay attention, itself a form of prostitution when offered for remuneration, stems from collective recognition of her phenomenal influence in the world.

Madonna is a woman of historic significance, the triumphant feisty Whore in a tradition to which any self-respecting woman might aspire – if she were not afraid of looking or acting like a *whore*. As Mary Joe Frug put it, 'Anti-prostitution rules terrorize the female body' (1992: 133). Like 'Dyke,' the word 'Whore' is far more powerful when reclaimed and used proudly as a self-reference by women who have earned the accolade than when used as a conventional epithet by those with no understanding or sense of humour. Many of the strongest women in the history of the world have been Whores by one definition or another, public women who took their power, overcame the indifference or contempt of contemporaries, and gained their respect or their fear. Madonna, speaking of Eva Perón, who was accused by her opposition of being a whore, says in her defence: 'the aristocrats and most men ... were completely frightened by the kind of power that she had. And it's always easy, it's the most obvious and predictable way out, to call a woman a whore and imply that she has no morals and no integrity and no talent. And God knows, I can relate to that. It's the oldest trick in the book' (quoted in Udovitch, 1997: 98).

In the Western tradition, the 'whore' epithet has not always been reserved to mean the selling of sex services. Laura Gowing writes of how in sixteenth-century England, 'the word "whore" could be made a symbol for every kind of female misbehaviour' (1994: 29), just as the current U.S. inner-city vernacular 'ho' has gendered meanings apart from sexual connotation. As we approach the end of another millennium, Madonna has successfully trashed every vestigial tradition of public feminine propriety; she has been unruly in the extreme. In other times and places she would have been burned at a stake for the historical equivalent of what she has done on stages and in front of cameras as a young twentieth-century superstar. Instead, given her impeccable sense of timing, she has made a revolving trend of herself in the fashions and rhythms of popular culture. She is a Whore rather than simply a whore, because she figured out how to maximize her talents to phenomenal material advantage, and to radically transgress gender scripts and beat back the censors. In the large picture, her courage benefits women.

In an article on the operatic figure of Carmen, Dick Pels and Aya Crébas discuss the myth of the femme fatale, who is 'the personification of the exotic-erotic, the sphinx who inevitably destroys those unfortunates who succumb to her irresistible charms.' Madonna may have never destroyed anyone – to the contrary, perhaps – but she is described as 'an old-fashioned fatal, vampish type' (Pels and Crébas, 1991: 339, 368 n2). Because such women reject morality-based gender roles, they are treated as 'fair game.' 'While the woman who refuses to submit to the prevailing code of modesty and dependence may therefore feel that she has escaped the constricting "game" of conventional femininity and become free as a bird, she thereby runs the risk of becoming "fair game" in quite another sense ... [At the same time], whorishness becomes sexual frankness ... Social stigmas still potent in the 1950s – evinced by epithets like tramp, vixen or hussy – seem to have become the compliments of the 1980s' (ibid., 340, 346).

As Marx laid it out so clearly, within capitalism it's uncommon to find paid work that doesn't require the prostitution of one asset or another, and it's even more uncommon to be compensated adequately (much less excessively) for one's time and labour, whether or not it's meaningful work. Madonna seems clearer than most of us about what she's willing to sell, and better equipped to locate her own market and to set her own terms. When called a 'whore' or a 'prostitute,' as she frequently is, both disparagingly and with respect, it isn't about selling physical sex. It's about using the body and sexual symbols to capitalize on a consumer society built from and for active libidos. But the Whore, with a capital W, is also a metaphor for the dazzling, triumphant power she exhibits in her work, having made her way to the top of a male-dominant industry and, most extraordinarily, by having maintained control over her many careers at every stage of the journey . She uses her assets, not to seek favours or to submit, but to command, and to maintain through representation the prerogatives of free speech, sexual choices, and agency. She owns her body.

If I had published something about Madonna when she first burst onto the global youth stages, it would have been a different story. I would not have been at all ambivalent. I would have identified her as a strong role model for adolescent girls. She was obviously a disciplined, talented, and well-trained dancer, who rapidly acquired effective songwriting skills, and eventually a voice of note. And she had a captivating presence on the movie screen. But, even more, she was an attitude, an event, a transient phenomenon whom no one I knew in the 1980s took too seriously, because fads don't last. We were wrong. In the mid-1990s, she's still a major cultural force, who for well over a decade has steadily expanded her music/video/film/book empire. Every time a critic notes that her sales are lagging and suggests that she's seen her day, she springs back with a new, creative hook.

Madonna's ubiquitous international presence was underscored in Canada when she was featured in a twenty-four-hour marathon of Madonna videos on the MuchMusic channel (16 January 1992). On 29 November 1994, her thirty-sixth year, the U.S. Fox Network telecast a docudrama, *Madonna: Innocence Lost,* based on Christopher Andersen's biography (1991) and creating a fleeting career for Terumi Mathews, a well-directed Madonna clone. Relatedly, the numbers of academic articles and trade books referencing or focusing on Madonna-as-icon have increased since 1992.

Through audio, video, photography, film, and print, Madonna has been permanently inscribed on the culture, and she is not stopping here. If only because of her particular effect on an entire generation globally, she is worth thinking about, and her work is worth paying attention to, reflexively, in her own time. Through her varied and constantly changing creative personas, Madonna both reflects and helps to invent social values and body-centred cultural trends which are commercially constructed in the context of the United States, and which are distributed as ideology throughout the world.

PAYING ATTENTION

Passive, mindless escape is sufficient reason for me to immerse myself in magazines, movies, soap operas, novels, or music. But when I'm passive in my reading/viewing/listening, I get hooked into the banal sentimentality of it; I cry over soap operas, even when I don't know the characters. When I catch myself getting sucked into feeling sorry for rich, lying, manipulative, exploitive, cruel, shallow, snobbish, phony soap-opera queens, I feel betrayed and embarrassed by myself. If I consciously scrutinize what I'm hearing or seeing, I notice things, such as how even the few sort-of virtuous (if not interesting) female characters on U.S. television soap operas (the good wives) frequently tell lies, among their other lapses from madonna-virtue. The cynicism of the writers is expressed in the ways the characters routinely manipulate, deceive, and torment each other. That the characters of Shakespeare (whose own work has constituted popular culture at various stages of history) have done the same thing is not reassuring.

We can pay attention to pop culture as a way of being ritually neutralized, entertained, and intentionally distracted from pressures and troubles, and, at the same time exercise critical awareness and become more discriminating about what we're willing to take into our personal brain, heart, and body rhythms. If we view the work critically, we can appreciate artistry, even while rejecting the message; we can admire a performer aesthetically without appreciating everything about her material; we can get lost in a story while resisting (by mentally rewriting) its ideological subtext. We can exercise the double vision of simultaneously processing the artist's intention and our own responses, responses constructed from our ways of receiving or reading into the work and investing ourselves in it. When we're open-minded enough to receive something for which we have no frame of reference, and in which we find no point of recognition, we may learn something *or* we may rush to read into it something altogether inappropriate in terms of the artist's intentions. I am confident that I am occasionally guilty of this failure of perception where Madonna is concerned; I'm aware that I don't always understand her.

Middle- and working-class youth, especially males, are the key target group of popular-music advertising. Commonly at this age, for reasons both biological and sociological, the boys are interested in sex, the girls with finding a steady mate, and music is a great accompaniment to and means of expressing both (often conflicting) activities. Industries decide which fare to offer: the kids decide which of the offerings will be a hit. They're the ones who make millionaires of some and paupers of others, even when the latter are as talented as the former. On the cutting edge of the postmodern Western world, young people from their teens into their thirties, are deciding through electronic communications which fare will be offered, and they are producing and exchanging their own musical goods away from the mass market; these underground markets constitute the genesis of the new commercial forms the mass market will take.

For purposes of interpretation and analysis in some of the chapters ahead, I must sometimes explicitly speculate on Madonna's reasons, but I'm in no position to understand her. I'm on firmer ground when I consider the ways I see her as she presents herself, and as she is being received by and affecting our world. Although she is a self-crafted public person – for whom being analysed by strangers is an occupational hazard – she reminds us that she is also a sensitive, vulnerable person, who is asking, not to be criticized, but to be either appreciated or ignored. And I do appreciate Madonna, as a result of paying attention to her. She offers herself as a kaleidoscopic commodity for which a broad spectrum of the consuming public has a steady devotion or recurring curiosity. I'm interested in all our reasons.

Madonna is in no way a fixed identity. What may be an accurate, if partial, description of the public Madonna today is passé by tomorrow. She's a non-static, high-energy work-in-progress, a non-linear self-production who leaps from one persona to another in sometimes seamless and sometimes jagged segues, transgressing conventions, deconstructing and disrupting familiar codes. She is maturing, the times are changing, and she will forever find new ways to express herself.

Upon publication of this book its contents will be history, residue from Madonna's public beginnings – before the baby, before *Evita* – nuggets of stories of herself in process, critical observations and analyses of her significance to those who are drawn to her as to neon light. Neon, unlike natural light, does not usually hold out the promise of enlightenment, but it does seem to promise a good time, and in that the young Madonna delivered big-time.

2

Who Is This Madonna?

On the one side of the ancient Madonna/Whore dichotomy, the Madonna of the male imagination is the purest of women, embodying the patriarchal ideal of the passive, eternal Virgin. The glamorized Whore, on the other hand, who signifies resistance, is presented through the fictions of bad-girl images as asserting herself as an independent agent with entertainment value. As exemplified in the 1930s by Mae West, who was any man's equal, she takes charge of her body, capitalizing on its capacity to spring male fantasy. This whore of the imagination is a woman in business for herself; she would rather exploit and satirize the sexual objectification of women for material advantage than give herself up to the passive-dependent imperatives and quiet dangers of madonna-like femininity. These were the choices in the world to which Madonna was born.

Madonna came by her ironic name honestly. Named for her mother, Madonna Louise Veronica Ciccone was born at the Mercy Hospital in Bay City, Michigan, on 16 August 1958, a Leo. By age twenty-five, Madonna was able to capitalize on her name and transform the madonna image from pure, self-sacrificing mother of pure goodness to satirical exhibitionist and sexual hedonist. She came out as the antithesis of the socially committed 'folk madonnas' of the sixties, epitomized by the three Js – Joan Baez, Joni Mitchell, and Judy Collins – who, despite their humour and cavorting, managed to emit the 'aura of a saint,' and who appealed to 'liberals, freethinkers and socialists' because their 'virtue was simplicity: no artifice, no kitsch, no get-down funk' (Pavletich, 1980: 51).

Madonna exploited myths and stereotypes of both seductive child-woman and provocative grown-up whore. With style and keen marketing skills, and in her themes, she managed to smash the madonna/whore paradigm of polarized sacred innocence and profane evil. No image is sacred. No image is evil. She deconstructed the reductionist, binary categories, and in the process encouraged fans to be as outrageously expressive as their sexual knowledge and capacity for display would allow them. She defiled patriarchal sex and religious symbols and at the same time paid homage to them. The contradictions balance out a widely disparate mass of fans.

Her career opened wide during her 'grunge' period in the mid-1980s, which set a major teenage fashion trend while giving no clues that in 1995 Madonna would be named 'Most Fashionable Artist' at the Fashion and Music Awards in New York. She's a follower of high fashion in the tradition of prominent nineteenth-century Whores, and she pays dearly for the clothing, make-up, hairdressing, and other superficial beauty aids which are requisite to her career. She milked nostalgia in older generations with her reprises of glamorous, voluptuous stars from the past whose celebrity was built on comedic sexuality. In retro mode, she posed as Jean Harlow and variations on 1920s flappers: the *Dictionary of American Slang* defines 'flapper' as 'typically a young woman characterized by a cynical attitude, a frank interest in sex, a penchant for daring fashions' – which describes Madonna, and also speaks to 1995 fashions. Television fall advertising for designer Oscar de la Renta, for example, focused on the '"New" Femininity,' which is straight, old-fashioned Freud. The announcer, a female, narrates voice-over, while, on screen, sleekly coiffed and sexily dressed models, minimalist in their fashions but immodestly aggressive in style, strut and turn. The narrator's voice says, very smoothly but authoritatively, 'The woman is the seducer rather than the one being seduced' (aired on CBS on 19 September 1995 and intermittently thereafter). This is a Madonna message.

When recognizably imitative in her early career, Madonna appeared most often as Marilyn Monroe, with the caveat that, unlike Monroe, Madonna would not be a victim. Her first widely seen impersonation was in her video 'Material Girl' (1985), based on Monroe's diamond-seeking 1950s sexpot in *Gentlemen Prefer Blondes*, a film that was itself a mockery of gender roles. In Madonna's version, the girl doesn't lust for wealth; she goes for true love with the suitor who looks like an ordinary working guy with a battered pickup truck (Kaplan, 1987: 33, 120, 125).

Whereas Marilyn Monroe strategically achieved icon status in part by letting her breasts extend softly from a body that promised easy comfort (before the age of fitness), Madonna charged forth aggressively with cone-shaped breast armour created by bad-boy designer Jean-Paul Gaultier. Even when wearing sensuous gowns and glittering jewellery, and obviously imitating Monroe via her hair, costume, make-up, décolletage, and posturing (as at the 1990 Academy Awards ceremony, to which she was appropriately accompanied by superstar gender-bender Michael Jackson), Madonna brings armour to the enterprise. Her sharp physical angles, dancer's muscles, and jabbing wit give her an edge that is more challenging than invitational. Like Grace Jones, who also wears metal 'lingerie', she seems not to be seeking soft and bemused intimacy with her fans, *à la* Monroe, but control over them.

Academics, as well as journalists, take an interest in Madonna because she is a distinct cultural force, herself a pastiche of changing values. She crosses cultural and moral boundaries with the energy of an electronic rock'n'roll amazon *cum* dancer, movie actor, producer, songwriter, investor, film- and video-maker, author, and fashion trend–setter. She goes for the risks, and publicly rejoices in censorship, which defines her next challenge. She utterly desentimentalizes sex.

Madonna is not the ideal of a romanticized past or the prototype of a fantasized future: she is strictly here-and-now. In 1992, her skill and savvy won her a $60-million five-year contract with Time Warner. She appears to write her own ticket, with real talent buttressed by marketing ingenuity. She owns a major multimedia corporation, Maverick Entertainment, which is signing promising young talent. 'I do what I want,' she says. 'I'm the boss' (Devaney, 1992: 28).

As a public person, Madonna comes across as what Funk and Wagnalls call an 'upstart,' defined as 'one who has suddenly risen from a humble position to one of wealth or importance and is usually arrogant in tone or bearing.' As I see her, she's a vibrant, sassy, dynamic, bright, predictably unpredictable, creative, charismatic, talented presence – who is sometimes crudely contemptuous, arrogant indeed. But her energy and outrageousness may draw our attention even if we don't like her, or she disgusts us, or we worry about her decadent influence on the moral fibre of the planet.

In 1990 one of the leading U.S. business journals, *Forbes* magazine, featured her on the cover as America's number-one businesswoman. She had by then earned more than $500 million in sales for Time Warner. In that year only seven entertainers, all male, generated more money than she did. Since leaving Michigan in the late 1970s, she's purchased homes in three power cities, Manhattan, Los Angeles, and Miami, where she houses world-renowned art collections and circulates with high society. She is routinely on the covers of globally distributed magazines – women's, men's, and teenagers'. In 1990, *Glamour* magazine appointed her Woman of the Year. The same year, *Ladies' Home Journal*, a traditionally conservative magazine, included her with Barbara Bush, the then-president's wife, and Supreme Court Justice Sandra Day O'Connor as among the year's most powerful women in the United States (Andersen, 1991: 345).

By 1993, her celebrity came from the concern, as headlined by *McCall's* magazine, 'How to Protect Your Children from Madonna' (January 1993). She has made a career of being offensive to moralists, and renegade fans by the millions have cheered her on. As a fledgling economic enterprise in the 1980s, Madonna stood alone in a competitive industry in which just over 10 per cent of albums sold and videos on the U.S. Music TeleVision channel (MTV) were by women (Kaplan, 1987: 115). In her myriad successes, she's in a league with industry moguls. She has more power than anyone around her. When asked in an interview for a teen magazine 'Who's your best friend in the whole world?' she replied, 'Me' (*Young and Modern*, 1993: 48). By 1994, at age thirty-six, she had personally amassed $190 million; that year, in an *Esquire* magazine interview with Norman Mailer, she remarked on the isolation generated by the fame that produces such wealth: 'when you perform and there's a hundred thousand people in a stadium, and they're all there because of you ... the responsibility of entertaining that many people in two hours is daunting and exhausting ... Then you go up to your hotel room, and you can't go out because you're too famous ... Yes, everyone adores you in a kind of mass-energy way, but then you're absolutely separated from humanity. It's the most bizarre irony, don't you think?' (Mailer, 1994: 49).

Madonna's career took off in the mid-1980s, when she was still being dismissed as a passing fad and trivialized as a studio-created singer whose first two albums – *Madonna* (1983) and *Like a Virgin* (1984) – were products of engineering ingenuity. Some ingenuity: 'Like a Virgin,' the title track, sold 11 million copies (Gaar, 1992: 334). Her third album, *True Blue* (1986), sold 17 million copies and was a critical as well as popular success. At a time when women were achieving token gains in every avenue of the music industry, and rock artists like Joan Jett were taking charge of their own careers, with *True Blue* Madonna became her own co-producer. It was the world's top-selling 1986 pop album, number one in twenty-one nations. Every subsequent album, to 1995, has reached the Top Ten, with as many as five cuts on singles charts at a given time. In Madonna's early days of success, women's rock groups like the Go-Go's and the Bangles, among many others (beginning with Fanny in the 1960s), came and went as women fought for space. Madonna, who wraps her celebrity around her Self in every medium she crashes, has shown herself to have the mix of clear goals, backing, individualistic grit, and the resilience required for balance and staying power in the entertainment industry.

Launched by Music TeleVision on 1 August 1981 (Gaar, 1992: 323), round-the-clock music video was a logical outcome of lip-synched promotional film-clips, movies featuring rock'n'roll, and popular performers featured on early television variety and dance programs. Along with Cyndi Lauper, a great talent whose feminist values may have short-circuited what might otherwise have been a sustained high-voltage career, and Tina Turner, the most durable of the guiding lights among commercial rock'n'roll women,

Madonna helped pioneer music video. One of her first promotional clips, 'Borderline' (1984), included a nude statue showing male genitalia, just a hint of what was to come. In 'Bad Girl' (1992), Madonna's character smokes too many cigarettes, drinks alcohol, and is watched by an eerie character played by Christopher Walken; she engages in alienated sex, confesses 'I'm not happy,' and in the end she's dead. Not for a minute has Madonna played it safe in her subject-matter.

Madonna is now an acknowledged master of video, which rapidly became the commercial music industry's primary marketing mechanism, as well as a more complex system of musical expression. Norman Mailer, who calls Madonna 'our greatest living female artist,' remarks on her 'high intelligence' and calls her 'the premier artist of music video [which] might be the only new popular art form in American life' (1994: 56).

In her early videos Madonna emerged as an attitude to be reckoned with, and her message seemed clearly aimed at young girls. A lot of older bad girls were likewise cheered by her irreverence; they were also confounded by her contradictions. For example, in 'Papa Don't Preach' (1986), a pregnant teenager defies her father (played by Danny Aiello) and decides to keep her baby. The defiance was encouraging, but the song was widely interpreted as an anti-abortion statement. For this she was praised by anti-abortionists, who otherwise abhor Madonna, and protested by abortion-rights activists alarmed at the spectre of a growing generation of young single mothers on the path to permanent poverty for themselves and their children (Andersen, 1991: 221).

Three decades earlier, Marilyn Monroe presented images of irreverent receptivity, teasing men into believing she adored and needed them. She was born in 1926 and died in 1962 at age thirty-six (when Madonna was four years old and her mother was dying). Marilyn Monroe's death touched the soul of her nation; her sin was her sex, and in effect it killed her. The sex goddess, whose body was a freak gift of nature, died the tragic female martyr's sacrificial death, before entropy could take its course and age her voluptuous beauty. Madonna challenges women, no less than men, to be irreverently assertive. She asserts a 'woman's right to pleasure without guilt or moral recriminations, sex as fun rather than something which should be taken too seriously' (Garratt, 1986: 13). Madonna's sexualized personas seldom suggest a tragic ending; only rarely does she capitalize on women's vulnerability.

Less a work of nature than a purposefully self-created work of art, Madonna has moulded herself from the materials of a plastic society. We would expect her to conquer the exigencies of old age with the same brassy rudeness with which she conquered the exigencies of being a working-class white girl who wanted to be in show business. She was a straight-A student throughout high school, in the top 2 per cent of her class, and reportedly has an IQ over 140. She studied and taught dance (Gaar, 1992: 333), and was the founder of the high-school drama club and took the lead in every production (Andersen, 1991: 38).

For one and a half years, she studied dance at the University of Michigan, on a scholarship obtained for her by her dance teacher, Christopher Flynn. In her early days in New York (and briefly in Paris) as an aspiring rock singer, dancer, and actress, Madonna honed the technique of focusing on herself in a way that compelled others to pay attention to her. In 1980 she acted in *A Certain Sacrifice*, demonstrating naked poise in a violent film which she later denounced (Andersen 1991: 75). She became the shimmering subject and object of her own gaze, as refracted by the camera. She thrust her middle finger into the air and proceeded to both expropriate and defy mainstream pop, black, and Latino music formulas.

Among the many entrepreneurs who discovered Madonna during her early career, Seymour Stein, head of Sire Records (who later 'discovered' Madonna's friend k.d. lang), seemed to have been particulary attuned to Madonna's transgressive sexual power. He could see that she could have appeal for gays and lesbians without being threatening to heterosexuals (Starr, 1994: 203). Stein's prescience paid off, and by now Madonna has demonstrated more than adequately that she has the talent, personality, power, body, brains, courage, constancy, and staff (especially, for many years, publicist Liz Rosenberg and manager Freddy DeMann) to hold or recapture an audience. Her appeal crosses a cultural and, to some extent, generational spectrum. Even when I think I've outgrown her, she turns my head because she's changed, again.

More than most women in the late twentieth century, Madonna creates choices on her own terms, and holds power which befits the mythical Whore. As super-fan Camille Paglia puts it, 'I perceive Madonna's strutting sexual exhibitionism not as cheapness or triviality but as the full, florid expression of the whore's ancient rule over men' (1992: 11). Madonna channels sexual titillation through every technological venue of the mass media, and has influenced the lives of millions of young people globally. On the negative side, she reifies harmful gender myths: to boys she says that girls' bodies are for the taking, and that girls like to receive *and* inflict pain; to girls she says that boys can be seduced and controlled. At the same time, she breaks with these old scripts through gender-bending performances.

For example, in a 1986 video, 'Open Your Heart,' Madonna plays a peep-show porn worker, entertaining very pathetic men in their little booths. She then metamorphoses from the slutty character to an attractive androgyne who joins up with a young boy wearing a grey suit to match her own, whom she kisses sweetly on the lips before they laughingly skip down the road, hand in hand, into a wholesome country scene. For this video she was criticized both for playing the whore and for glorifying child abuse. In my reading, the kiss was innocent and her relationship with the boy was reciprocally, playfully respectful, and not suggestive of sexual intent or power plays – as a distinct alternative to a world in which pathetic men sit in boxes and put coins in boxes for peeks at sexy women writhing pathetically in boxes of their own.

In this video I see Madonna smashing dirty sex secrets by bringing the camera into the peep show, and then following a path of renewed innocence with the familiar referents of children and nature. As I read it, the little boy who scampers off into the countryside with Madonna is not likely to become a peep-show customer when he grows up, and for me that's the point of the advice to 'open your heart' – to get out of those closed, claustrophobic, dangerous, lonely fear closets, find a friend, and appreciate natural beauty and simple joy.

Like postmodernists in academia and cutting-edge media, Madonna uses both experimental and conventional devices to take it all apart, mix it up, and make new sense of it. Rigorous attention to context has elevated the potential for authenticity of representation in both cultural performance and scholarly research. Identity politics as an expression of context is framed overtly by one's individual world-view as a product of one's collective, historical social identity. By contrast, media entertainments promote a fractured kind of decontextualized and detached individualism. Frith observes that 'the most astute video stars, like Madonna, give meaning to their ever-changing imagery in the narrative of their own careers' (1988: 216). As if seeking synthesis, Madonna 'pastes the traditional virgin onto the traditional whore, hoping to get rid of a polarity that no longer makes sense' (Kaplan, 1987: 133). Her appeal is grounded in her contradictions.

3

Grist for Feminist Thinking

Feminists, given the diversity of our social, political, and personal identities and agendas, have had mixed views in appraising Madonna's value or harm to women and young people in her early career, and her defiance of or collusion with patriarchal cultural traditions. On the one hand, Madonna's celebration of myriad sexual identities breaks down taboos and clears more cultural space for sex as a human commonplace with significant variations. On the other hand, a young person learning about sex from Madonna in the late 1980s and early 1990s could easily have formed the impression that everyday sex includes multiple partners, 'seductive' children, and sadomasochism with dark meanings underscored by religious symbols.

The issues of sadomasochism and sexual adventurism are divisive among feminists, and there is no agreement at all concerning pornography or censorship (cf. Willis, 1983; Lacombe, 1994; Easton, 1994). Advocating a 'feminist sexual ethics' which recognizes sexual diversity, but which is cognizant of the effects of power relations, Mariana Valverde stated in 1985 that 'it would be a contradiction in terms to develop a "feminist morality," a code of rights and wrongs based on some arbitrary notion of individual feminist virtue' (203). This is not, however, to reduce feminism to moral relativism of the kind that obstructed early international feminist protests against cliterodectomies, sex-based selective abortion, and suttee practices. It may be a woman's 'choice' to torture her daughter and pre-empt her daughter's chances for sexual pleasure; abort only female foetuses; or throw herself on her dead husband's funeral pyre, to be burned alive. But these are choices based on inherited, coercive, culturally imposed sex/gender principles that are harmful to women and children, and are antithetical to any conceivable definition of feminism.

Some self-identified feminists, notably sex educator, author, and activist Pat Califia (1980, 1981), have engaged in defences of consensual adult sadomasochism. Referring to herself as a sex radical, Gayle Rubin, in her classic 1984 essay, considers essentialist-feminist anti-porn rhetoric to be in collusion with the right wing, and the invocation of inflammatory S/M symbols as a means of protesting pornography to be a dangerous trend which denies women's desires. She exults that, although the second-wave 'women's movement may have produced some of the most retrogressive sexual thinking this side of the Vatican ... it has also produced an exciting, innovative ... defense of sexual pleasure and erotic justice' (1984: 298, 302). Critical of certain 'exciting' innovations, and echoing Audre Lorde (1987), Celia Kitzinger remarks that 'taking pleasure in sex scenes which enact power struggles, or which play with the symbols of fascism, may reflect the measure of our complicity in our own and other people's oppression' (1994: 197).

Kitzinger acknowledges the growing confessional evidence that many women have masochistic fantasies (just as Freud proclaimed, but for very different reasons), deriving pleasure from being subordinate in sexual relations, whether between a woman and man, or two women. She discusses reasons for women's reluctance to acknowledge those fantasies. In Madonna's S/M performances, she was, in effect, sending the message that 'whatever turns you on' is okay. (Madonna also, however, later insisted that she herself did not engage in S/M practices, and that her sadomasochistic representations were strictly theatrical, playful, ironic performance, and that she was just having fun with it.) As Kitzinger discusses, 'We live in a culture in which sex is defined in terms of dominance and submission' (1994: 204). Power imbalance was central to the erotic in the modern age, and in every age power abuse is deliberately eroticized not only in pornography, but in everyday lives. The images of pain-loving women are generally by, for, and about men, but according to their own testimony some women do want to feel overpowered (Friday, 1973), just as some women apparently want to be dominant.

One might reasonably expect most feminists, with Valverde (1985), to condemn the patriarchal, capitalist, and racist structures, socializations, and abuses that produce (and capitalize on) alienated desires. In her discussion of pornography, Dany Lacombe (1994: 62) problematizes this social-constructionist position, which suggests that women have been 'manipulated by a totalizing system of oppression.' In Lacombe's strongly argued anti-censorship position, feminists who isolate certain chosen sexual practices as perverse, and dismiss felt needs as 'false consciousness,' are delegitimizing diversity and the fact of choice and human agency. The beauty of Madonna is that she couldn't pass *any* test of political correctness. Relative to the justificatory claim of consensus in S/M, Drucilla Cornell states: 'Within the sadomasochistic system of gender representation in which the masculine is on top and the feminine is on the bottom, the only alternative is reversal of *power*. One is either a slave, or a master. The political goal of empowerment can only be obtained by reversing the hierarchy. But the hierarchy is not dismantled, even if women were to take the upper position ... our political struggle for power must be informed by a challenge to phallic logic itself' (1993: 100).

As a young girl Madonna wanted to be a movie star, or a nun, like her teachers at Catholic school. She saw them as powerful women, 'superstars ... superhuman, beautiful, fantastic people.' At the same time, she remembers the nuns punishing her for 'mouthing off' by washing her mouth out with soap; when that didn't silence her, they taped her mouth shut (Andersen, 1991: 27). She rebelled, in her words, 'against the church [and the] laws decreed by my father, which were dictated through the church ... I never told the priest what I thought I'd really done wrong. I'd make up other, smaller crimes ... I don't practice Catholicism now. The Catholic Church completely frowns on sex ... Catholicism is extremely sexist' (Fisher, 1991: 39–40).

Like that of many Protestant religions, Catholic morality orders all of life as good or evil, dichotimized. In traditional Catholic societies, women who offended against gender proprieties were called 'whores,' even when they didn't exchange their sex for material gain. Madonna markets contradictions, the profane, wannabe nun who disdains sexual boundaries and chauvinist moralities but who, at the same time, was quick to protest the sacrilege when Sinéad O'Connor tore in half a picture of the Pope on the popular satirical *Saturday Night Live* television program. Madonna subsequently went on the show, on 16 January 1993, and tore in half a photo of middle-aged Joey Buttafuoco (whose teenage mistress, at his bidding, shot his wife), mocking O'Connor with the admonition to 'fight the real enemy.' Given Madonna's own sacrilegious use of Catholic symbols and her criticisms of the Church, one can wonder at this perhaps hypocritical gesture even while appreciating her sideline feminism, which challenges the morality codes, if not the hierarchy, of the Church.

Like O'Connor, Madonna appears to be a compulsive icon-smasher, and she spent a good part of 1993 defending her right to rub national flags against her crotch during her concerts on her 'Girlie Show' tour. Citizens and politicians in Australia, Puerto Rico, Brazil, Germany, and Thailand attempted to ban her live concerts and TV videos on the grounds of obscenity (*Vancouver Sun*, 28 September 1993: C6). Given the active sex trades in each of these countries, this is a remarkable charge. In Australia she also offended Aboriginal elders 'when she played with a "didgeridoo," a long tube-like wind instrument traditionally untouched by women' (*Vancouver Sun*, 30 November 1993: C6).

In common with punks of the 1980s, Madonna finger-flipped every social convention, but she did it from within the realm of acquired privilege. Madonna appears to celebrate human diversity in her themes and with the singers, dancers, and crews she hires to work on records, tours, and videos – African Americans and Latinos, young and old, gays and lesbians, and so forth. But at bottom, her work is so Madonna-centred that she doesn't take the fact of difference into account. In a discussion of punk culture and feminism, Kathleen Pirrie Adams notes how punk girls disdained middle-class-victim imagery in a way that promoted feminist independence, but denied important realities of difference that left some girls getting hurt and feeling like failures. As Pirrie Adams analyses it, 'escape from the 'victim scenario,' with its implicit renunciation of categorical gender oppositions, often mobilized a rhetoric of individual self-assertion that tended towards an obscuring of actual historical differences: in capacities, resources, confidence, and opportunity' (1991: 26).

On the one hand, Madonna advocates freedom from socially constructed sexual hang-ups, which presumes a natural sexuality that can be recovered. On the other hand, she is creatively and critically aware that she is herself constructing and commercially producing contemporary sexual knowledges. She isn't seeking original 'truth' so much as she is reiterating variations on anti-establishment truths for fun and profit, at the risk of being distinctly anti-feminist. With the October 1992 *Vanity Fair* spread of Madonna posed as a seductress of approximately twelve years of age (Orth, 1992), and the publication the same year of her masculine-gaze soft-porn book, *Sex* (Madonna, 1992), the media space she commanded exploded. Both mainstream and gay bookstores had difficulty meeting the demand (Griffin, 1992a: B7). As one store owner accurately predicted, Madonna 'is able to create such interest in herself and her sexuality [her book] will be the biggest thing of the year' (quoted in Griffin, 1992b: A3).

In her sexual advocacies, Madonna represents the most permissive and least judgmental end of the pop-culture sexual-liberation spectrum. She poses effective resistance to the opposite pole, as represented by Miss California 1996, third runner-up to Miss America, who proclaimed in the globally broadcast ceremony (16 September 1995) that her platform is to promote sexual abstinence. She represents a movement of chastity clubs among conservative and religious adolescents and young adults (especially girls), coinciding functionally with AIDS risk and family-values rhetoric. Madonna works actively to promote AIDS prevention. But her view of sex is that it is dangerous to hide it, suppress it, and pretend it isn't a real and compelling desire, which is going to be acted out by young people however much others might protest.

Madonna's fascination with lust and unfettered passion, sometimes violent, sometimes fanciful, even sometimes romantic but seldom uncomplicated was publicly displayed at every turn in the early 1990s. At the party to launch the *Sex* book, the decor was reported as resembling 'a dungeon worthy of the Marquis de Sade, featuring models in leather and mesh, acting out fantasies with whips, handcuffs and heavy-duty chains.' Madonna, shelving her dominatrix leather and paraphernalia, came dressed as a voluptuous Heidi, clutching a toy lamb (*People*, 1992: 57).

In her *Vanity Fair* photo layout, Madonna cheerfully exploits the seductive, provocative, child sex-kitten image without any apparent consciousness of how she might be colluding with actual child abuse. She wears bobby sox, a short child's dress (with bulging décolletage), and pigtails, and postures herself and sets her facial expressions in coy Lolita come-ons. This photo spread is viewed by bell hooks as an 'opportunistic attempt to sustain the image that she can be forever young' (1994: 12), compounding feminist issues of child abuse with issues of ageing and femininity.

Prior to the appearance of the *Sex* and *Vanity Fair* publications in 1992, Susan McClary suggested that perhaps Madonna was a healthy breakthrough, that what North American pop culture needed was a 'woman musician who can create images of desire without the demand within the discourse itself that she be destroyed' (1990: 5) – a girl who likes sex and doesn't get punished for it. Indeed, this attitude is her primary attraction to her fans and her critics alike: the bad girl who is rewarded for her sins. But with the *Vanity Fair* photos and the *Sex* book, Madonna lost a lot of her older fans and credibility; 1992 was the year of Madonna's breakthrough from playing primarily to an adolescent audience to going for a much more lucrative R-rating.

It's easy to agree with Madonna's pronouncements about (safe) sex as something to be celebrated, free of hang-ups or external constraints. The question is how S/M props – symbols of force – can be complementary to or representative of the celebration of consensual sex or liberation of any kind. Rather than deconstructing the phallus as parody, she adopts it as her instrument of gender resistance, which is as nonsensical as a feminist wanting to be a man. Feminisms by definition are grounded in women's experiences. Similarly, in the *Sex* book well-known heterosexual women assume 'lesbian' or bisexual postures from the perspective of a male-identified gaze for the apparent purpose of entertaining men. Madonna's style in this period suggests more interest in rebelling against women than in rebelling against women's pre-scribed roles *vis-à-vis* men, and tells us nothing at all about Madonna's own desires.

While trying and failing to understand S/M as feminist practice, an entirely second-hand, academic endeavour on my part, I came upon a self-admonition from Josef Breuer, Freud's colleague, who had difficulty with all Freud's sex talk: 'But what have my taste and my feeling about what is seemly and what is unseemly to do with the question of what is true?' (quoted in Cuddihy, 1987: n. 90). As for Madonna's playful treatment of sadomasochism, which emerged long after I had begun this project and befuddled me, she did indeed make commonplace that which I and many others had avoided as something we didn't want to see, hear, or even know about.

I've now been persuaded in theory, by people who know, that someone who has been abused, or who has unresolved control issues with parents or other authority figures, might feel empow-ered by being in control with a willing partner. Someone who has been controlling could learn surrender. It could be mutually cathartic to negotiate the terms and to trade places, or to know up front that the one on the bottom is in charge, or to explicitly take into account the issues of power present in most sexual encoun-ters. Some people may be drawn to sadomasochism for 'therapeu-tic' catharsis, acting out desires to give or receive pain in a negoti-ated environment. According to one beautiful, intelligent woman of my acquaintance who prostitutes as a dominatrix, the men who come to her are very clearly seeking therapy. She and others believe that controlled S/M diverts men who might otherwise commit rape. This is similar to the pornography catharsis theory, but the evidence is contradictory. On the one hand, rapists and killers who are addicted to porn as a turn-on and guide, like Ted Bundy, crave progressively more violent porn to satisfy their fantasies, and finally search out live bodies to assault and destroy. On the other hand, most consumers of pornography are not rapists or killers.

Madonna's early career was built around her being a bad girl. In many respects the 'bad girl' image was a euphemism for 'working-class girl,' and it was more from class bias than sexual prudishness that she was so harshly criticized. Nevertheless, she played up aggressive sexuality as her *modus operandi*, and her bad-girl image reached its apex when she tuned into S/M as entertainment. She defended herself on the grounds that, if men can do it, so can she, which from her point of view is a kind of feminism.

The notion of S/M as *feminist* practice is contested in part because the very word 'feminism' has become troublesome and takes on a reactionary connotation in certain circles. I use the word (though increasingly with defensiveness or a need to explain what I mean by it) because it has for three decades held deep, mul-tidimensional personal and political meanings for me. It identifies grassroots, political, theoretically informed activist movements of women struggling for rights, freedoms, and justice all over the globe, as well as academic and community theorists and research-ers who are themselves often publicly activist. The infinite varieties of feminism all share in common (with infinite particularities) an active challenge to sex/gender inequities and power abuses. In this broadly defined feminist context, games of power which sig-nify pain and oppression are hard to grasp as sexual liberation; why would women who critique power abuses wish to dominate men or one another? It's very much a subjectively informed dilemma. Given that so many activist feminists have been focused on reducing male violence, the notion that women can find plea-sure in deliberately inflicted pain, or simulations thereof, is not easy for everyone to understand either viscerally or intellectually. If one consents to being abused, is one therefore not abused? Does the reach for desire's goal (to dominate or to be overpowered) supersede the actual or symbolic harm caused by the humiliation? What do we make of, as Jon Simons says in his discussion of Fou-cault, 'the invention of new pleasures, utilizing the unruliness of desires that might be denounced but cannot quite be ignored' (1995: 100)? From the vantage point of gender consciousness, we need to ask *whose* pleasures? *whose* unruly desires?

The ecstatic high of the S/M experience, when achieved, is

described as 'out-of-mind-and-body' and as transgressing the 'boundaries of the self' (ibid.). This potentiality can explain the attraction of bondage for men who feel culturally or familially pressured to aspire towards privileged masculinity, men seeking an antidote to the compulsion to cultivate the persona of an individualized, commanding Self, to be in control in every situation, and to not recoil from violence when it is the 'manly' thing to do. This doesn't explain in positive terms, beyond phallic envy, what the appeal would be for Others, for Woman, who by the terms of the Enlightenment was refused Selfhood. Women might well appreciate opportunities to experience dominance, but few women need practice at the experience of subordination. Pleasures involving scripted pain, slave symbols like leather collars, and tools of torture or confinement do not transgress so much as feed in the shadows of hierarchical, patriarchal power relations which are built on exclusion, subjugation, and pain (cf. Linden et al., 1982).

Richard von Krafft-Ebing, the titled German neurologist and psychiatrist who late in the nineteenth century coined the term 'masochism,' defined it as 'the wish to suffer pain and be subjected to force' (1886: 86). From his point of view, joined by that of Freud, women are masochistic by nature. In the absence of any structural analysis of socialization and power relations, this would explain why women have been mainstay parishioners in those religious bodies which are most sadistic or punitive in their orientation. Among Christians, Madonna's Catholic Church in particular has celebrated (and inflicted) suffering, and women must suffer by virtue of being women, by having descended from Eve. This widely accepted theologically based condemnation, evidenced historically by the material reality of power relations, created conditions for men to be sadists. Bram Dijkstra observes of the nineteenth century that 'men everywhere came to demand that marriage be the continuous enactment of a master-slave ritual that would fulfill in fantasy their search for a power which escaped them in real life ... Physicians, sexual researchers, and anthropologists came running in to prove that ever since the world began and wherever humanity had settled, woman's natural pleasure was to suffer' (1986: 116). Contemporary practices don't always hinge on fixed gender roles. Roles can change any time in a fluid exchange of eroticized power. But when Madonna says in interviews, regarding sadomasochism, that mutual consent is the key, she is denying the reality that women and men do not commonly share the same notion of or resources requisite to consent, and that imbalanced power dynamics privilege the male's interpretation and sense of rights.

Mariana Valverde comments that 'there is not much creativity in the constant breaking of taboos' unless it is accompanied by 'an examination of why certain things are taboos and not others' (Valverde, 1985: 201). She goes on to analyse a hypothetical scenario: 'If a woman truly wants to wear high heels and a corset and be tied to her bed by a macho man in cowboy boots, we are not given a way to understand her "honest" desire as being socially instilled. I certainly would not want to "shame" the woman or tell her not to do what she wants to do. But I would not call her activity part of women's liberation. The content of her desire was produced by sexism. In enacting it she is perhaps being "a naughty girl" and challenging Puritanism, but gender relations remain intact' (ibid.).

This point of view follows from the work of Michel Foucault, for whom 'the knowing subject is not the producer of knowledge but rather one of its effects' (Braidotti, 1991: 79). My difficulty in understanding sadomasochism, 'intergenerational sex,' or any other sexual pleasure based on actual or re-enacted power imbalance as feminist practice may put me in Paglia's category of the puritanical feminist. I do, in writing about this, feel a bit like Jerry Falwell scolding and wagging my finger at an unrepentant Larry Flynt. But despite respected friends who passionately challenge the limits of my understanding and the obstinance of my will, I don't comprehend the liberatory quality of Madonna's S/M representations in the *Sex* book. It may simply be a generational problem. It no longer alarms me that some feminists enjoy S/M activity (though Madonna says she doesn't, that for her it's only about performance), but I can't interpret it as feminist practice any more than going to church is apt to be feminist practice, even though many feminists go to church – a practice which may or may not inform their feminism but not derive from it.

The diversity among feminists in our material conditions, familied experiences, and social identities and values has caused problems in attempts to define 'shared moral and political principles,' and in attempts to agree on what constitutes politically correct sexuality (cf. Dimen, 1984: 140). It may be anti-feminist to even raise the question. Those of us defending ourselves against charges of puritanism in our reactions against representations of pleasure in pain and/or confinement see those conditions as a concrete as well as symbolic anti-feminist game of eroticizing degradation and abuse. Just as some women who have been raped and beaten apparently find relief or ecstasy in sadomasochism, others are repelled by the violent echoing catalysed by the imagery: to my knowledge, the consent factor is never present in the memory of being unwillingly assaulted, however much others may insist she wanted it. Fear cannot produce legitimate consent.

That Madonna would cheerfully pose as a sexualized, seductive preadolescent in pigtails challenges her identification with feminism, but Paglia says, 'Madonna is the true feminist. She exposes the puritanism and suffocating ideology of [North American] feminism, which is stuck in an adolescent whining mode' (1992: 4). Maybe, but I think the issues raised by sadomasochistic representations are much more political and problematic than either Paglia or Madonna allows. Most seriously in terms of potential consequences, they both overestimate the ironic sophistication of those youth on whom Madonna has had the greatest influence. Further, in these times of global neo-Nazi proliferations, I heed hooks's assessment of the implications of Madonna's *Sex* book: 'Madonna's appropriation of the identity of the European actress Dita and of her Germanic couture is an obvious gesture connecting her to a culture of fascism, Nazism, and white supremacy, particularly as it is linked to sexual hedonism' (1994: 19). Given the historical surfeit of totalitarian governments, persecutions, and holocausts, it's anachronistic to isolate Germany as a singularly guilty nation. Further, the 'Germanic couture' of some of the photos consists simply of a studded leather bikini with net stockings, and variations thereof. For the most part, at least half of Dita/Madonna is naked. But hooks's point is well taken. Even allowing for the wide range of ideologies in the name of feminism, by any plausible definition feminism would be incompatible with 'fascism, Nazism, and white supremacy.' It's just not entirely clear that Madonna is guilty of formulating these associations in the *Sex* book so much as she is enacting love-making or sex-taking in every possible configuration, including that of soft sadomasochism as a trendy, leather, counter-cultural phenomenon in the early 1990s, to which she contributed legitimacy. Her steady gift is anticipating the next trend and presenting herself as a mainstream prototype.

Madonna herself is apparently neither antagonistic towards nor informed about contemporary women's movements, and all the different points of view that travel in the name of feminism. As an *artiste* she has no particular responsibility to study feminist theories, or even to think about these things. Nevertheless, in 1987 she opened herself up to interrogation when she expressed qualified identification with a feminist orientation: 'I don't think about the work I do in terms of feminism. I certainly feel that I give women strength and hope, particularly young women. So in that respect, I feel my behavior is feminist, or my art is feminist. But I'm certainly not militant about it, nor do I exactly premeditate it' (quoted in Gilmore, 1987: 87).

Seven years later, in 1994, Norman Mailer used an interview with Madonna to release more of his notorious rancour against feminists. He suggests that her formidable, 'ugly' Jean-Paul Gaultier breast cones invoked age-old fears in men that women will take over entirely, and withdraw their nurturing, soft bodies. In the world of his fears, 'you get the equivalent of a Stalin or a Hitler among the women ... I can see the day when a hundred male slaves will be kept alive and milked every day and the stuff will be put in semen banks to keep the race going. No more than a hundred men will have to be maintained alive at any time' (1994: 50). From listening to what they say, I am confident that many disheartened women, especially among heterosexual women who struggle unsuccessfully day to day in their intimate relations with men, would find some fantasy pleasure in Mailer's fears. But after his prolonged lament on how her metal breasts signify a concession to mythical man-hating feminists (who deprive men of natural succour), Madonna, with pointed irony, lumps Mailer with the feminists as having a limited sense of women's power: 'My whole thing is you use all you have, *all* you have, your sexuality, your femininity, your – any testosterone you have inside of you, your intellect – use whatever you have ...' (Mailer, 1994: 50). Taking her own power for her own purposes, Madonna renders both feminist and anti-feminist critics irrelevant. She came in with her own agenda, which corresponded with a generational shift in feminist identities. The cultural tension between her feminist and anti-feminist critics produces precisely the cultural opening for Madonna and other forthrightly risqué female performers. The legitimacy of female sexual assertiveness is renegotiated. The norms are sufficiently challenged that genuine choices assert themselves.

Even when she plays softly to loving themes, Madonna projects an independence of mind which can be readily identified with a particular idiosyncratic and individualistic feminist outlook. As Lisa Lewis suggests, 'it is her ability to represent gender experience symbolically in the characters she creates that provides points of identification for a female audience' (1990: 104). In 1985, two seventeen-year-old girls quoted in *Time* magazine offer examples of how she had this kind of influence early in her career: 'She's sexy but she doesn't need men ... she's kind of there by herself' and 'She gives us ideas. It's really women's lib, not being afraid of what guys think' (Skow, 1985: 59). Agreeing with them, my goddaughter, Merunka, a university science student, says of Madonna, 'I hate it when people criticize her and say that she's a whore ... I really looked up to her as a kid. I still do.' Madonna herself suggests that women and girls who have self-respect don't need to worry about men's opinions. And yet she appears to direct her gaze to men in the posture of one who, in fact, does seek to gain their approval, even as she defies their authority.

With reference to the oft-cited work of John Fiske (1987), Susan Bordo observes: 'For the "wanna-bes," Madonna modeled the possibility of a female heterosexuality that was independent of patriarchal control, a sexuality that defied rather than rejected the male gaze, teasing it with her *own* gaze, deliberately trashy and vulgar, challenging anyone to call her a whore, and ultimately not giving a damn what judgements might be made of her' (1993: 282–3). Although this is a persuasive characterization, few young girls are likely, in their lifetime, to have the luxury of 'not giving a damn' about other people's (and especially men's) judgments. Girls and women have been locked up throughout history for being 'trashy and vulgar' (Chesney-Lind and Shelden, 1992; Faith, 1993b). It's encouraging to think that Madonna might be envisioning a world wherein females will be 'independent of patriarchal control,' but she rarely lets us see that vision in her art. Her attachment to hierarchy (as long as she's on top) contradicts her challenge to patriarchal relations, which can accommodate token women in high places.

The word 'pornography' derives from the Greek words *pornē* and *graphō,* meaning 'the writing of prostitutes'. As periodically debated and defined by feminists, the media, the religious right, legislatures, and the courts, in its modern usage the word carries the connotations of obscenity, degradation, sin, physical exploitation, and obstruction to women's and children's equality (cf. Lacombe, 1994). Madonna, who very successfully sold her versions of pornography in the commercial marketplace, has written herself on the culture at large. She has inscribed her sexual identities on the psyches of millions of children, adolescents, and adults in dozens of nations, on half a dozen continents. Some of her best work is deeply erotic; much of it is comically parodic or dramatic exposition of the worst clichés about sex; and much of it, by design or effect, pornographically exploits, and even celebrates, the dominance–submission model which has resulted, in the real world, in women's and children's victimization. That women can be on top is not reassuring.

'Whore' is claimed as a subversive category by those already labelled and condemned in much the same way that lesbian-feminists of a certain sensibility appropriated the epithets 'dyke' and 'queer,' as proud identity statements. I claim for Madonna a label she would probably reject for herself. In my reading of her, she sees herself as an artist commited to the *artifice* of performance. She uses her artful pretences to expose the hypocrisies and vanities of non-artful conventions. At the same time, she never exceeds that which the most libertarian components of her broad audience are prepared to tolerate. Her staged transgressions are profitable, not because they sometimes challenge hegemonic power relations, but because they so often do not.

I celebrate Madonna's border-crossings, but her mis/representations are effectively parodic only in those moments when she loses herself and fleetingly suspends her role-playing to become that which she parodies, and perhaps desires as identification. In these priceless moments, on record, stage, video, or film, she displaces the artificial terms of engagement with her subject. She is most convincing to me when she appears taken in by her own invention of Self, and in that process she becomes that which she strives to illuminate through invention or imitation. She is, in such moments, proving that she can act.

The issue of feminism is recurrent. Because Madonna apparently considers her work to be consistent with the goals of women's movements, she is openly perplexed by feminists who criticize her. Her perplexity is shared by other 'sexual dissidents' (Dollimore, 1991). As Madonna says, 'Being a sexual being does not cancel out being a feminist' (MuchMusic, 1996). She also protests what she perceives as differential treatment based on sex/gender: 'I get so much bad press for being overtly sexual ... When someone like Prince, Elvis, or Jagger does the same thing, they are being honest, sensual human beings. But when I do it: "Oh, please. Madonna, you're setting the women's movement back a million years,"' (Andersen, 1991: 157).

At least in theory, most feminists seem to agree that imitating masculinist postures can't constitute liberation for either women or men. For example, the struggle of some women for the right to combat duty in war is often supported by feminists in principle, but many others oppose legitimizing a destructively masculinist tradition. That is, simply transgressing the feminine doesn't constitute feminism. Madonna's performance in particular 'is emblematic of the confused way women are represented in popular culture' (Danuta Walters, 1995: 3). Responses to Madonna similarly reveal not only clear identity differences among her spectators, but the confusions of trying to correlate identity formations with popular representations of the options. Sexual fantasies and fetishes in Madonna's work may be her own, or they may be contrived, borrowed, or inspired by muses. They appear liberated only because it is a woman expressing them. Coward discusses how 'publicly sanctioned fantasies confirm men's power, women's subordination' (1985: 203). Women's fantasies, in whatever different shapes they may take, and whether represented by male or female performers, are only beginning to make it onto the public stage. Women who put themselves out there, as Madonna has done, women who are doing it for themselves, can be seen only as role reversals defined by a masculine standard. To be accepted by the amorphous 'mainstream,' outrageous women must present themselves as mockery or satire – the lip-biting, eyeball-rolling, tongue-in-cheek messages that 'she doesn't really mean it.' Spectators are left to their own devices.

Madonna routinely puts a cheerful spin on her work, and her campier routines in the late 1980s borrowed heavily from gay camp, the prototype, instead of from the much less stylized lesbian camp then emerging in venues that were less accessible than gay clubs. Elspeth Probyn points out that 'one of camp's most obvious and serious pleasures is precisely the way in which any truth becomes yet another conceit to be played with' (1992: 505). I live in a neighbourhood in Vancouver's West End which is heavily populated by gays to whom both straight and gay merchants cater and where camp is highly valued. Evidence that she's appreciated by those from whom she borrows is that one routinely hears her music being played in commercial establishments up and down the street.

Dollimore says of camp: 'it is situated at the point of emergence of the artificial from the real, culture from nature – or rather when and where the real collapses into artifice, nature into culture; camp restores vitality to artifice, and vice versa, deriving the artificial from, and feeding it back into or as, the real. The reality is the pleasure of unreality' (1991: 312). Madonna's images of women 'loving' women mimic *un*real stereotypes of glam-butch women poised with masculine props. In the more glamorous routines, she appears as if in drag, which is part of her appeal to camp culture in the tradition of Judy Garland and Bette Midler. In imitating gay camp and drag culture, masters of gender deceit through parody of women, Madonna imitates the master imitators. She strikes poses which imitate camp, which imitates women (or some variation thereof), and, in the process, transgresses gender and (imitations of) heterosexuality. As stated by Judith Butler in 1990, '*in imitating gender, drag implicitly reveals the imitative structure of gender itself – as well as its contingency*' (137, emphasis in original). In this sense, Madonna is working for women resisting indoctrinations of femininity, women who break the mould. But, as Butler commented more recently, 'there is no necessary relation between drag and subversion' (1993: 125). There's nothing new in women imitating men's representations of women. Consonant with Butler's analysis, drag may service the same gender norms it disparages: 'drag is a site of a certain ambivalence, one which reflects the more general situation of being implicated in the regimes of power by which one is constituted and, hence, of being implicated in the very regimes of power that one opposes' (ibid.).

Safe drag produced as 'high het entertainment,' of which Madonna's work has been representative, has the effect of fortifying 'the heterosexual regime' (ibid., 126), in part because it is understood to be play-acting. Straight drag films such as *Victor/Victoria; To Wong Foo, Thanks for Everything, Julie Newmar;* and *Birdcage* evoke heterosexual hilarity and offer straight people a catharsis for unexamined gender anxieties, but such films have nothing or little to do with a gay world or sensibility, and can be highly offensive to gays (cf. Russo, 1987). Gay drag is more dangerous to the status quo precisely because it contests the legitimacy of heterosexual presumption.

The French postmodernist scholar Michel Foucault (see chapter 4) effectively challenged the category 'homosexual' as epistemologically inadequate (1988: 292), which is also true of the category 'lesbian.' In this vein, gay culture exposes the inadequacy of 'heterosexuality' as the category of sexual hegemony. In his wake, Butler (1993) convincingly demonstrates that the historical attempt to establish heterosexuality as a cultural imperative is flawed precisely because heterosexuality, as the standard order, can flourish as conscious intent only when its (oppositional) antithesis, homosexuality, is present and recognizable as the (deviant) alternative Other. To the modern world, heterosexuality (as one of two male sexual inventions; the hermaphrodite is elided) was the reactionary and repressive response to homosexuality as an omnipresent, looming possibility. Cornell (1991: 99), following Foucault's colleague Derrida, takes the view that it is the opposition itself, the great sexual divide, which delimits sexual expression. On the one hand, this point is buttressed by the growing 'bi-' community, in which Madonna, with public vacillations, has conditionally and tentatively (and superficially) positioned herself. On the other hand, the 'bi-' category is still contained within dualistic thinking. By simply substituting 'both' for 'either,' '*bi*sexuality' perpetrates the myth that Sex is a continent with just two nations, and although one can perhaps hold dual citizenship, it is likely that one nation or the other will emerge as the superpower.

Freedom, in any radical, utopian sense, would not require the precondition of choice between two unequal, or even parallel, sexual expressions. But sexually independent women, in particular, have needed the category 'lesbian' to distinguish themselves not only from the imperatives of heterosexual femininity, but also from homosexuality in all its masculinist variations. Lesbian feminists have had the prescience to challenge, via their lifestyles, butch–femme variations of the conventional hetero–homo dyad in forming their sexual identities. Women with power imbued by having or lacking a particular skin colour, heritage, or material advantage that propagates competitive individualism and reproduces power imbalances, proved by example (as do Madonna and her artificially queer peers in the contemporary scenario) that neither virtue nor flaw is rooted in genitalia.

The race/class/gender triad (and *age*) has imposed complicating factors *vis-à-vis* differences among women, and feminist deconstructionists have contested the viability of the very notion of 'woman' as a coherent category. Anti-hierarchical and anti-racist feminists do not wish to simply reverse or reproduce power mandates, and they have generally welcomed these debates and admonitions as essential to the integrity of human struggles for freedom and transformation. That is, no one can be free until all are free and until difference (with material equality) is honoured as birthright, intentionality, and choice instead of rejected as a sin, curse, or unlucky inheritance. (As Cornell says, in defence of sex/gender difference, 'Only by taking off from within sexual difference can we "affirm" the feminine': 1991: 100.) Meanwhile, there is no universal map for how to get to that state, there is no singular conception of freedom, and there is no truth to the idea of linear, irreversible progress towards that destination.

In certain extended-freedom zones in the United States in the 1970s, a 'woman-loving-woman' ethos emerged which encouraged women to love, nurture, express, and assert their own and their sisters' strengths and choices as women, not as a negative absence of phallus, but as the affirmative possibility of womanness. As attested by the early enthusiasm for Adrienne Rich's notion of a *continuum* of lesbianism (contra compulsory heterosexuality), the absence of rule-making concerning sexual practice enabled 'straight' women to cross the borders: raising their consciousness and working with and for women by day, and sleeping with their personal exception to the oppressor by night. Many of these women, after finding the nerve to experiment with women sexually, discovered that they could feel more passionately 'at home' with other women than with their sexual 'complement.' (This is something that also happens with women in sex-segregated cultures, including Western convents and prisons, but that is another story: cf. Faith, 1993b.) Being with women felt less like a choice than like a recognition and long overdue homecoming. But it couldn't have happened in such large numbers without feminist analyses and burgeoning women's communities.

Liberatory and self-affirming collectivities of '70s 'women-identified women' formed communities supporting elaborated cultural enclaves such as the 'women's music' concert, festival, and recording network, as discussed in chapter 1. These feminist communities provided ample space for learning and making choices about one's sexuality. But for some women it was the culture itself, even more than isolated couplings of sexual passion (which, like most passions, often entailed too-painful complications and endings),

that offered a refuge. (A few notable women who became vociferous feminist activists and proponents of lesbian separatism later
did turn-abouts and re-entered heterosexual unions. They re-
treated ostensibly for the purpose of having children or 'normaliz-
ing' their families, but one can hope for their sake that they also
had heterosexual desires.) Those of us who were confident in our
choices and secure in our political outlook generated for ourselves
a reassuring social margin within which self-defined, resistant identity could be celebrated as a positive rather than a negative
response to hegemonic culture. As Madonna presents herself, this
political commitment can be simply passed over.

Although Madonna often seems to be self-identified with gay
men (as opposed to feminists/lesbians), she similarly fails to satisfy
a gay standard. Most recently, from within gay culture(s) Madonna
has provoked detractors who objected to the *Sex* book. John Champagne points out the conventionality and homophobia of the book
in that, in all the pages, a penis appears only once, and it's flaccid.
The bottom line, for most 'community standard' censorship
boards, is an erect penis, and, for all we know, almost all
Madonna's men could be eunuchs. From Champagne's 'sex radical' perspective, 'on some level, [the book] is just not foul enough.
For many readers, it is exceedingly banal, serving up mostly familiar, almost lethargic fantasies in an arty kind of softcore porn style'
(1993: 126, 116). Madonna is not paradox so much as she is an
eclectic set of layered contradictions, at once stealing from, resisting, reinforcing and neutralizing stereotypes. Self-identified sex
radicals of the 1990s are antithetical to the 1970s radical feminists,
who insisted then, and do so now, on an analysis of sex/gender
power relations in their critique of and campaigns against pornography and violence against women and children. While acknowledging inequitable power relations, postmodern sex radicals are
'liberal' in so far as they defend pornography and any sexual practice on principle, if not with enthusiasm, including sadomasochism
and paedophilia (cf. Modleski, 1991: 152; Rubin, 1984). They are
not transforming sexuality so much as legitimizing dominance–
submission models.

As an aggressive producer of and model for what I read as pornography, Madonna has carried her apparent contradictions to the limit. She protests that her work is *not* pornographic, emphasizing that no one in her projects is ever depicted as being forced to submit to anything, no one is shown to be subjected to violence, despite the visual presence of leather, chain, and rope tying her to the bed with all four limbs spread-eagle. In fact, the appearance of coercion is present in a number of pictures in the *Sex* book, and if irony is intended, it is lost in the delivery. Nevertheless, Madonna's mantra on this subject is: 'The issue is consent, mutual consent' (*Newsweek*, 1992: 103).

Historically, the issue of consent has been a loophole for men charged with rape; rapists have been held not accountable on the grounds that they believed the women consented, and a 'no' was ingenuously interpreted to mean a coyly feminine 'yes.' Until the 1980s, Western courts generally failed to recognize substantive, informal, entrenched gender imbalances, which complicate the issues of equality and consent. Authentic consent can't be rendered when one party has legitimized power over the other. The symbolic line between consensual S/M erotica, and hard pornography which aggressively glorifies force and power abuse, cannot be as simply drawn in practice as Madonna might wish.

Unlike Paglia, I can't feel or think about pornography at large as a healthy cultural sign of masculine vitality from which all of society can benefit. To me her enthusiasm reads like a fatalist acquiescence to masculinist hegemony. Paglia projects her postmodern identity onto Madonna, whom she describes as 'slutty' – among other intended compliments. She says, 'I regard Madonna as my weird double – like her, I'm forcing a reassessment of every single cultural assumption at the present moment' (Dwyer, 1992: 77). Madonna lost feminist fans with her pornography, but in Paglia's view the book was simply poorly produced: '*Sex* is a tacky, horrible mess, full of important but completely undeveloped ideas ... in three hours I could have headed off a lot of the stupid things that are in there. She needs me' (ibid.: 78). I assume Paglia is referring to portions of the text, which is a strange mélange of wise advice and nympho chatter. She alters voice with different type or handwriting, complete with crossed-out words. Some of it is beautiful writing, some of it is not. The photos, on the other hand, are stunning, but redundant. Madonna is at the centre. Everyone, across a wide range of actors, is 'making love' to her, one on one, in threesomes, or in crowds, in every kind of setting, including on top of a pinball machine – which recalls the uncomfortable memory of a gang rape in a pool hall in Massachusetts. (In the 1988 Hollywood version of this grim story, *The Accused,* Jodie Foster played the victim and was awarded an Oscar for her profoundly multifaceted performance.) Often as not, when Madonna's alone in a photograph, she's making love to herself and to her beautifully sculptured body, fully exposed. The photos are stunning as photos, and Madonna is often stunning in them.

Despite grousings about Madonna's short-sightedness, Paglia gives way to unbridled enthusiasm for Madonna as a woman with as much liberated gumption as Paglia herself:

Madonna has a far profounder vision of sex than do the feminists. She sees both the animality and the artifice. Changing her costume style and hair color virtually every month, Madonna embodies the eternal values of beauty and pleasure. Feminism says, 'No more masks.' Madonna says we are nothing but masks. Through her enormous impact on young women around the world, Madonna is the future of feminism ... Madonna, role model to millions of girls worldwide, has cured the ills of feminism by reasserting woman's command of the sexual realm ... Madonna's most enduring cultural contribution may be that she has introduced ravishing visual beauty and a lush Mediterranean sensuality into parched, pinched, word-drunk Anglo-Saxon feminism. (1992: 5, 11, 13)

Paglia is in good company among academic renegades and cultural critics in regarding Madonna as a significant social force worthy of academic scrutiny. Harvard, UCLA, Rutgers, Princeton, and the University of Texas were among the first U.S. universities to bring Madonna into the curriculum, in a range of courses concerned, respectively, with deconstruction of fixed female identities; her significance in twentieth-century musicology; her influence on popular culture; the role of glamour in mass media; and her effect on teenagers. Not surprisingly, traditional scholars disdain such study as 'the basket-weaving of the '90s' (*Montreal Gazette*, 1992: E4). However, scholars concerned with the gender complexities of contemporary popular culture recognize Madonna as a key figure (cf. Kaplan, 1987; Lewis, 1990; Schwichtenberg, 1993). More inclusively and emblematically, a journalism course at the University of Colorado, 'Gender and Performance: Madonna Undressed,' focused on critical analyses of contemporary social issues (*Vancouver Sun*, 10 January 1993), putting a light on Madonna as a universally heeded commercial artist whose work both signifies and resists the grounds of cultural bewilderment.

In addition to developing curricula which centre Madonna as a symbolic vehicle for advancing cultural knowledge, scholars have engaged in research which sets Madonna as a 'paradigm case' through which research subjects' own identities can be concretely signified. For example, 332 college students were shown two of her videos ('Papa Don't Preach' and 'Open Your Heart'), and then given open-ended questions to determine which of them loved Madonna, which hated her, and which were 'somewhat' Madonna fans. The group most likely to hate Madonna were those 'most likely to identify themselves as feminists ... [*but* who] did not include sexual freedom in their definition of the term *feminism*' (Schulze, White, and Brown, 1993: 29–30).

In another study of students' reactions to Madonna, the researchers learned that different generalized ethnic groups formed different readings of her work. Asians tended to be distant in their appraisal, without identification with the images she presents. Hispanic, Latinâ/o, and Mexican-American respondents varied in their views, but generally commented on what they saw as representations of machisma in her work. African-American students, upon viewing the video 'Like a Prayer,' affirmed that she had dramatized 'the kind of racial injustice that goes on in the real world.' Many of the European-heritage students, for their part, failed to see the significance of racial issues in her work, although they recognized their experience in her depictions of (hetero-)sexual relations (Nakayama and Penaloza, 1993). Such studies give indicators that Madonna's fans, as much as her detractors, bring a multiplicity of interpretations to her work, according to the consonance or transgression they experience in her representations of the cultures with which they identify.

By the early 1990s, in her mid-thirties and a decade after her career took off, Madonna was receiving more attention than ever from the print media. This included a collection of Madonna dreams experienced by fifty women aged thirteen to sixty-one who love her (Turner, 1993), and *The I Hate Madonna Handbook* for people who love to hate her (Rosenzweig, 1994). Unauthorized biographies (all by men, to date) have appeared from time to time, perhaps prematurely, given her age (cf. Andersen, 1991; James, 1991; Bego, 1985 and 1993). To many media watchers and producers to the mid-1990s, she was a frivolity, a sexy, tantalizing bitch. In contrast, to many of those of her fans who personally identify with some aspect of her presentation of self, she signifies the 'insurrection of subjugated voices,' to use Foucault's phrase, as well as brilliant artistry.

Through a circuitous stream of discovery, which asks for your patience, I came upon what may be a useful insight about Madonna. In an article on Foucault's concern with 'the ancient care of the self,' Davidson (1994) discusses Pierre Hadot's interpretation of Seneca the Younger, the Stoic philosopher, Roman statesman, and dramatist who was Nero's tutor and chief minister before committing suicide in the year a.d. 65, under charges of treason. Davidson quotes Hadot: '*the true self of each individual transcends each individual*' (emphasis added). In Foucauldian terms, 'the care of the self does not take the form of a pose or posture, of the fashioning of oneself into a dramatic character ... it is, instead, the sculpting of oneself as a statue, the scraping away of what is superfluous and extraneous to oneself ... the art of taking away' (129–30). This is not unlike the testimony of transsexuals as to how they go about shedding cloaks of gendered social prescriptions (and corresponding physical attributes) incompatible with their personal sex/gender identity. They do not emerge with a new or changed identity, but rather with an external identity now consistent with that of the inner being.

This is the Foucauldian way, and it also describes Michelangelo's method as a Renaissance sculptor. And despite Foucault's own rejection of 'humanism,' it also describes the ideals of the Enlightenment Man. With elements of sex/gender defiance, Madonna both betrays and refracts these overlapping traditions. As I see her, Madonna has first cultivated herself almost accidentally from the materials of her society as she found them, and then, with great deliberation, has pushed the boundaries from within. As a *human* being, and therefore lacking immaculate perception, she produced and continually reproduces and reshapes a distinctive Self which incites and allows her to surpass herself, to transform herself (or selves), in such a way as to keep herself *apart* from the collectivity of both 'women' and 'feminism.' In this process she has repeatedly risked commercial suicide before rising again in the mainstream, malestream market, and her bare-assed courage has radically changed the face of 'woman' as performer and as entertainment commodity.

4
The Scholar and the Showgirl

With this chapter, in particular, I aim to bridge some of the artificial boundaries between academic and popular cultures, and the chapter is intended for the reader not already fluent in the work of Michel Foucault. Madonna the showgirl has been the subject of study in many universities. Although she doesn't present herself as an intellectual, I liken substantive aspects of her work to that of a path-breaking scholar. I'm not interested in engaging here in old Foucauldian debates, but rather in showing how very similar threads of inquiry circulate in very different cultural settings. Foucault's vocabulary circulated far beyond universities, and was absorbed into the fabric of popular culture. Using a different vernacular, Madonna has addressed some of the questions framed by Foucault. In their respective contexts, they have both illuminated the sex, knowledge, power, and identity preoccupations of their times in a style unique to their social locations.

My initial interest in Madonna's interventions in popular culture coincided with my study of Michel Foucault's controversial confrontations with modern scholarship (for details of his life and academic career see biographers Eribon, 1991; Miller, 1993; and, especially, Macey, 1994). In my view, Madonna's global impact on mainstream pop culture is analogous to Michel Foucault's influence on international pop-academic culture. Although they have addressed very different audiences, I see commonalities in their character and in the ways they have worked and affected people.

Foucault died in 1984, but I none the less often speak of him in the present tense because his work is still very much alive. Similarly, Madonna's work has reached a crossroads in the mid-1990s; when I speak of her in the present tense, it is with reference to the first decade of her career.

Madonna and Foucault are both rebels who entertain and educate on issues of sexual regulation, confinement, power, and the construction of 'truths.' Both resist and challenge received knowledges and ideas, especially concerning sexuality. Working in antithetical cultural milieux, they both take their power through the very discourses they resist. They are both intensely involved in thinking through and acting out the construction of Self.

Most conspicuously in common they both attempt to demystify sex, Foucault as a gay man who derided the term 'homosexual' as epistemologically inadequate. He 'refused his subjection' and 'resisted being bound to an identity that was defined in the nineteenth century according to a supposedly sexual nature ... What is crucial is the conscious choice to be gay and to live one's life differently ...' (1988: 292). The difference includes building new forms of culture, community, friendship, ethics, and subjectivity. Contrary to those gay men in particular who hold homosexuality to be a biological given, Foucault recognizes both hetero- and homosexuality as an invention, 'created rather than discovered in oneself' (Simons, 1995: 97). The young, bawdy Madonna, as an act of creativity, masqueraded as a sexual adventurist who defies all categories while defending heterosexuality in the substance of her work. Her postured performances often appeal, from an older woman's often admiring perspective, less to the visceral senses than to the critical or ironic mind.

Mixing metaphors, just as Lenny Bruce repeated dirty words until he'd shaken the dirt out of them, so did Madonna take the teeth out of sex, through sheer, playful repetitive excess in her representations of it. Both Madonna and Foucault have been excessive and irreverent in their displays, and this has been part of their appeal (including appeal borne from repugnance). The excess can be interpreted both as part of their mimicry of the straight and narrow worlds from which they separated (but with which they were/are interdependent) and simply as straightforward mirroring of the extreme possibilities.

Foucault's treatment of the Victorian preoccupation with sex (1978), and his scholarly evisceration of ancient Greek male sexuality (1985), lend significant weight to a rash of academic work in the past decade on the social construction of sexualities. He deconstructed ways by which 'modern puritanism imposed its triple edict of taboo, nonexistence, and silence' (1978: 4–5). He overturned 'the notion of sexual instincts and the myth of their repression' (Harland, 1987: 157). He drew criticism for refusing to disavow groups which advocate 'inter-generational erotica' (Macey, 1994). He had the same partner for several decades before his death. He also, on visits to California in the 1970s, sought out sexual adventures in gay bath-houses (Miller, 1993). He took sex as a social phenomenon very seriously, devoting much time to earnestly researching and writing about the structures, discourses, and active (commonly masculinist) human processes that produced it in its various forms. He said in 1984, ironically the year of his death, 'We have to understand that with our desires, through our desires, go new forms of relationships, new forms of love, new forms of creation. Sex is not a fatality; it's a possibility for creative life' (quoted in Weeks, 1991: 166). However, he also said, in the previous year, 'I am much more interested in problems about techniques of the self and things like that ... Sex is boring' (quoted in de Lauretis, 1994: 298).

Madonna likewise suggested in interviews that sex is boring. The irony is terrific, given the attention she and Foucault each gave to sex. Foucault's own observation, as paraphrased by Richard Harland, is that through constant babble about sex, 'the object thus created is sexuality or the idea of sex, a cultural object that imposes itself on bodies ... Instead of sex as desire, we now have a desire for sex – as something which is in itself desirable' (Harland, 1987: 158). This is the vicarious function served by Madonna, the enactment of desire for sex. In the following remark, Harland is characterizing Foucault's view of sex in 'the Orient,' and he could as well be describing Madonna: 'Instead of sex as a servant of nature or a centre of truth, this is sexuality as an erotic art, a kind of playing, creative and deliberately artificial' (ibid.: 160).

Madonna surely privileged artificial sex in her early public work, and her sexual poses played on the folly of too much earnestness about sex. She revelled in sex as the basest common denominator in human experience, yet presented sex as avant-garde guerrilla theatre, protesting every prohibition and regulation. Like Foucault, she has taken sex apart, documented sex, and attached sex to moral codes, in her case the cross, which as jewellery has become more a sexy fashion piece than a statement of religious conviction. She let audiences see their sexes, and especially their controlling attitudes towards their own and others' bodies, as absurd, dangerous, and ideologically invested. Foucault explicated the ways by which sexuality is informed by issues of power. Madonna exploits sexualized images as a power statement. She struts around with bawdy verve, but only rarely admits to old-fashioned two-person sex as a lusty but also spiritual pleasure that might go deep into the soul. In Madonna's world, it appears that mechanical sex can be as imaginatively engineered as mechanical music. Yet she also represents the desiring subject, a theme to which Foucault gave major attention. Foucault, concerned with power *of* the body and power *over* the body, wrote the text on the power relations of sexuality, and Madonna provided embodied illustrations.

Madonna's mother died during her childhood, and she was one of six siblings – Anthony, Martin, Madonna, Paula, Christopher, and Melanie – who were raised as strict Catholics by their Italian father, an engineer. (She is variously represented by journalists as both working-class and middle-class in her upbringing; she identifies with the working class.) Two years following the death of her mother, Madonna's father married Joan Gustafson, the woman he had hired to assist with the household, and she bore two more Ciccone children, Jennifer and Mario. The spunky third child and the eldest of three girls of the original six, Madonna was noted by siblings for her maternal as well as highly individualistic ways, and by her teachers for her creativity and inclination to perform. As a teenager she was posing enthusiastically for cameras, she was an acrobatic cheerleader, and she cultivated a then-unearned reputation for being bad (*Time*, 1985: 61; Andersen, 1991).

Foucault came from an affluent French family, his father a renowned surgeon. He was a brilliant scholar all through school; he received a privileged education and built his notable academic career on uncommon opportunities. After an illustrious high-school career, Madonna lost interest in academics during her second year at the University of Michigan, even though she was making top marks and starring in university productions. With encouragement from her artistic mentor, ballet teacher, and friend Christopher Flynn, she ran off to New York in 1978 (with $37 in her pocket), and went to work promoting herself (Andersen, 1991: 40–53). Years later, still friends with Flynn, she lost him to AIDS.

By early adulthood, Foucault, too, had moved away from the conventional wisdoms of his social environment to the edges of possibilities for resistance. James Miller characterizes Foucault's vision of the contemporary intellectual 'as a kind of elusive guerrilla warrior, hard to pin down, always on the prowl' (1993: 189). This would also be an accurate observation of Madonna's artistry. Scholars are suspect as intellectual dilettantes when they eschew specialization and leap around the disciplines, as Foucault did, indulging yesterday in philosophy, today in history, tomorrow in criminology, and taking none of them seriously as Authority. And, until they've paid their dues in one medium or another, performers aren't supposed to zip between songwriting/singing/recording, dancing and acting, modelling, filmmaking, book-publishing, and so on, as Madonna did from the start – in the shadow of other contemporary, diversified iconoclastic superstars, including Whoopi Goldberg, Bette Midler, Barbra Streisand, Lily Tomlin, and Oprah Winfrey.

Foucault was introduced to U.S. intellectuals in 1963 by Susan Sontag, in an essay on Marguerite Duras (cited by Macey, 1994: 160). In 1970, Foucault was granted the anti-disciplinary and self-named Chair of History of Systems of Thought, at the prestigious Collège de France in Paris. He held this singular position until his death from AIDS fourteen years later, at age fifty-seven. He had, by 1970, been teaching for many years in universities throughout Europe, and lecturing all over the world. His prodigious published works were translated into every dominant and dozens of other languages, and wherever he spoke the room was filled beyond capacity. For example, more than 2,000 people crowded a hall in Berkeley when he gave a lecture there in 1983, with the title 'The Culture of the Self' (Macey, 1994: 456).

Predictably (given his break with the French Communist Party) and paradoxically (given his support of proletarian struggles), Foucault's work hasn't been allowed to circulate in certain socialist countries, such as Cuba and Albania. But he is everywhere else, even though the European Foucauldian fad of the 1970s and '80s has passed and never really got started in North America, despite his being continually referenced. He is firmly entrenched, his concepts absorbed into academic and popular vernacular in discussions of the meaning of discourses, the ways that power circulates and is resisted, and especially the relationship between power and knowledge – erroneously clichéd as 'knowledge *is* power.' More accurately, people with social power have the ability to impose their will and enforce their view of the world as 'truth' and 'knowledge,' though always, already meeting resistance (Faith, 1994).

In a very different milieu, attracting millions more people than any academic could ever reach, Madonna is likewise central to the cultures she inhabits and global in her sustained impact. As described by *Rolling Stone* magazine in 1987, she was (and is, to the mid-1990s) 'the most notorious living blonde in the modern world' (Gilmore, 1987: 37) – though she is sometimes not blonde. Foucault's genealogical method of history 'would systematically break down identities, revealing them to be so many masks' (Macey, 1994: 232), which also describes Madonna's mode of performance. Of masks, Foucault says 'we are difference ... our reason is the difference of discourses, our history the difference of times, our selves the difference of masks' (quoted by Flynn, 1994: 44).

Foucault showed how the practice of confession, usually about sex, was transferred from the Church to the psychiatrist; Madonna dissects sex and the confessional as entertainment. Foucault recognizes the Self as 'a transitory and contingent result of power relations that constitute it' (Simons, 1995: 47), but, with reference to the Greeks, Foucault examines 'the government of the self by the self in its articulation with relations to others' (quoted by David-son, 1994: 11). This means working on one's self as an ethical and ascetic imperative affecting others, while constructing new forms of community that challenge the élitist male individualism that was inherited from the Enlightenment and entrenched within capital-ist economies. Madonna is exceptionally individualistic, but she is also exceptionally disciplined as a creative imperative. She presents her selves as costume, as flashy works of art; Foucault's notion is that the 'care of the self' is transformative, and thereby surpasses the self (1986).

Both Foucault and Madonna are renegades from sexual con-straints and identities, yet both are stubbornly androcentric in their images and perspectives – which has caused problems with feminists for both of them. It's predictable, in the best of times, that male scholars will focus on male subjects. Foucault was cogni-zant of the political significance of women's movements. Before he died he was preparing work on the sexual pathologization of woman, as an outcome of late eighteenth-century medical dis-course which informed Freud's view of 'hysterics' (Foucault, 1989: 144). A politically astute gay man, he did not denigrate women with the condescensions so common among his academic peers, but in his published histories of madness (1965), prisons (1977), and sexuality (1978, 1985, 1986), for example, he is utterly andro-centric in his gender-blindness. His failure to articulate the signifi-cance of sex/gender to power relations is striking – given his expansive insights into discursive power–knowledge relations more generally. His scant references to women, though never denigrat-ing in any obvious way, are imbued with the curious tone of acknowledging the Other (Faith, 1994).

It is even more problematic when a female public figure is male-centred in her projections of sexuality, exploiting dangerous cli-chés about women. In sexy guises, Madonna satirizes myriad ste-reotypes of women, as if she is both seeking to attract male viewers and, at the same time, making fun of their vulnerability to female guile. Her subtexts may well be messages to women about taking charge by using the traditional tricks of the trade. However, her often contradictory content regarding female independence is conveyed through the layered lenses of one who knows she is being observed by male power. When she is most transparent, Madonna directs herself to the male gaze.

Foucault employs Jeremy Bentham's eighteenth-century 'panopticon' prison model as a way of explaining how we are constantly under the gaze of authority. We know they're there, but because we can't always see those who hold us under surveillance, we internalize the surveillance and become our own guards, monitoring our own behaviours to avoid the risk of being seen in a transgression. Madonna's performance suggests that she has internalized the male gaze, and postures herself to meet that look with her own. She faces it head-on, accepting its challenge. For this very reason, her feminist ironies, as the rebellious female, may be lost to accommodationist reconstructions of gender relations, where a woman has to vamp to be seen. And yet, as observed by Susan McClary as a strength, 'she flaunts as critique her own unmistakably feminine ending' (1991: 33). In this respect, McClary compares Madonna and the discursive power of Laurie Anderson's music performances, in which Anderson presents herself as 'deriving power from being a *knowing* "object" of the male gaze' (ibid.: 139, emphasis in original).

There isn't anything explicit in Foucault's work to suggest that he would necessarily, generically, prefer men's judgments over women's, and he had intellectual, political, and close personal friendships with women such as Michelle Perrot, Arlette Farge, Danièlle Rancière, Hélène Cixous, Catherine von Bülow, and Simone Signoret (Macey, 1994). But he may not have appreciated Madonna's approach to liberation, except as theatre. Certainly he was cognizant of the importance of popular culture and recognized rock music 'as a cultural form which constitutes "a way of life", fashioning attitudes and responses beyond musical taste' (Simons, 1995: 96). One of the reasons he admired women's liberation movements was that, in contrast to (early homosexual) men's movements, its proponents are not preoccupied with sexual discourses; they examine all the complexities of life and take a holistic view of women's experiences (Faith, 1994). This does not describe Madonna. With Foucault, paradoxically, she observes a world that tells us to look to sex to 'tell us our truth, or rather, the deeply buried truth of that truth about ourselves which we think we possess in our immediate consciousness' (Foucault, 1978: 69). They both critically expose belief in a sexual repository of truth to be a historical construction, which they take apart for us, but in which they themselves take part as performance and scholarship.

Foucault cultivated a distinguished scholar-activist Self, and Madonna cultivated a distinctive artist-exhibitionist Self. Each has a magnetism for both the male and the female gaze. In photographs they both often direct their gaze straight-ahead, hard with the glint of authority, scrutinizing the spectator. They are both very aware of their own power, and Madonna, in particular, does not seem disturbed by it. Foucault suggests that one must 'struggle against fascism' and he refers to 'the fascism in us all, in our heads and in our everyday behavior, the fascism that causes us to love power, to desire the very thing that dominates and exploits us' (quoted by Bernauer and Mahon, 1994: 154–5).

Both Foucault and Madonna devote themselves to sex-related taboo issues. Madonna may very well make adult heterosexual men, in particular, uneasy (which in itself could be an aphrodisiac). But despite strenuous efforts from many quarters to censor her, she has not been silenced; nor, except as masquerade, does she lower her head and avert the direct male gaze, as is the wont of feminine custom. 'The ability to scrutinize is premised on power. Indeed the look confers power; women's inability to return such a critical and aggressive look is a sign of subordination, of being the recipient of another's assessment ... The aesthetic appeal of women disguises a preference for *looking* at women's bodies, for keeping women separate, at a distance, and the ability to do this' (Coward, 1985: 75–6). Madonna stared her viewer in the face, inviting everyone – men, women; white, of colour; young, old; hetero, homo – to look at her body in its multifarious sexual possibilities, with all the risks implied by the invitation and by her cynicism.

Like Foucault, Madonna demonstrates social conscience. Among other causes, she has worked on behalf of AIDS research, having lost close friends to the epidemic, including her mentor Christopher Flynn and one of her best friends, Martin Burgoyne.

Although often irreverent for the cameras, and inarticulate as an interviewee, in other interviews she can be dignified and serious, such as in her focus on safe sex on ABC's *Nightline* during a discussion of censorship as it was affecting her own work (3 December 1990). She effectively deflected the bigotry that dismissed AIDS as a 'gay disease' by emphasizing accurately that the pandemic was spreading most rapidly among heterosexuals (Henderson, 1993: 110). Her work, in whatever medium, is living testimony to her commitment to freedom of expression *and* to good health – though her performances and *Sex* book don't suggest that safe sex is at the front of her characters' minds, when they feel desire.

Mariana Valverde discusses sexuality as a social process, 'not a ready-made force lurking in the primeval depths of our feminine being ... We are trying to create a sexual culture of resistance, which is an integral part of the feminist project' (1987: 203). Madonna is a contradiction in that, on the one hand, she graphically demonstrates how sexual categories are socially constructed, and, on the other hand, she inserts essentialist attitudes, suggesting that if one can become liberated from moral judgments and fears, one's *true* sexuality will emerge. Foucault was critical of this Reichian orientation, as well as the Freudian notion of repression, which, real or not, has been the perpetual target of Madonna's strategic attacks.

Judith Butler points out the 'tendency to think that sexuality is either constructed or determined, to think that if it is constructed, it is in some sense free, and if it is determined, it is in some sense fixed' (1993: 94). Foucault, too, saw the complexities that preclude simple dichomotous explanations. He saw the infant, not as a free, unfettered, and uncontaminated being, but as a totally vulnerable dependent whose eventual, adult imperative would be to strip away all the past influences, the acquired contaminating layers of disciplinary inscriptions, as a steady, conscious maturation process of taking power.

Foucault, like Madonna, looked to sexuality as a key site of revolutionary resistance. He did not view sexual identity in causal or teleological terms, but rather, in effect, in terms of human discourses, artfulness, and social organization. On the one hand, the possibilities for liberatory sexuality excited Foucault and, from his view, as Bernauer and Mahon put it (1994: 149), 'the logic of sex is the key to personal identity in our time.' On the other hand, 'normalization' is a social process which severely restricts sexual possibilities. Both Foucault and Madonna have defended sadomasochism as a way of, in Foucault's words, 'inventing new possibilities of pleasure' (Macey, 1994: 368) – which, as he saw it, was a way of eroticizing power roles as distinct from liberating natural desires. He spoke of 'limit-experiences,' experiments in which the individual self absolves itself as subject, transgressing the rules of sex and power to take it to the limit, to the very edge of death itself.

Foucault's lifestyle was not that of a hedonist, though he was an extremist, living 'the extremes of asceticism and Dionysian excess ... stretching human experience to its outermost limits ... [transcending] the conventional dichotomies of consciousness and unconsciousness, life and death, reason and madness, pleasure and pain, truth and fiction' (Deutschmann, 1994: 290). In their routine lives, apparently, both Foucault and (pre-motherhood) Madonna lived like monks, excessively devoted to the disciplines of their work, and they both explored maximum possibilities for how to interpret the pleasure principle. Unlike Madonna, Foucault, who lived through the Second World War, was spartan in his personal tastes. In painful struggles he defended the rights of resistance groups in many countries, including labourers, prisoners, gays, students and other political dissidents. A French Communist in his young adult years, he was later adopted by the conservatives, but (unlike Madonna, who presents herself as a sexual libertarian) he appeared to be a (non-doctrinaire, non-violent) anarchist, resistant even to that label. As he put it, 'It's true that I prefer not to identify myself and that I'm amused by the diversity of the ways I've been judged and classified' (quoted in Macey, 1994: xix). Foucault barricaded himself with dissident students protesting state limits on liberatory education, and was beaten on the head with the batons of the French police for protesting labour practices. Madonna's public beatings have come from critics who have scathingly dismissed her work.

Both Foucault and Madonna have been censored and indicted

by critics for immorality, and both express a conflicted relationship with the Catholic faith of their upbringings. They share a commitment to 'liberation from all restrictions on pleasure and power' (MacCannell and MacCannell, 1993: 229), and, as lapsed or recovering Catholics commonly testify, the Church has been a powerfully restrictive force. Of her religious beliefs, Madonna says, iterating a basic impulse of women's spirituality movements, and reiterating the theme of her song 'Secret': 'I like the idea that God is in all of us, but to me, the ultimate form of prayer, if God is in each of us, is to be kind to one another ...' (Mailer, 1994: 55). With this admonition she is advising, 'Do as I say, not as you've seen me do'; her honest capacity for cruelty was striking in her film *Truth or Dare*. And yet she is commonly praised by directors, producers, co-workers, and friends as in every way sweet, considerate, and cooperative.

Madonna and Foucault have both resisted status-quo cultural values and have revealed the resistances and contradictions inherent in power relations while reaping the harvests of capitalist economies. Both adapted to the strict hierarchies of their professions, and vigorously engaged in self-promotion with the powers-that-be while at the same time deviating from every norm: Foucault with the quiet dignity that behooves the 'academy,' and Madonna with the low-chakra high energy that dominates youth culture. Each has played the part of the provocateur, posing more imaginative sexual possibilities than is normally permitted by contemporary gate-keeping guardians of morality; each is repopularizing body titillations from ages past. Neither follows the Platonic hierarchy of worthy pursuits, which places sexual desire at the bottom of the scale – because, in Plato's view, unlike the most worthy pursuits, namely, eternity, truth, and beauty, the human body rapidly decays, is transient, and is utterly insignificant in the larger picture. In the spirit of secular feminism in a postmodern age, both Madonna as an artist and Foucault as a scholar take the socially constructed body seriously indeed.

Both Madonna and Foucault took control of their professional careers, and both have capitalized on criticisms from those whose conventions they have disdained. Foucault 'was notoriously intolerant of criticism' and harboured grudges (Macey, 1994: 144, 337). For all her public bluster, Madonna candidly shows what I think is a healthy sensitivity towards criticism, and a reasonable desire for respect as an artist. Like all triumphant souls, Madonna and Foucault both denied legitimacy and power to critics who would silence them. Without missing a beat, no matter what the nature of the attacks, they just kept working. In Foucault's case, his very transient body expired at age fifty-seven in 1984, which, for Madonna at age 26, was a banner year. He understood that 'the scientific and technical world ... is our real world' (Macey, 1994: 171), and she was making his point through the scientific world of communications technology. In pop culture, Madonna *is* the real world.

5

Identity: Sex, Religion, and Difference

Issues of identity politics, as related to racialism, ethnicity, class, sex, and age, are potent in Madonna's representations. She represents identities which she can know only vicariously. Fundamental to early 'identity politics' was the assumption that 'there was a direct correlation between one's social location and one's political position ... [But] identity itself is complex, contradictory, and shifting and does not unproblematically reveal itself in a specific politics' (Giroux, 1993: 173).

Madonna's peculiarity is that she has cruised so freely through so many cultural terrains. She has been a 'cult' figure within self-propelling subcultures just as she became a major superstar in mainstream pop media globally. In particular she was a touchstone for young fans exploring sexual identity outside the traditional categories. They are 'learning to remember their bodies in a critique of gender that is autonomous of gay liberation and feminism' (Patton, 1993: 86). The 1960s and 1970s gay and lesbian movements, and 1980s and 1990s debates on political correctness, are not recognized as relevant to these upstart gender rebels (cf. Whisman, 1993; Stein, 1993). The idea of someone like Lenny Bruce going to prison for using slang sex words in public now seems ludicrous, a dead issue from an anachronistic time half a century ago.

As for the older, politically committed gay community, 'she inhabits gay consciousness as a popular guest, despite her status elsewhere as cultural proprietor' (Henderson, 1993: 109), or, as otherwise stated, 'she has won for herself an unlimited ticket for subcultural tourism – she can visit any exotic locale she likes, but she doesn't have to live there, (Tetzlaff, 1993: 259). Further, as Diana Fuss recognizes, 'identification with the Other is neither a necessary precondition nor an inevitable outcome of imitation' (1995: 153). As bell hooks puts it, Madonna 'occupies the space of the white cultural imperialist, taking on the mantle of the white colonial adventurer moving into the wilderness of black culture (gay and straight), [and] of white gay subculture' (1994: 20). Among white mainstream entertainers, Madonna is hardly alone in this tendency: David Byrne and Paul Simon, for example, have also taken bad raps for capitalizing on the 'exotic'. Reinforcing the point, but interpreting it as representative of postmodern culture, Elayne Rapping says, 'there is no more "inside" and "outside," no more clear boundary between high and low, mainstream and alternative culture. Artists today move easily in and out of these categories ...' (1994: 276). By centring herself as a straight woman in a gay-male scenario, Madonna neutralized the categories with the liberal message that it's okay to play around with people who are gay, as opposed to it's okay to be gay. Although she says 'there are times I really feel bisexual' (Mailer, 1994: 52), she has made it clear that she herself is 'not a lesbian' (cf. Fisher, 1991: 36), that it was all an act.

From the beginning, Madonna drew heavily on gay and queer cultures as creative inspiration and as a reliable pool of paying customers. She delivered a loud and clear message to youth at large to express themselves, to claim their bodies as their own to do with safely as they will, without moral constraints beyond not causing harm to others. Even understanding that performers are by definition acting, it would be hard to accept that she didn't really mean it when, with many different voices, she told girls to take charge of their own lives. That message, as I read it, was never that to be sexually liberated one must be engaged with queer life; that position may be defensible, but her work doesn't offer the evidence. What her work says to me is that, when all the myths are exposed and lose their grip on our conscience, sex in its myriad variations is at least as deserving of our indulgence as any other earthly pleasure.

As Foucault demonstrates in his (male) sexuality histories (1978,

1985, 1986), and as Jeffery Weeks (1991) argues persuasively, gene theories regarding sexual orientation are insufficient explanations as a cause of 'homosexuality,' which is a foundation for being 'gay' and which is, by either name, different from being a 'lesbian' or a 'dyke,' all of which are different from being 'bisexual,' 'transgender,' 'pansexual,' 'transsexual,' 'transvestite,' or 'queer.' None of these contemporary terms is adequate to express what is being lived. All of them are fluid as categories. The evidence is plentiful that, whatever one's predispositions might be, dominant sexual practices are socially constructed and, in the main, culturally coerced, which is why so many gays and lesbians have been/are in opposite-sex marriages, usually prior to recognizing or acting on their choices, preferences, or 'natural' urges. Gary Kinsman has written a strong analysis of the ways by which the contemporary state exercises controls over sexual intimacies and identities (1987). Another Canadian, Holly Devor, has lucidly elaborated the gender complications that arise from hegemonic sex-role scripts and efforts to locate sexual identity scientifically in genes and chromosomes (1989). In the end, the hateful aggressiveness with which same-sex activity has been officially attacked historically in the Western world attests to the profound fears that accompany 'normal' sexuality.

Practices of heterosexual intimacy are structurally laden with power imbalances that may or may not be resolvable within the dyad. This does not have to do only with the myths of universal, hormonally determined sex-based difference: aggressive can't-help-themselves penises, or passive always-waiting-to-receive vaginas. Sexual practices are subject to the same historical forces, contradictions, and resistances as other phenomena which affect social identities. The declaration of one's sex/gender identity has become an active component of contemporary social practices, whether rationalized hegemonically as 'being/doing what comes naturally' (either gay or straight) or, antithetically, consciously constructed from what are perceived as the choices. Sexual preference is commonly experienced as genetic by older homosexuals and young gays in particular, and, as well, by many old dykes and new queers who have 'always' known they were lesbians, although to date no one has discovered or conjured a gene unique to lesbians. One might as easily locate a *feminist* gene which mitigates against the heterosexual imperative, or a compelling genetic impulse towards adventure, non-conformity, creative use of imagination, and passion which may or may not be tied to sexual eroticism, or may simply be felt as a need to not be trapped in a subordinate gender role. Conversely, in this hypothesis, egalitarian gay men could be endowed with a gene which mitigates against social coercion to assume a posture of social superiority *vis-à-vis* intimate partners.

All we can know for sure is that, given a rigid dualism upheld by social institutions, some of us know ourselves to be significantly 'different' from the norm. Gail Vines concludes from her research on hormones that essentialist and genetic causal theories are significantly flawed scientifically and in their sociological inferences; 'simplistic biological explanations take sexuality ... out of its lived context. The tragedy is that these ideas, as they filter into our consciousness, may make us more likely to behave as if we really were sexually driven automatons – intent not on relationship but on mere physical couplings, genital *frisson*, with the sex object of our choice' (1993: 123).

For people who believe they were 'born that way,' whose recollections of their childhoods and adolescence support that presumption, and who endured lifetimes of persecution (including homosexuals who, in the 1940s, were marked with the pink triangle and were among the first to be exterminated by the Nazis), this 'preference' which forced people into repressive, claustrophobic closets is not experienced as choice. Many such individuals have been subjected to (usually unsuccessful) psychiatric 'cures' of this 'genetic abnormality,' which is based entirely on the ideological presumption of the naturalness of universal heterosexuality. Sexual identity as a choice may very well be influenced by genetic factors, but, as the history of homosexuality since the ancient Greeks has shown, 'choice' is invariably situated within very particular social and cultural conditions, and woe to the one who makes the wrong choice. Among women, there would never have been a 'love that knows no name' had there not also been strong Church, State, and medical sanctions which entrenched male-dominant heterosexuality as the norm, the given, with all else as deviant Other.

Self-identity, which may be fictional, is gendered, and may or may not be consonant with circumstances, attitudes, or behaviours. It is a conscious choice, to the extent that our subjectivity is our own, and we can claim ourselves as knowing subjects. Self-identity has to do with freedom and dignity, in the most fundamental sense. This self-knowing is what Madonna projects, but not always convincingly, and, as for her heterosexuality, 'if you know who you are, you don't need to signify,' as said by a lovable, old-timer butch dyke in a state prison. My friend was disdainful of the 'flaunting' of the sexual appetites of young first-timer 'JTOs' (jailhouse turn-outs), who were experiencing both prison and sex with a girl for the first time, and strutting around the gloomy prison in an obnoxiously aggressive state of sexual ecstasy and conversion enlightenment.

Stein points out that 'often it seems as though the only performers who are "allowed" to speak lesbianism are those, such as Madonna, whose heterosexuality is seen as unwavering' (1993: 65). This view is reiterated by the director of an AIDS organization: 'Madonna has done a good job of talking about sex and sexual orientation, and so has Garth Brooks. But these are straight people, who don't have a lot to lose' (quoted in Starr, 1994: 199).

Judith Butler recognizes that 'gay and lesbian subjects do not wield the social power, the signifying power, to abject heterosexuality in an efficacious way' (1993: 112). And this assertion from a conversation between two queers about Madonna's appropriation of gay culture underscores the significance of this point: 'her celebrity is constructed, in however complex a way, as *heterosexual*. She can be as queer as she wants to, but only because we know she's not' (Crimp and Warner, 1993: 95). It appears that Madonna's own agenda is to break down the categories and dispense with dualities. She's attracted to cultural margins without which the dominant categories would be without meaning, but she doesn't refuse the sex/gender dichotomy so much as capitalize on it as a career tool – which can be exploited, challenged, or ignored, as she wishes.

Heterosexual hostilities and gender wars aside, Madonna routinely makes a show of loving men. As described by Jackie Stacey,

Madonna represents 'the "assertive style" of heterosexual spectacle, inviting masculine consumption' (1989: 127). But Madonna's
tongue is in her cheek, and her female fans accept her impersonations of sexy women 'as a knowing wink, a gesture of empowerment' (McClary, 1990: 6). Fiske agrees that 'Madonna utters quite
different meanings for her teenage girl fans and her *Playboy*-reader
fans, who each find in her quite different pertinences to their different positions in the patriarchal social order' (1989: 146). Just as
Madonna is excessive in her representations, so are her fans
(fanatic, by definition) excessive in their attributions of meanings
to her work which she may or may not have intended. Her reputation is that 'men are terrified of [her], which is part of the reason
young women love her so' (Garratt, 1986: 12). However, this
doesn't square with her prominent, perennial presence on TV
music channels, of which the targeted demographic is primarily
young, white males (Lewis, 1990). Nor would it follow that she
would appear on the cover of adult men's magazines if she didn't
sell to men. If she does terrify them, they must like the feeling.

As a diva, Madonna has more in common with dynamic black
performers like Josephine Baker and Ethel Waters of the 1920s
than with the white goddesses she has imitated in drag. Baker and
Waters, unlike Madonna, had to break through racist barriers
(Baker expatriated to France) to succeed as multidimensioned
international entertainers. Like them, the young Madonna lacked
the 'class' to present herself as a detached aristocratic diva. Also
like them, her campy haughtiness separated her both from her
roots and from her aspirations to use her star power to 'inspire'
her audience. In her early years in the limelight, she didn't inspire
so much as energize and amuse, although young women were certainly inspired to emulate her independence and fashions. Donald
Bogle, in a study of the history of black female superstars, identifies
features (here briefly paraphrased) of a singer–dancer theatrical-
diva style that could as well apply to Madonna: dazzling, elegant
extravagance; live-wire humour; a cool, unembarrassed attitude;
sparkling costumes; lack of shame of their bodies; spicy and
naughty repartee with the audience, which, at the same time, sus-
tains distance between them. 'So they have strolled, strutted,

stomped, and sashayed like crazy, attitudinizing all over the place. They have liked showing off, speaking up for their rights, shouting out to the world that they were women born for luxury and that they had no intention of holding back ... [They are] champion[s] of rebelliousness and self-assertion' (Bogle, 1980: 15).

In fact, Madonna's fabulous diva eclecticism may one day be her Achilles' heel. In her videos, other characters are *de facto* subordinate to Madonna's, which is problematic when blacks, Latinos, gays, and women are in those roles. Difference is obliterated, neutralized. Difference itself is constitutive of identity and cannot be erased without discrimination. In an analysis of Madonna's appropriation of African-American imagery, hooks (1992) observes how (unlike Sandra Bernhard, who acknowledges the sources of her material) Madonna takes what she likes and uses it as her own, an observation which is echoed by Goldsby: 'Part of Madonna's glitter and glee is that she's a cultural robber baron, taking what she wants from wherever she roams, incorporating it into her rhetoric of self-presentation without so much as an ethical doubt as to the political implications of her gestures' (1993: 125). Yet again, one feels compelled to point out that virtually all artists roam and gather inspiration where they find it, incorporating it into their work as their own. Hybrid culture is an inevitable by-product of mass media. Cultural rip-off is a particularly serious problem when the rich are stealing from the poor, so to speak, but the problem is less about Madonna than it is about the racism, homophobia and class inequities, of which 'popular entertainment' takes full, shameless advantage.

The gender-bending elements of Madonna's work are still fashionable in the 1990s and, as discussed by Baudrillard, are 'symptomatic of our era' – when it is generally agreed by transgressors that the reinvention of sexual identity makes possible the reconceptualization of every other freedom to which one might aspire. Baudrillard viewed transsexuals as 'the end of binary differences' (Braidotti, 1991: 122–3), which are already disrupted by the fact of gay, lesbian, and bisexual cultures. The appeal of gay (male) culture to Madonna is not mysterious if one accepts John Rechy's description: 'The law tells us we're criminals so we've become defiant outlaws. Psychologists demand we be sick and so we've become obsessed with physical beauty. Religion insists we're sinners and so we've become soulful sensualists. The result is the unique, sensual, feeling, elegant sensibility of the sexual outlaw' (quoted by Dollimore, 1991: 215). It is the positive self-shaped reward of this construction, not the exclusion, labelling, suffering, and condemnation which precede it, that attracts Madonna, although Dollimore challenges the notion of a 'homosexual sensibility' which could be isolated in any meaningful way (1991: 308). Madonna's attraction to African-American and Latin cultures seems likewise based on aesthetics, sensuality, and dis-identification with the narrowness and sterility of so much of mainstream culture. By association, she frees herself from the limits of her own identity, but in her oft-reiterated rejection of lesbianism she imposes other limits and ensures stability for herself within the matrix of heterosexuality, as a 'natural' refuge or confinement.

No one can attempt to represent someone else's experience, style, or knowledge without risking criticism for appropriation, but, in Madonna's defence, her musical borrowings reveal her respect for her sources, even if she doesn't explicitly acknowledge them. She crosses so many cultural borders in her work that, to the uncritical viewer or listener, she 'becomes' whomever she represents in any given moment – for sheer lack of any tangible clues as to whom she might be without costumes and props. Jeffrey Weeks discusses how most of us 'live with a variety of potentially contradictory identities, which battle within us for allegiance' (1991: 184). Madonna presents contradictory identities as parodic performance. She conveys affection for the myriad subjects she caricatures without conveying whether she situates herself within any of her representations.

Madonna's signifying props over time – in turn grunge, boy-toy, glamour-nostalgia, gal-pal, leather, schoolgirl, or vamp – blur together, and she may be all of it or none of it. To the mix she adds actors, dancers, and back-up singers whose colours and attitudes signify the diverse cultures from which Madonna derives her inspirations. From young, prancing gay men she took voguing, striking a pose, and turned it into an urban craze. Later she took on hip hop. As Dollimore states, 'In the escape from sexual oppression and sexual repression individuals have often, like [André] Gide, crossed divisions of class and race' (1991: 337–8). This identity amorphousness, layering, or multiplicity, with the possibility of power and control represented by Madonna in most of her mutations, is a significant reason for her popularity – given the fractured, fragmented, disempowered, and resistant identities that characterize the postmodern age. Henry Giroux speaks of these times:

As we move into an age in which cultural space becomes unfixed, unsettled, porous, and hybrid, it becomes increasingly difficult either to defend notions of singular identity or to deny that different groups, communities, and people are increasingly bound to each other in a myriad of complex relationships. Modes of representation that legitimated a world of strict cultural separation, collective identities, and rigid boundaries seem hopelessly outdated as the urban landscape is being redrawn within new and shifting borders of identity, race, and ethnicity. (1994: 79)

By the 1990s, Madonna has come into her own as a songwriter whose glittery presentation doesn't preclude meaningful lyrical content. Musically she has similarly matured, moving from structurally simple, compellingly repetitive, danceable rhythms, to songs daring to change keys and tempo, so as to tell a story. With little musical training when she started her career, she's learned by doing it, from teachers along the way, and through collaboration with skilled composers. Patrick Leonard said of Madonna, as a writing partner, 'she's a brilliant writer ... I've never worked with a better lyricist or a more prolific singer. Almost every vocal that she does is first take ... In a few hours the song is written and the vocal is done' (quoted in Zollo and Odegard, 1989: 37).

Produced by Mary Lambert, who was involved in much of Madonna's most successful early work, the video 'Like a Prayer' (1989) was one of Madonna's first striking achievements as a co-songwriter (with Leonard); it was reassuringly more melodic and harmonic than her earlier work (as was true, to a degree, of all the songs on the album by the same name). This complex, non-linear video includes images of Madonna with crucifixion wounds on her hands; a rape/murder by four white men of a woman who resembles Madonna; the rape blamed on an innocent black man, who was attempting to help the victim, while Madonna, intimidated by one of the actual rapists, flees the scene. She seeks refuge in a Catholic church, where she falls asleep on a pew and dreams. Later we see Madonna dancing in protest before a field of burning Ku Klux Klan crosses, and myriad other transgressive representations of sexual guilt and innocence, and the chaos, horror, and brutality of racism.

In this surreal, quick-cut video, Madonna's prince (and sexual lure), the falsely accused black man from the street, is living counterpart to a mesmerizing statue (in the church) of an African-Peruvian saint, St Martin de Porres (McClary, 1990: 21), who, in the seventeenth century, gave aid to African slaves transported to Peru. In a dream, she brings the statue to life by kissing his feet, which, although perhaps intended as a gesture of reverence and supplication, can be viewed, as well, as sacrilege when the scene becomes explicitly sexualized and they make love on the altar. In the analysis of Ronald Scott, who respects Madonna's treatment of racism in 'Like a Prayer,' she appropriately positions the church as a 'safe haven from the racist assaults that have threatened blacks throughout their history' (1993: 71). In an ebony/ivory configuration of female strength, a black angel-woman appears in a sky–dream sequence to give Madonna's character reassurance.

Internal scenes in this dramatic piece feature an African-American gospel choir (the Andraé Crouch Choir), whose ecstatic and cathartic energy subverts the emotionally stifling ambience of the Roman church which contains them. While Madonna was growing up under the discipline of Catholicism, she became attracted to the popular offshoot genres that grew from the music in black churches. In the video, the juxtaposition of the two moods (and modes) of worship, accented by the sexist and racist violence beyond, is shocking in its incongruity.

Madonna's transgressions offer resistance and symbolic resolution to bigoted and racist stereotypes, while simultaneously capitalizing on them. For example, the stereotype of the ubiquitous black

predator/rapist is exploited by Madonna and, until the conclusion, may be read either uncritically (racist satisfaction on the part
of spectators predisposed to receive stereotypes) or as a critical
deconstruction of the ideologies that sustain racist stereotypes. In
the end, awake now, Madonna's character goes to the police. Her
testimony frees the wrongly accused black man and they leave the
jail together.

Through the ages, artists in every medium have mixed up religion, sex, violence, and racialism. Madonna did not invent this formula, and indeed one can look to the Church itself as the earliest
harbinger of such imagery. Neverthless, because of her lurid treatment of religious iconography, the Vatican banned and condemned the 'Like a Prayer' video as 'blasphemous' and urged a
boycott of her concerts. This is the same Church which, in pre-
modern times, excommunicated women who became actresses
(Greenberg, 1988: 320–1, n.126). After lobbying by the fundamen-
talist American Family Association in protest against 'Like a
Prayer,' Pepsi dropped a $5-million contract with her, creating
enormous publicity (Carpenter, 1992).

One reviewer, convinced that Madonna hasn't 'recovered' from
Catholicism, points to the continuity of her religious references:
'She calls herself Madonna [reasonably, since it's her given name],
she used to wear crosses and rosary beads, she used to sing about
being a virgin, and now she's finding a spiritual solace in prayers.
You can make up your own mind' (Bakshi, 1989: 14). Rather than
demonstrating an attachment to the Church, Madonna took the
traditional religious basis of pornography and extended it to a
deconstructive articulation of sex, desire, and faith, altogether
undermining the sources of her inspiration. When asked 'What is
it about bondage and S&M that's interesting to you?' she replied:

Maybe it's my Catholic upbringing. When I was growing up there were
certain things people did for penance; I know people that slept on coat
hangers or kneeled on uncooked rice on the floor, and prayed for hours
... There was some ecstasy involved in that.

And the whole thing of crucifixion – the idea of being tied up. It's sur-
rendering yourself to someone ... I mean, there's a lot of pain-equals-

pleasure in the Catholic Church. And that is also associated with bondage and S&M ... But let me just preface all of this by saying that for me, it's always about mutual consent, never about being forced or taking advantage of someone. (*Newsweek*, 1992: 102–3)

Madonna speaks of ecstasy, which in Weber's observation is a means to acquiring a new soul, the rebirthing of self (1946: 279). It was Max Weber who proposed the sublimation theory, that (in Margareta Bertilsson's words) 'when religion loses its hold on people the only means of salvation left to them is the religion of erotic love.' But in this confining framework, 'eroticism ... is intimately attached to brutality. The more sublimated the culture of eroticism, the more brutal is the act of love.' The short-term benefit of erotic salvation is that it's democratic, anyone can attain it, unlike the stringent requirements for religious salvation, which is reserved for those who deprive, discipline, torment themselves, and suffer in order to earn their place in heaven. In the absence of God's guilt-producing commands, humans freely 'confront one another ... as a means to one another's lust and passion.' Instead of sharing in the collective identity of a community of restraint, people become individual means to one another's ends (Bertilsson, 1991: 303–4). Weber recognized that, just as ecstasy can be an instrument of salvation, so can it be an instrument of self-deification.

In 1964, while working in France, I went to Barcelona during the Easter parades. Men wearing scraps of raggedy cloth dragged enormous, rough-hewn crosses for miles, subjected themselves to self-whippings, and otherwise punished their own bleeding bodies, until, at the end, they fell to the ground in agonized pain and exhaustion. This religious masochism was impressive as a rite of penance, but it surely didn't evoke a sexual connection; rather, it glorified suffering for its own sake as a choice of individual humility and conscience on behalf of the slain Christ. The experience may have been one of ecstasy, but, if so, it didn't show. Madonna's treatment of sex/violence is closer to that of the Russian Khlysty movement in the early eighteenth century, whereby people seeking spiritual elevation whipped each other while engaged in provocative, ritual dancing. The only sex they condoned was that which occurred between people who were not married to each other (George, 1995: 284). Detachment defined the terms of pleasure.

And again, in terms of Madonna's rationalization for the recurrent S/M imagery in her work, the idea of mutual consent is a dangerous one, because it presumes equal power and the choice of consent. As Cornell admonishes, in the sadomasochistic model of (hetero)sexuality, the only alternative presented for women is 'reversal of *power*' (1991: 132, emphasis in original). 'The sado-masochistic system of gender identity is ... confirmed at the same time that it is supposedly being rejected. Without an ethical affirmation of the feminine which involves a different way of envisioning political struggle itself, we cannot slip beyond the replication of hierarchy inherent in the master/slave dialectic' (ibid.). The bottom line is that, as the beginning of a new millennium approaches, few women enjoy the luxury of being able to 'consent' to games of power.

When racial identity is factored into the equation, the power issues become even more volatile. In her *Sex* book, for example, a photo that may have been intended to signify a liberated race- and gender-blind sexual experience instead looks pornographic: a very white and blonde Madonna is positioned above a prostrate black man who is confined by a leather studded collar around his neck, to which is attached a chain held tightly by Dita/Madonna, who also wields a whip. He is licking her ankle: the dominance–submission posturing is evocative of slave imagery. At the same time, in another photo Madonna is kneeling before a black man who is upright and awaiting her pleasuring; she appears to be shaving off his pubic hair. And in yet another series of photos, a naked Madonna is sandwiched between a black man in a swimsuit and a naked black woman, both making love to her – the perfect Oreo. On almost every page, Madonna stands out from other characters because she's the only blonde woman. The others, with their dark hair, and often dark skin, provide the contrast that makes Madonna shine, with her fair skin and glistening blondeness.

Madonna grew up in a large Italian family in a small home in the Harrington Hills neighbourhood of Pontiac, a Detroit suburb, and later in Rochester, a more affluent community. Motown was her

primary musical influence – along with classical music (from studying ballet), and the music of Phillip Glass, Aaron Copland, and jazz
masters (from studying modern dance: Zollo and Odegard, 1989:
9). When she arrived in New York, still a teenager, she trained with
the junior company of the Alvin Ailey American Dance Center, and
worked with co-founder Pearl Lane (Gaar, 1992: 335). She co-wrote
her first hit, 'Everybody' (1982), with Steve Bray, African-American
musician, producer, and old boyfriend, with whom she continued
to work over the years. Her first two albums were co-produced by
respected African-American producers Reggie Lucas and Nile
Rodgers, and she 'has a clear track record of appealing to black
audiences'; in 1984, Madonna and Boy George were the only white
artists to rank in the top fifty 'black' albums of the year (Scott, 1993:
63). She co-wrote 'Justify My Love' (1990) with Lenny Kravitz.
Although her music is generally found in the Pop section of record
stores, she is also commonly found in the Soul/Dance sections, in
the company of primarily African-heritage soul artists. She has
recently been produced by Kenneth 'Babyface' Edmonds, the most
acclaimed artist/producer of 1996. White audiences, in particular,
liked the hip hop and street rhythms that Madonna brought to
'white' music. Nevertheless, she has been charged with insensitivity
in her appropriations of black and Latino musical styles.

In hooks's analysis, Madonna's 'envy of blackness,' apparently
wanting to be black (or Latina), 'is a sign of white privilege' which
denies the pain and white oppression behind the soul of blackness:
'White folks who do not see black pain never really understand the
complexity of black pleasure. And it is no wonder then that when
they attempt to imitate the joy in living which they see as the
"essence" of soul and blackness, their cultural productions may
have an air of sham and falseness that may titillate and even move
white audiences yet leave many black folks cold' (1992: 158).

Elvis Presley's profits from Big Mama Thornton's 'Hound Dog'
is a classic example of white entertainers reaping fortunes from the
work of black songwriters and performers. Madonna hasn't stolen
others' songs. She has layered her own pop sounds with the R&B,
gay disco, and Latin rhythms, colours, and slangs of the street,
which identify her, superficially, with exoticized underclass minor-

ity cultures. While on *The Arsenio Hall Show* to promote the film *Dick Tracy*, Madonna insulted Arsenio's haircut, to which he later replied in print· 'You have borrowed our sound but not our sensibilities, so don't make an attempt to tell me how I should look' (Andersen, 1991· 326). Jackie Goldsby notes how white Madonna is rewarded with money and status for pseudo-lesbian S/M posturing, while someone like Vanessa Williams, the first black woman to win the Miss America contest (1983), lost her title and years of work when *Penthouse* magazine published photos of her in soft lesbo-erotic poses (Goldsby, 1993).

Hooks discusses how the 'blonde beauty' standard oppresses black women, and she qualifiedly appreciates Madonna for 'the way she deconstructs the myth of "natural" white girl beauty by exposing the extent to which it can be and is usually artificially constructed and maintained. She mocks the conventional racist defined beauty ideal even as she rigorously strives to embody it' (1992· 159). This is akin to Butler's analysis of the ways that parodic performance subverts heterosexuality, demonstrating that there is no natural, original, essential gender identity (1990). This assumes that the parody is recognized as parody, or the excess of mimicry, and not perceived as mere or exaggerated imitation of gender as inborn and fixed. In some of her work, Madonna succeeds utterly in transgressing essentialist notions of gender/sex/race; in other work, more subtly, she reinscribes those notions on the culture, which diminishes her transgressions.

Madonna is accused of colonizing black culture to enhance her own image as a 'bad' white girl, as in her crotch-grabbing *à la* Michael Jackson – the undisputed master of problematizing colour identity with artifice. As discussed by bell hooks (1992), Madonna subtly presents African-American back-up singers as stereotyped 'mammy' figures whose job is to take care of Madonna. In hooks's view, 'tragically, all that is transgressive and potentially empowering to feminist women and men about Madonna's work may be undermined by all that it contains that is reactionary and in no way unconventional or new' (1992: 164). Yet hooks hasn't given up on Madonna as empowering to women, and clearly Madonna's identity cannot be contained by any politic.

6

Liberated Sex Crusader?

The fascinating paradox of sexual identities is that they are both artificial and essential, arbitrary but forceful, invented categories which nevertheless provide the basic directions by which we navigate the shoals of personal need and social relationships. (Weeks, 1991: 5)

The sex-secretive conservatism of the 1950s was mitigated in part by the surging popularity, among men, of Hugh Hefner's soft-porn *Playboy* magazine, which both directly and indirectly anticipated the 'free love' rhetoric of the 1960s. In practice, 'love' was translated to mean 'sex,' and although sex may have become more freely available to men, the women who gave it to them often paid heavily in consequences.

Mainstream legitimacy of sex talk came with the 1970 publication of Masters and Johnson's study of human sexuality. As Virginia Johnson stated in a 1992 interview, the purpose of their research and sex-therapy work was 'to put ourselves out of business, to make such cultural changes that sex would no longer be a sin and something to be feared' (Fried, 1992: 142). Masters and Johnson's liberationist goal, though limited by heterosexist presumptions, has been shared by many over the millennia, as expressed in the twentieth century by artists, writers, performers, social critics, activists, scholars, and therapists. Anxiety about sex can be measured by the barometers of popular (dominant, mainstream) culture, which in our times is increasingly awash with sexualized youth imagery. As Foucault illustrated, even in the nineteenth century, when moralist

Victorians are presumed to have repressed non-procreative sex and talk about it, popular culture and professional speech suggested preoccupation with it (1978).

Madonna has been compared with the sexually (performatively) creative Prince (or the androgynous symbol formerly known as Prince), following a trail cleared by many male gender-bender music superstars, especially David Bowie, Elton John, and Boy George. Over time, the diverse musical artists Joan Armatrading, Laurie Anderson, Annie Lennox, Tracy Chapman, k.d. lang, and Melissa Etheridge, among others, likewise projected androgynous sensuality in their stage appearances. Each of them has been subversive in the ways they have infused their work, to varying degrees, with recognition of sex/gender choice and invention. Despite her forays into sexual ambiguity, ambivalence, and role construction, ultimately Madonna has been much more flamboyantly engaged with artifice than any of these women (although Annie Lennox and k.d. lang have certainly pushed the edges). For over a decade, Madonna has been the vain, proud, and wilful queen of spectacle. Boy George may have described her best when he said of Madonna's performance and public persona that she's a 'gay man trapped in a woman's body' (1995).

As TV-video became the dominant music outlet in the 1980s, 'natural' women such as Patti LaBelle, Joni Mitchell, the Pointer Sisters, Carole King, Aretha Franklin, Linda Ronstadt, Gladys Knight, and Roberta Flack, all hugely popular through the 1970s, gradually lost their places on youth stages. The same problem beset livewires such as Chaka Khan and Donna Summer, the latter of whom was a gospel singer before becoming a nasty disco queen feeding heartily on gay culture. She later reconverted and formed an alliance with the 'Christian' Anita Bryant, an old Miss America who suggested in a *Playboy* interview in the mid-1970s, when gays were dancing to Summer, that homosexuals should be executed (not a new idea).

New performing songwriter–singers of artful substance and stylistic innovation did break through in the 1980s, including Jane Siberry (Canada), Suzanne Vega (New York), and Sinéad O'Connor (Ireland). But the vogue of the decade were sexy dancer/

vocalists, and, within a rainbow spectra of superstars, Madonna kept company on the charts with Tina Turner, as the ever-young matriarch of the art, and Gloria Estefan, Janet Jackson, and Paula Abdul.

Probably more than any other music performer with wide exposure through visual media, Madonna most consistently brings the body out of the shadows and into the light of the open marketplace. A superb dancer, Madonna celebrates the self-sculpted human body, and being naked in the world is one of her ways of shedding her 'ultra-conventional Catholic' upbringing. She modelled nude for art classes while beginning her career, which taught her to think of her body 'as a work of art.' Her lack of self-consciousness is refreshing, and explains her ability to break taboos fearlessly. She says, in regard to the photo shoots for her *Sex* book, that 'the high point was taking off my clothes and running through the streets naked ... I felt like a little girl. It was a rush. I felt like I was on a roller coaster, I couldn't stop giggling ... The idea of taking off your clothes and running through the streets naked is very liberating ... I think everybody should run through the streets [naked] at least once ... If you can do that, chances are you can have a lot of fun in other areas of your life' (*Vancouver Sun*, 5 February 1994: B3).

With an uncanny ability to translate contemporary sexual uncertainties, desires, and fears into commercial art, Madonna knows how to market products that burst through boundaries. Just as a notion or practice approaches the line from perversity or obscenity to acceptable titillation, she has been there to express it, to capture the eager audience. In her early interviews she repeated *ad infinitum* that her purpose was to liberate people from their sexual hang-ups, which gave her a certain one-dimensionality. Her film work to 1995 was all about sex. She represents the 'loose woman,' even in *A League of Their Own* (1992), directed by Penny Marshall, an engagingly wholesome story about a women's softball team in the 1940s. Amidst a group of sheltered, innocent young women, Madonna's character wryly uses an erotic paperback to teach an unschooled teammate how to read.

Elayne Rapping, describing Madonna's on-stage performance,

speaks of her humour, irreverence, and lust; her celebration of 'female freedom from sexist constraint'; her 'sexual bravado,' and 'unbounded sexual energy and aggressiveness' – all of which preclude the possibility of her being misunderstood as an exploited 'sexual object' (1994: 55). Rapping goes on: 'She is so at ease with her sexual power, so fearless of its effect on others, so outrageously candid and open that she stands as a living symbol of the liberating power of breaking social taboos' (ibid.).

Sex appeared to be Madonna's very obvious *raison d'être* throughout her first decade as a performer, though she occasionally protested that this was a problem of audience perception. For example, she claims that her song 'Like a Virgin' is *not* about sex; it's about fresh new beginnings (Gilmore, 1987: 38). Expressing disappointment that the video was misinterpreted as juvenile bimbo lust, Madonna said the real point was the character's strength, that sexy women can also have substance. She says in an interview that, given that she wore lingerie in the video and danced erotically with a seductive attitude, 'it might have seemed like I was behaving in a stereotypical way [, but in fact] I was also masterminding it. I was in control of everything I was doing, and I think that when people realized that, it confused them. You *can* be sexy and strong at the same time ... Sex is equated with power in a way. ... It's scary for men that women would have that power, and I think it's scary for women to have that power – or to have that power and be sexy at the same time' (quoted in Gilmore, 1987: 87).

Young Madonna's protests that she wasn't all about sex were less than convincing when she called her publishing company Slutco, talked about sex incessantly, represented it as both high and low drama in her work, and in other ways implied that she has a prodigious sexual appetite or, at least, an ironic obsession with it. Madonna said of herself, ingenuously, 'Everyone probably thinks I'm a raving nymphomaniac, that I have an insatiable appetite, when the truth is, I'd rather read a book' (quoted in France, 1992: 104). She doesn't say whether it might be a book about sex, but she has said, in her *Sex* book and elsewhere, that her 'dick' is in her brain, as her explanation for why she doesn't need the 'physical apparatus' to experience phallic power. In the opinion of 'sexpert'

Susie Bright, 'being a very public and willing sex maniac is the most original, radical, and courageous thing that Madonna Ciccone has ever done' (1993: 86).

In her documentary film *Truth or Dare*, directed by Alek Keshishian (1991), Madonna let herself be seen as a dominatrix with her dancers and singers, though she says she thought of herself as being 'motherly' with them. Before each show she gathered the group together for a circle prayer and, in these and other documented scenes, her loving side is shown. She also chose to include abundant real-life bad-girl material which shows her off-stage as inexplicably arrogant, rude, hurtful, and cruelly disrespectful towards others, including her father, one of her brothers, a childhood friend, a gay dancer she outed, and Kevin Costner; when Costner came backstage to tell her he thought her show was real 'neat,' behind his back she made mock gagging gestures at his unhip turn of phrase. In the film she shows bully-pleasure at having the power to order people around, condescend to them, and express mean thoughts to or about anyone. This is her own presentation of Self, and I like to think that she reveals her dark side, not because she is oblivious of her own nastiness, but rather because she is committed to an honest portrayal.

When the film documents how the Toronto show of the 'Blond Ambition' tour, co-produced by her brother Chris Ciccone, is threatened by censors with cancellation (because she simulated sex on stage as part of her act), she is clearly pleased, knowing her tease value shoots up with every censorial pronouncement. Moreover, every threat of censorship, however weak in practice, puts her in good company with the victims of witch-hunts through the ages. Artists are trusted both to mirror life as they find it and to elevate the human spirit with their own creative visions. On either count, their work may threaten the status quo and lead to dangerous censorship decisions. Consider, for example (courtesy of Joann Field, Simon Fraser University Bookstore), just a few of the authors whose books have been banned over centuries for falling short of the standards of the moral guardians of various times and places: George Orwell, Mark Twain, William Faulkner, Mordecai Richler, bell hooks, Toni Morrison, Voltaire, John Steinbeck, Kurt Vonnegut, J.D. Salinger, Thomas Hobbes, Margaret Laurence, Dante, Ray Bradbury, Ernest Hemingway, Rudyard Kipling, Allen Ginsberg, Maya Angelou, Alice Munro, Oscar Wilde, William Golding, Shakespeare, Henry Miller, Ken Kesey, W.P. Kinsella, Andrea Dworkin, Thomas Hardy, Salman Rushdie, Marguerite Duras, Lillian Smith, D.H. Lawrence, Timothy Findley, Jane Rule, and children's authors Robert Munsch, Roald Dahl, and Maurice Sendak.

In Canada, in the 1990s, certain imported books (and tapes) are banned through arbitrary censorship exercised by Customs officials, not on the legal grounds of obscenity so much as on the grounds of an individual officer's attribution of generic obscenity to the communities for which the work is targeted. Thus, books related to sexual technique can be located in almost any library or bookstore, but books which are addressed to gay and lesbian bookstores are often intercepted, even when they're not about sex (Fuller and Blackley, 1995). Wherever censorship thrives in these times, it will be applied most consistently to those with the least political power, and Madonna is not among them.

Had Madonna lived a century earlier, she could not have been so outrageous. At the end of the nineteenth century, in London, the prostitution-abolitionist movement closed down 1,200 brothels over an eighteen-year period, and campaigned against sex publications, 'nude paintings, "immoral" plays and novels. A special target of their hatred was the music-hall, where working-class audiences enjoyed variety shows that included sexually explicit jokes and sketches and burlesque-type dances' (Roberts, 1993: 258). The moralists won the day, but music-halls are periodically revived and censorship battles are potentially part of every creative artist's occupational hazard. Money and fame afford political power, which is why attempts to censor Madonna have been unsuccessful. Madonna does not shrink from facing the censors; rather, despite their bluster, the censors seem afraid of her.

The 'Bonfire of the Vanities,' one of the great censorship events of all time, took place in 1498 in Italy, Madonna's ancestral homeland. Just six years earlier, the westward sailing of the Italian navigator and pirate Christopher Columbus led the imperialistic invasion of what the world now calls the Americas. This was the era of the

Renaissance, the post-medieval rebirth of classical culture and the arts which stressed beauty, balance, harmony, and (Man's) dignity. It was a time when 'respectable' women stayed in their homes. Prostitutes dyed their hair blonde to enhance their attractiveness, as the centuries-earlier Roman whores had done (Roberts, 1993: 102), and as Madonna and millions of other contemporary women have done.

When practised by renegades from hegemonic ideologies, censorship can backfire. The doomsday monk responsible for this bonfire, Girolamo Savonarola, was himself later hanged, and then burned in Florence's city square as a heretic. His awful crime, committed just two decades before Martin Luther led the rupture of Christianity, was criticizing the Roman Catholic adoption of pagan icons as religious symbols – the same iconographic symbols which Madonna parodied, and popularized as adornment. With support of the ruling Medici family (who also sheltered Michelangelo, ironically), before fatally losing favour, Savonarola became highly influential in Florentine society, and he loudly expressed his fury at the materialism, lust, and greed that had corrupted the Church and the rich patrons of Pope Alexander VI; he especially disapproved of depictions of the naked human body, which he considered obscene.

The famous marketplace bonfire instigated and ignited by Savonarola was fuelled with treasures which wealthy believers gave up to him willingly in their quest for redemption for having materialistic vanities and false idols: musical instruments, literature, fashionable garments, cosmetics, and countless, priceless works of art (including most of Botticelli's paintings) went up in smoke (George, 1995: 282–3), precipitating the submission of Savonarola's own body to the flames.

Almost half a millennium later yet another Italian would be threatened with censorship of *her* sacrilege and obscenities, a threat having the effect of designating her transgressions as authentic resistance. Indeed, the Italians of Madonna's heritage cancelled two concerts in her 1990 'Blond Ambition' tour because she was simulating sex on stage. Some of us might have wished for Madonna to be more critically- and consequentially-minded in her work, more mindful of the dynamics of power relations, and on those grounds more often self-censored for reasons very different from those of critics who condemn her. As gay novelist Terry Southern asked in the 1960s, himself a target of censors, 'At what point does the aesthetically-erotic, extended indefinitely, become offensive? Offensive not to the audience ... but to the [artist him/herself]?' (quoted by Krassner, 1996: 7).

Censors be damned, the pleasure–pain continuum was central to Madonna's early work, whether acting as a dominatrix, or dressed in drag and exploiting masculine power garb, or costumed as a preadolescent feminine seductress. She doesn't explicitly deny power imbalances, and she acknowledges power abuses in videos such as 'Like a Prayer,' where a saintly black man is wrongly accused of rape. She observes the violent desires that result from injustices, and for these desires she claims legitimacy. Desire itself may or may not be predicated on power relations, within which human beings struggle for their particular sense of self, voice, and place. But when the relations between 'partners' are unequal by definition, it's a set-up for abuse, whether or not that choice is taken. Madonna claims the violence, and then trivializes it through hardware symbols and posturings. Paradoxically, her singular characteristic as a blatant challenger to submissive female traditions is her ballsy femaleness. She doesn't seduce with soft femininity (although she's increasingly presenting herself that way in the mid-1990s). She orders everyone around, even in those rare times when she presents herself as a compliant receiver. As she says of her own autocracy in the studio, 'This is not a democracy' (Orth, 1992: 306).

Madonna doesn't seem to be saying, when in male drag, that she wants to be a man, any more than she seems to be saying, when dressed like Marilyn Monroe, that she wants to be that woman. She's a gender interventionist, disrupting conservative sex/gender scripts. At the same time, she interjects an ideology that presumes that avant-garde sex, in any configuration, is simply intended to push the boundaries of the existing practices. She doesn't present new ways of imagining sex, even when both subjects are female, but rather follows the model of role-play (masculine and feminine, conquest and submission, flirting and taking charge) that characterizes mainstream heterosexual imagery. She exhibits what de Lauretis calls 'the confusion of desire with identification' (1994: 116).

Even though she is said to be terrifying to men, when a 1992 English-Canadian poll asked men to name their first fantasy for a celebrity affair, Madonna took first place, virtually without competition (Wallace, 1993). In 1994, *Esquire* (August) and *Details* (December), mainstream men's magazines, featured Madonna on their covers in nearly naked S/M and ageing-prostitute poses. The *Esquire* hook was the Madonna interview by Norman Mailer, self-appointed arbiter of women's (hetero)sexual currency. There's clearly a male market for Madonna.

In her first decade, Madonna consistently put Sex in the centre of things by being aggressively female and using her breasts and groin strategically. In the masculinist tradition, only men are supposed to take what they want; females are supposed to entice males into wanting them. The public Madonna defies this custom, presenting herself as the *master* of her own sexual journeys. While she holds countless Madonna-wannabes in her thrall as a vicarious source of female power, when her fans show humble deference she stands back from their adulation. She said of young female fans in Japan, whose rituals of servility disarmed her, 'Sometimes it makes you feel like you're enslaving somebody, and that's a creepy feeling' (quoted in Gilmore, 1987: 38). In real life, then, it doesn't feel so good to her. Madonna disdains the weakness of the girls in the shadows, playing from a distance to those willing to follow her lead without contact. Yet she appears to be making light of enslavement in her film and print representations of sex, where, in a male-identified way, she assumes a dominant position.

In 1985, before her wedding to Sean Penn (which was invaded by photographers in helicopters), *Playboy* and *Penthouse* magazines both published nude photos of Madonna taken five years earlier, when she was a young, unknown, aspiring musician, dancer, and actress, working as an artist's model. She tried unsuccessfully to stop their publication of her bared self. It wasn't the nudity that disturbed her, but the loss of control of her image, and the inference that her talent was built on taking her clothes off. Marilyn Monroe was another of many women to be confronted, after achieving fame, with nude photos from her past. Madonna, for her part, turns shame on its head and has the last laugh. As one of the most powerful performers in the world, on her own terms, she self-produces equal-opportunity pornography featuring her sculpted body and down-and-dirty sex, which puts mere nudity in perspective.

'Justify My Love' (1990) and 'Erotica' (1992), among other Madonna videos temporarily banned from Music TeleVision, and *Truth or Dare* (1991), the documentary film of her 'Blond Ambition' tour, were read by conservatives, on the one hand, as narcissistic indulgences in contrived exhibitionism which exploited immoral (biracial and bisexual) fantasies. Her critics were cut from the same cloth as those who resisted the U.S. Supreme Court's decision in 1967 that the states could no longer outlaw interracial marriages. Women and men who identify as 'sex radicals,' on the other hand, exulted in Madonna's fiercely frank denunciations of repressive sexual (and racialized) barriers. She is not on the cutting edge so much as she is simulating a myriad of sexual identities already percolating in the real world. As eloquently discussed by Jeffrey Weeks, people are talking about 'sexual identity' as never before, and openly debating such issues as whether 'homosexuality' is a matter of diversity, plurality of truths, change, resistance, and choice, or of fixed identities, monolithic truths, imperatives, destiny, and genetics.

The very profusion of often confusing and conflicting voices, lyrical and anguished, biting and caring, romantic and cynical, repelling and appealing, contentious and collective, has marked the world of sexual politics as uniquely cacophonous and disturbing. (Weeks, 1991: 8)

So what do we mean when we use the term 'sexual identity'? Does it offer us the 'truth of our beings,' or is it an illusion? Is it a political trap that imprisons us into the rigid and exclusive categorizations of those arbiters of desire, the sexologists? Or is it a necessary myth, the pre-condition of personal stability? Is it a snare ... or a delusion, a cage ... or an opportunity? ... (ibid.: 69)

The 'Justify My Love' video features a glamorous and feminine (*à la* Monroe) Madonna as the dominant figure, centre stage, choreographing erotic play with subordinate, stylized-exotic characters across borders of colour, sex, culture, and ethnicity. She crashes the fiercely guarded gates separating black/white sexuality, producing erotica from that which is racist. Religion is in the picture (predictably) in the form of the ubiquitous crucifix, hanging from her lover's neck. The video, and the very danceable song, had become a queer anthem in gay clubs before the mainstream could see it on TV. At the end of the video, a message appears on the screen: 'Poor is the man / Whose pleasures depend / On the permission of another.'

In 'Justify My Love,' Madonna implicitly represents real-world power relations, but glosses over them to imagine a consensual world where all are equal – except for herself: as always, she's in charge. Mainstream feminists commonly recoil from the dominance – submission theme to which Madonna seems so attached. As Greenberg puts it, with reference to the ancient Greeks, they 'could not easily conceive of a relationship based on equality,' but, for the Greeks, male supremacy was a given (1988: 147). Contrary to this tradition, feminist resistance privileges equality in sexuality, as in all human interaction. Equality itself is eroticized (Valverde, 1985). However, in Henderson's arguably feminist-positive view of Madonna, the 'Justify My Love' video signifies the liberated '"bad girl" who refuses to secure her legitimacy by denying or relinquishing sexual agency,' and who uses her power to combat 'homophobia, racism, puritanism, and sexual violence' (1993: 115).

In Madonna's *Sex* book, her humour is pronounced, when, for example, she is photographed nonchalantly hitchhiking in high heels and carrying a purse, but otherwise stark naked in daylight on a street in Miami Beach. Like the elderly Sons of Freedom women whom I've encountered in prisons in my province, who parade naked to protest the materialism, vanity, and private ownership of modern life, so does Madonna, the original 'Material Girl,' point out the hypocrisy and silliness of people hiding from one another under their garments; underwear worn on the outside is resistance to concealments and hypocrisies. The Sons of Freedom women have reached a spiritual plateau which permits exposure with neither shame nor sexual inference. Madonna is differently, irreverently shameless, towards both sex and sexual authority. She celebrates sexual transgression as a documentarian as well as a titillator and provocateur.

With an immediate international demand, *Sex* (1992) 'became one of the fastest-selling books in Canadian history,' despite normally harsh Customs policies against literature depicting gay or lesbian sex (Toobin, 1994: 76). In Vancouver, in May 1993, six months after the book's release, 1,068 individuals still had holds on the Public Library's three copies of *Sex*, which meant that, if all the copies were returned within a week, those awaiting it could all read the book by late March 2001 (Wyman, 1993). There were similar line-ups at libraries wherever it was stocked, and bookstores couldn't keep up with sales.

An internationally acclaimed French art director, Fabien Baron, designed the book, which consists of 128 pages of Madonna in sexual poses with friends (including actors/models Isabella Rosellini, in drag, and Naomi Campbell), with a written narrative accompanying the photos. At least one serious text has already been published with a specific focus on the *Sex* book, and I quote from the introduction: 'Like the Gulf War, the trial of William Kennedy Smith, the confirmation hearings of Clarence Thomas, and the debate about gays and lesbians in the military, *Sex* was the sort of public spectacle which, while commonplace in North American culture, is nonetheless produced as an extraordinary event, even as a crisis' (Frank and Smith, 1993: 12).

It was the celebrity of the author that sold the book. Thanks to the publicity, the first printing of *Sex* netted Madonna in excess of $20 million (Orth, 1992: 298). On first printing, 750,000 copies of the book were produced, requiring three-quarters of a million pounds of aluminum for the covers, which were then heat-sealed in heavy mylar. The book measures approximately 10 by 13 inches and weighs 3 pounds; the package contains a remix CD of the title track to her album *Erotica*. The printing company wouldn't allow its name to appear in the book. The man who coordinated the production of the book, Nicholas Callaway, was candid in explaining that the complicated packaging had a phallic purpose: 'We wanted there to be an act of entering, of breaking and entering' (ibid. 302).

In the *Sex* book, Madonna and her friends engage in sex play that includes S/M accoutrements and posturing, and she appears inappropriately (though humorously) buck naked in ordinary public daytime settings. She celebrates exhibitionism and evokes images of 'consensual' violence in the name of sexual liberation. She breaks down the categories by presenting erotic partners in every configuration, breaking norms both in mainstream and in 'deviant' practices. Contrary to Adrienne Rich's 'lesbian continuum' (1983: 192), Madonna's women-in-bondage postures do not signify lesbians at any level of intimate friendship or sexual commitment, but rather offer porn caricatures for the heterosexual male gaze. Her representations are consistent with 'perverse' depictions of 'female homosexual-lesbianism,' using de Lauretis's distinction; they don't communicate 'lesbian subjectivity,' but rather are 'representation of desire heterosexually conceived, even as it is attributed to a woman for another' (1994: 77, 110). In discussing how women are 'cut off from the myths that could give the feminine meaning,' Drucilla Cornell asserts the Lacanian sense that women 'are silenced before the mystery of the ground of our own identity,' that women are 'appropriated by the imaginary feminine as it informs male fantasy' (1993: 75).

Madonna is the focus of the camera in *Sex*, and as the narrator she assumes the alter identity of 'Dita,' a European actress in leather. Madonna is the only blonde woman in the book; she separates herself, yet is the centre of every scene, even when she poses as an onlooker. No social context is established, just make-believe, detached moments of sex play recorded for all time as art. Nothing in the work challenges reactionary ideologies which threaten gay men and lesbians in the real world. Much of the narrative, in fact, is a bit inane. As a banal example: 'I let her french kiss me and smear my lipstick.' John Champagne comments on this failure of her words or images, ultimately, to transgress hegemonic sexual moralities in modern culture: 'what renders *Sex* not perverse enough is its particular deployment of the figure of Madonna and its accompanying star persona. Such a deployment threatens to make the "impure" world of the perverse useful for a contained consumption by homogeneous capitalist culture' (1993: 119).

Packaging and marketing for the 1992 *Sex* book were coldly invitational to censors, with the metal cover sealed in hard plastic, ominous symbols of dangerous content, and a 'warning' sticker ('Adults Only!,' it says) for those in doubt. The news media gave daily reports on where it was being censored. The CBC reported that, among many others who were prodded by citizens' groups to investigate the book's pornographic content, the sheriff in Cincinnati and the attorney general in Alberta both decided the book was okay, and could be stocked in public libraries. Libraries in North America reported removing the book, not because of censorship, but because the metal cover was coming off and the book was falling apart from overuse.

The book was banned from public distribution in Ireland and in some Australian states. In Japan, the English-language version went to the top of the best-seller list, because the Japanese-language version could be sold only after airbrushing to hide the photo of male genitalia (*Advocate*, 1992: 32). Nicholas Winterton, a Conservative member of British Parliament who appealed in vain to the 'obscene publications squad' to ban the book, said of *Sex*, 'This is a vile, obscene, pornographic book ... Filth of this kind should not be sold in our shops' (*Montreal Gazette*, 17 October 1992). In India the police seized the book at airports, and the *Times* of India editorialized that Madonna is a 'sex-bomb, a shock-baby, a waif who went wrong because that's the right-on gambit to stay on top of the charts' (*Vancouver Sun*, 3 November 1992: C3). Such press is good news for Madonna, whose fortunes and influence multiply each time she is declared a menace.

That so many anti-fans can't resist paying attention to her is testimony to Madonna's charisma. Her fans supply the fuel that powers her career and her critics provide the incentive for her to lead the children down ever stranger lanes. Journalists write long columns about her, at the same time decrying the attention she receives. As one writer said of *Sex*, concluding his loud and lengthy negative review, 'This book is probably best ignored ... anybody who loudly attacks it is only contributing to the phenomenon, the megahype ... The steamroller effect has taken hold ... Only one thing can halt the steamroller in its tracks: massive indifference. The grace of silence' (Abley, 1992: J4). Chris Dafoe, arts critic for the English-Canadian *Globe and Mail*, agreed in his own lengthy story that the time had come for a boycott of Madonna stories (1993). In fact, the media couldn't stop talking about Madonna's book, with special attention to its more daring features, such as the 'tattooed, bare-breasted lesbian skinheads' (*Vancouver Sun*, 10 September 1992: A3). The startling provocation of this photo is Madonna's exaggerated femininity in contrast to the queers, and her identity-distance from their intimacy. She maintains a similar distance in the Oreo shot, with oh-so-white Madonna sandwiched between Big Daddy Kane and Naomi Campbell.

Much of *Sex* is about Madonna's uncovered body – though with high-heeled shoes, gloves, belts, straps, purse, and a bunny tail. There she is, stark naked in her assiduously cultivated body, hitch-hiking, riding a bike, eating pizza, pumping gas – and kneeling over a dog in a way that invited speculation as to her meaning. That photo is unnerving, and others are worse, but the sexualized nakedness alone caused a stir: 'When the naked female form is being blatantly sexualized by a superstar woman, there is little hope of de-sexing it enough to allow women to walk the streets shirtless without attracting lascivious male attention. Until people like Madonna stop taking part in such exploitative eroticism, it's a hopeless cause' (*Vancouver Sun*, 19 October 1992: A10). Some of Madonna's poses in erotic clothing are more ominous than the naked shots. For example, she poses in a see-through bra with falling straps, held at the shoulders from behind by a good-looking man elderly enough to be her grandfather, who nuzzles her neck. In the next photo she's on his lap, bare-breasted and smoking, content while he handles her.

Hand-written narrative by Madonna's dominatrix alter ego, Dita, graphically describes sex acts, of which the accompanying photos offer visual representation. She presents a smorgasbord of poly-morphous perversity and sexual possibilities, including the one Madonna claims to abhor – performing oral sex on men. (In several photos with different partners, it is Madonna who is receiving it.) She observes of it, 'Who wants to choke? ... that's part of the whole humiliation thing of men with women' (Fisher, 1991: 120). She treats sadomasochist imagery as an amusement, by now an old theme.

On ABC's *Nightline*, in 1990, she defended scenes in the video 'Express Yourself' in which she is chained to a bed: 'Okay, I've chained myself ... I did it myself. I was chained to my desires ... There wasn't a man standing there making me do it. I do everything by my own volition. I'm in charge, okay?' It's just not obvious how choosing to chain one's self, as a way of taking one's power, can be interpreted as a signifier of liberation. Mary Joe Frug responded to Madonna's claim to be in charge: 'Although I believe Madonna's claim about herself, there are probably a number of people who won't. Anyone who looks as much like a sex worker as she does couldn't possibly be in charge of herself, they are likely to say; she is an example of exactly what [Catharine] MacKinnon means by a "walking embodiment of men's projected needs"' (1992: 132–3).

I emphasize Madonna's sexual outlandishness as the most conspicuous, compelling, pervasive aspect of her early work, but she has also shown a tender, feminine side which she similarly complicates for production value. For example, in the video 'Rain' (1993), Madonna is gentle, vulnerable, and sensual, her poetic nudity sweetly embodied within the romance of the song. And then suddenly, simultaneous with a persuasive performance of herself as innocent, desirous, and yielding, she makes the spectator conscious of her power by deconstructing the video in the process of its production. We see the crew at every stage of filming and recording her, in a multiplicity of gazes. In this hall of mirrors we see the crew itself being filmed as they film Madonna, who gazes back at them and, via the camera, performs to the imagined spectators beyond, who will, in delayed time, materialize as an audience unseen by Madonna through the loops of media technology, just as the cameras behind the cameras are unseen. She is the focal point of all this activity; she has the power.

With 'Rain' the spectator is carried back and forth from scrutiny of the production process to feeling the effects of a soft, appealing

Madonna in a simple romantic tale – which is all the more affecting because the tenderness contrasts with her more familiar raunchiness. The video within the video is minimalist compared with other Madonna videos, which tend towards visual flourish and complicated, layered story lines, settings, time frames, characters, fantasy/reality juxtapositions, and so on. Like all her productions, the 'Rain' video within the setting of video production is layered with visual signals that elevate and expand the sound and meaning. She makes the point that there is a lot more to her music than meets the ear. Her music is great to dance to, but radio/audio couldn't contain her. Detached from her embodiment, neither her voice nor her lyrics begin to convey the theatrical richness of her conceptual imagination in the way that her live performances and well-produced videos have done.

Madonna's video success continued in 1994–5 with 'Take a Bow' (1994) (from the album *Bedtime Stories*), which made her top winner at the 1995 U.S. Music and Television Awards, and 'Human Nature,' which ranked ninth in the Top Twenty Singles of 1995 (Aaron, 1996: 88). Her abundant talent as a visual artist is evident in these, as in previous works, although she returns to familiar imagery. 'Take a Bow,' co-written with her album co-producer, the talent powerhouse Babyface, tells of a tragic love affair with a toreador, a *de facto* romantic figure. Filmed in a 500-year-old building, the oldest bullfighting ring in Spain, the video indulges Madonna's ongoing infatuation with Spanish symbolism and passion, a sensibility graphically displayed since her lullabye 'La Isla Bonita,' produced on video in 1987.

'Human Nature' (1995) reissues black leather and rope scenarios, market-wise S/M props which, to the mid-1990s, sustained her bad-girl image and kept her interesting to those attracted to or intrigued by her fetishes. This song is Madonna's response to the press beatings over her *Sex* book and her four-letter display on David Letterman's *Late Show* (see chapter 9). Her sex 'obsessions' had become tiresome to her critics, but to paraphrase an arguable remark I recall hearing from David Bowie in an MTV interview, 'It's the artist, not the critic, who makes the culture'; it's the *making* of human culture that is the point here.

To her critics, Madonna sang impudently 'Did I say something wrong? – Oops ... I didn't know we couldn't talk about sex. I'm not sorry – it's Human Nature.' Cultural anthropologists, postmodernist philosophers, historians, sex/gender theorists, and many others have recognized that there can be no such thing as 'human nature,' not even where sex is concerned. Conquering nature was Enlightenment Man's imperative. Generic Man has defied nature in every way beyond the necessary (to life) biological functions of being conceived (in or out of a womb), growing as a foetus in a womb (or some reasonable facsimile), coming out and detaching from the umbilical cord, breathing, eating/drinking, sleeping, relieving bodily waste – and even after all that constant upkeep, eventually, like any living organism, the body dies anyway. Sexual desire, if not need, would seem to be universal, but there are extremely different means of expressing it. Adopting the Freudian (three-monkeys) strategy of denial of childhood sexual abuse by fathers and other male relatives, it was purported by anthropologists into the 1970s that there was just one universal taboo: 'incest.' With the smashing of the myth of children's safety within their home, we are left with no universal cultural taboos, even though every culture at any stage in history has many taboos of its own. The boundary makers and the boundaries themselves appear only when they are transgressed, and shift when the transgressions are sufficiently numerous and diverse to suggest that there can be nothing 'natural' about being 'human.' We make it up as we go along, though not usually under conditions of our choosing.

This song about 'Human Nature' is a story of sex invested, perhaps unwittingly, with *masculinist*, as opposed to masculine, values. Her idea of 'human nature' is embedded in what she clearly perceives as the inextricable relationship between sex and violence. And she goes on to sing, 'I'm not apologizing. Would it sound better if I was a man? I have no regrets. Absolutely no regrets.' In a vocal track under her sweetly sardonic melody line, her own voice whispers incessantly, 'I'm not sorry, I'm not sorry,' and for punctuation she states her proverbial message: 'Express yourself. Don't repress yourself.' We get it. This woman is not repentant.

As for whether Madonna is a *liberated* sex crusader, her performance suggests that she is herself liberated from the fears that commonly inhibit women's sexual expressions. And for over ten years, she was most clearly a sex crusader. For those who have already come of age sexually, and who take their sex fears too seriously, Madonna's saucy irreverence could be liberating indeed.

7

A Careening Career

Her phenomenal mass appeal and exceptional staying power notwithstanding, mainstream arts and music critics were only occasionally enthusiastic about Madonna's talents in her first decade as a superstar. As a musical *artiste* she was often thumbed-down shortsightedly by the men who are the Critics, even though admired for her daring style and startling business acumen. For example, reiterating a common attitude, *Montreal Gazette* music reviewer Mark LePage said of *Erotica*, her 1992 album, 'After all the ranting and ogling is done, it comes down to bad girl/good girl. That is, when Madonna's bad, she's good; and when she's good, she's so very, very banal' (1992; E1). Another typical reviewer, from the *New York Times*, dismissed her music as 'short on melody and long on crunching beats, cool in attitude but steamy with sexual bravado' (Holden, 1992). And, of course, sex sells. In July 1989, Madonna had already had fifteen Top Five singles in a row, surpassing the Beatles (Andersen, 1991: 298), and soon it was sixteen consecutive hits. Each album she has issued throughout her career has gone to the Top Ten on the charts, and over time she has become as much substance as style.

Madonna's music, as of 1992, consisted of five albums, plus soundtracks and collections, totalling on average 10 million album sales per year of primarily danceable tunes. By year's end, 1995, she had produced three more albums, mixes of powerful musicality and formula fluff. She exasperates reviewers, who can't easily type her music, but her eclecticism may be a strength, as observed by musicologist Susan McClary: 'Madonna's refusal of definition goes beyond the paradox of her name, her persona, her visual imagery. It also produces brave new musical procedures' (1990: 12). In explaining her diverse sources, Madonna says, 'I've listened to so many different kinds of music all my life ... I'm sure it's everything that I've ever heard. And then it comes out in my own bastardized fashion. What I am is what I've digested throughout my life. What comes out of me ... I just think it's all stored up' (Zollo and Odegard, 1989: 8). The body-waste/anality metaphor, likely unintentional, is Madonna-like. But the face-value observation that her music reflects the composite of her multicultural musical influences and identities explains her appeal to widely diverse audiences. Her history-making success is based in part on her border-crossing, her inclusivity of address.

Smashing in her first widely viewed film, Susan Seidelman's low-budget *Desperately Seeking Susan* (1985), Madonna received great reviews and her character was the key reason why the film was so appealing to women. Madonna's first cover story for *Rolling Stone* (9 May 1985) came out just as the film was released, and she was on the cover of *Time* magazine (27 May 1985) just following. Preadolescents and teenagers adopted Susan's (Madonna's) clothes and hairstyle, and critics treated Madonna with serious respect for the only time in her early film career. The following year they punished her with ridicule for her role as a missionary in *Shanghai Surprise* (1986), in which she co-starred with her then-husband Sean Penn. (Not incidentally, they were not allowed to film in Shanghai, because the officials considered her to be 'a whore.') Although she apparently liked her next film, *Who's That Girl?* (1987), she was harshly criticized for it; it lost millions and went to video after three months. The film *Bloodhounds of Broadway* (1988) was considered such a failure it went straight to video, and was never distributed to theatres. These films may not warrant defending, but it's hardly fair to hold Madonna responsible. (Likewise, her wild success in *Desperately Seeking Susan* was due in no small measure to the director Seidelman and to her co-star, Rosanna Arquette.)

Her most surprising professional turn in the 1980s was to act in David Mamet's *Speed the Plow* (1988), setting a Broadway record for advance opening-night ticket sales (Andersen, 1991, 274–5). As it turned out, the play did not herald the start of a serious theatre career, any more than her pre-*Evita* films augured well for a celluloid career, even though her acting was sometimes very strong.

Receiving decent, if not enthusiastic, reviews for the blockbuster *Dick Tracy* (1991), Madonna played Warren Beatty's sexy sidekick Breathless Mahoney (and off-screen companion). But her best achievement in connection with the film was the album it inspired, *I'm Breathless*, with strong vocals ranging from disco ('Vogue') to Broadway fare. She was also complimented for her fleeting appearance in Woody Allen's *Shadows and Fog* (1991), and for her small but significant role in *A League of Their Own* (1992). Reviewers of the 1993 R-rated *Body of Evidence*, in which Madonna's lead character is charged with killing a man with her lethal sexual powers, again concluded that Madonna can't act, but fans disagreed and I agree with the fans. Her performance (and/or the direction) may be uneven, but her best scenes in that film rank with the best of the other serious cinema anti-feminist 'super-bitch white killer-beauty' genre that sprang up with the Glenn Close character in *Fatal Attraction* (1987), and has recurred frequently since, notably with Sharon Stone's character in *Basic Instinct* (1992; Faith, 1993a: 265).

In 1995, she appeared in *Blue in the Face*, a quirky, star-studded art film with Harvey Keitel, Jim Jarmusch, Lou Reed, Roseanne, Michael J. Fox, RuPaul, Mira Sorvino, Lily Tomlin, and others. (For whatever reason, it never showed up in Vancouver, so I missed it.) Madonna's other 1995 film venture, *Four Rooms*, came and went. Four different writer/directors developed the film on the familiar premise that very different lives are being lived out in four rooms in a Los Angeles hotel. Allison Anders directed the first segment, casting Madonna as one of a coven of sexy witches. Predictably, none of the critics was enthusiastic about the film, and Madonna's presence in it was scarcely acknowledged. In 1996 she had at least two more films in the works: *Evita*, and *Girl 6*, directed by Spike Lee, with, again, a crowd of mostly quirky actors (including Halle Berry, Naomi Campbell, Debi Mazar, Ron Silver, Quentin Tarantino, and John Turturro); true to form, Madonna plays a caricatured madam.

As her performances in *Evita* and other films have demonstrated, saying that she *can't* act is simply wrong. Her recurrent failures with film critics rest in part on the musical Madonna's *poseur*
mode of expression, which she extends to film. She is theatrically
masked, instead of entering and moving the character through her
own being and inviting the audience to join her there. This is what
film requires of an actor, moving into the character and letting the
character move within the actor, unlike the stage, where it's a performer's job to go out to the audience and project assertively.
Aggressive projection of five minutes' worth of a character, even a
tender character, can work seamlessly with Madonna's music and
lyrics. Each song is a little play of her own design, and she may
project half a dozen attitudes in an hour.

Her difficulty in gaining momentum in film related to this difference between acting as masquerade and acting as displacement
of self. Madonna's Self, though multifaceted, looms larger than
the Self of any of her film or music characters. Some of her film
roles (for example, the nun in *Shanghai Surprise* and the dominatrix in *Body of Evidence*) have seemed utterly contrived and opportunistic, as a way to capitalize on fetish themes that also appeared in
her videos and in the *Sex* book, rather than bringing authentic life
to a character, which is what actors do when they're effective, and
which is what Madonna does with Eva Perón.

Madonna takes justifiable pride in being in control of her
career, but the extent to which she's a control freak may contrib-
ute to the actuality or the perception that, in film, 'she can't allow
herself the emotional nakedness of the craft' (LePage, 1993; E1).
Madonna herself says, 'I accept the fact that making movies is
about a collaboration and requires a certain amount of surrender
...' (McLeod, 1993: 15). She must surrender not only to the identity
of the character, but also to the writer, director, costumer, set
designer, make-up person, and so on, who collectively decide how
her character will look and be portrayed, a process which is further
complicated by dynamics with co-stars. By contrast, her myriad
masks as a performance artist–musician, in which she holds uncon-
tested centre stage, are her own creations or collaborations built
around Madonna's own persona. The very word 'persona' means

'mask.' Clearly, when it's her own conception and she's in control, she can effectively act any part. But 'the masquerade is never quite successful; or rather, it is successful *as* a masquerade – not an embodiment' (de Lauretis, 1994: 103). It is acting seen as acting, which works only if the star is performing in her own name. In her own name she can be 'excessively excessive.' She can use layered parody to mimic herself, 'flaunt [her own] performance as performance [,and] unmask all identity as drag' (Fuss, 1995: 81, n. 27).

Mastering the technique of masquerade and playful excess mimicry is Madonna's forte. But the skills required for masquerade or mimcry don't transfer easily to playing a role the actor didn't invent, which requires seamless acting not seen as acting. Her universal fame *as Madonna* has made her a key and ready target of the paparazzi; she is recognized virtually everywhere, and, given her outrageous presentation of self (selves), she has strong love–hate effects on people. Preconceived notions of who Madonna is may overwhelm an audience's ability to see her as a character independent of Madonna, and one can't attribute her slow start in the movies to Madonna's own limitations. The quality of Madonna's work on *Evita*, although in many ways it is a vehicle tailored to suit her, is sufficient proof that Madonna's been learning from experience how to enter and embody a character. The part had been close to her heart for years, so she was well invested in it. And because it's a musical, she's in her native element. In chapter 9, more will be said about *Evita*, because it signifies a turning-point in her career – particularly because she was pregnant while filming, and the baby arrived just two months before the film's release.

In the mid-1990s, Madonna's artistry has begun to match the level of her already achieved celebrity, but commercial culture has never relied on artistry to satisfy its goals. What is it, then, in addition to her talents, hard work, and millions in promotional budgets, that, for over a decade, has attracted so many millions of fans across the globe? Her bad-girl attitudes and posturings? her spectacular productions and phenomenal energy? her marketing genius? her prescient timing, and ability to tap into the cutting-edge pulse of popular culture? her pornographic provocations?

her contrived rudeness and bratty self-centredness as a young woman? This last point probably explains her early appeal to young people: she was a vicarious freedom ride for kids who have parents, teachers, older siblings, superior-acting friends, play-ground bullies, street bullies, police, welfare workers, and many other people telling them what to do. She's been the first rebel pony out of the stall, the leader of the pack.

This quality of always being ahead of the game was very evident from the beginning, in *Desperately Seeking Susan*. Rosanna Arquette's character, Roberta, takes on the identity of the hipster bad-girl Susan, played by Madonna. Roberta is torn between returning to her predictable husband and safe, suburban home, and staying with her new lover and the street excitement of an off-beat life signified by her idol Susan, who, as played by Madonna, is described by a male reviewer as 'an empress of trash, a libidinous but untouchable she-wolf' (Schruers, 1985: 32), and by a female reviewer as 'a free spirit who does as she pleases and most defi-nitely controls her own sexuality' (Rapping, 1994: 278). In one tell-ing scene, Roberta is in a magician's box, presenting the illusion that her body is being sawed in half. This scene is a key metaphor for the story, and also for desires invoked in the film's fanatical young female audiences, who soon after were perfecting Susan's image in Madonna look-alike contests at malls across the United States – constructing a link 'between the empowered, free, public world of the star and the powerless, constrained, private world of the teenager' (Fiske, 1989: 149). Roberta signifies the female dilemma of having to choose between being a madonna (domesti-cated woman) and being a whore (in-charge woman), being split apart. Madonna's Susan character signifies ambivalence resolved; faced with a binary choice, she'll play the Whore.

Like most news dailies and other publications, the *Montreal Gazette* runs the regular, obligatory Madonna stories. They went beyond that convention in October 1992, when they established a 'Madonna Hotline,' encouraging 'the public' to express opinions about her book *Sex*, and the *Vanity Fair* layout of Madonna posing as a seductive preadolescent. Of the 200 people who called in dur-ing the course of a week, 65 per cent approved of her work. Comments from a random selection of callers, as reported by the *Gazette* (31 October 1992: E7), did not generally indicate the age or sex of the person speaking, but one can recognize attitudinal distinctions in many of the comments that suggest male or female, teenage or adult. It is apparent, first of all, that the contradictions of Madonna do not go unnoticed:

I think she exploits women's bodies ... but she is very smart and intelligent and I love her.

The thing I don't like about her is that she is vulgar ... but I like her music ... she is very creative.

She is the best and she is trying to portray that you have to be in control and that there is nothing wrong in being gay or bi or black or white; I mean you can have sex with whoever you want as long as you take precautions and have safe sex and wear a condom. Then it's alright.

If Madonna wants to go around naked then she should do what she wants.

I don't think she cares whether we love her or hate her as long as we remember what she does.

More common messages on the Madonna Hotline were unabashed testimonies of either love or hate. The majority of callers, who simply love her, said such things as the following:

She should run for politics and should be Prime Minister.

I love her ... she is so sexy ... this is what the English community needs.

She is a good example. Our society is sexually repressed and she brings out people's true sexuality.

Madonna is the best and always will be. I adore her.

She is super-cool. One hell of a woman.

There is nothing I would change about her.

A disproportionate number of the complimentary calls were in fact back-handed and cynical in their references to age and trends. For example:

Her trendiness is getting boring.

She looks great for her age [Madonna was then thirty-four].

... a legend in her own time, and for her age she looks really good.

She feels she has to be different because she is getting old.

I'm fifteen and I have been listening to her since I was six.

However much she demonstrates that the artistic spirit is her moving force, when Madonna attends fastidiously to $60-million negotiations, it can only be concluded that the money also matters. (She tells how she was competitive in school because she and her siblings received a quarter for every 'A' on their report cards, and she wanted to get the most money: MuchMusic, 1996). She knows how to invest her money in work she cares about, and is one of the world's major collectors of both modern art and antiques. Few people in the world would have difficulty finding ways to disperse huge sums of money, 'wisely' or otherwise. Besides maintaining three homes, Madonna gives money to worthy causes, especially AIDS-related. Her 'Blond Ambition' tour alone raised $10 million for AIDS research. Artistic integrity and financial success do not have to be oppositional, even for principled performers, but bitter callers to the hotline accuse her of prostituting herself, figuratively speaking.

I think Madonna is a very clever money-making whore.

... she does it mainly for her ego and the money.

... a good example of somebody who will do anything for money.

Madonna prostitutes herself ... I think she is sucking everyone in.

All she is is a modern form of prostitution ... where a person has to sell everything she has to make a buck.

She is so rich she is bored and she is looking for ways to entertain herself. She irritates me.

If you are thinking of buying the book [*Sex*], then take that [U.S.] $60 and donate it to a worthwhile charity. [Alternatively, a cartoonist depicts two old codgers in front of a bookstore window displaying the *Sex* book and the price tag: one says to the other, 'Heck, for that kind of money you can get the real thing': *Newsweek*, 2 November 1992: 43.]

To some who called the Madonna Hotline, she is beneath contempt, but still compelling enough to induce them to make the call and express their opinion about her. The more scathing comments on Madonna and her work are evidence of the energy people give to her, even when they don't approve of her. Moralists, in particular, find her a magnetic target for their wrath, and she doesn't hide from them. One caller lamented that 'humanity is in a sad state when we direct so much attention to her and waste so much time and energy on her,' while giving attention, time, and energy to her. Other outraged callers were less philosophical in their tone, to wit:

I think she is disgusting and has problems and should see a psychiatrist.

I am sick of her... I hate her. She is a [disgrace] to humankind and to women.

... a very bad influence on children.

... just presents more stereotypes of women as [mindless] sex objects.

She is disgusting and immoral.

... she abuses the power she has and she degrades society.

She's dirt.

Such unqualified hostility came from a small minority of the callers, but the vociferousness of their wrath in the face of her mass popularity represents the extreme end of a continuum of judgments against her, from feminists to right-wingers.

These sounds of protest, all told, make barely a ripple in Madonna's career, and are more likely to enhance than disrupt her star value, which continues to grow. As one example: for approximately sixty major Hollywood celebrities, primarily actors, the average cost in 1995 of an autographed photo was about U.S. $65, the price for a Tom Cruise, for example. There are only seven stars whose autographed photos cost more than $100: Demi Moore ($110), Arnold Schwarzenegger ($110), Michelle Pfeiffer ($125), Harrison Ford ($150), Jodie Foster ($150), Julia Roberts ($195) – all movie stars – and Madonna, who is way ahead of the pack at $250 (*Premiere*, 1995: 102).

Madonna appears to be constantly on the move, emitting energy, taking it all in at a glance, and being seen, channelling her hyper energy and ambition into high productivity. One gathers from her interviews that she's well organized and that she works with competent, dedicated, nurturing people who cheerfully tend to her personal and professional needs. She's had the benefit of career-boosters, such as Dan Gilroy, who in New York gave her a home and led the first band she played with, Breakfast Club, and who, with his brother Ed, facilitated her start as a singer, drummer, and songwriter. She then started a band called, in succession, The Millionaires, Modern Dance, Emanon (no name), and Emmy, the last of which stuck. The drummer was Steve Bray, an African-American musician/songwriter from Michigan who for a time was her boyfriend (Lewis, 1990: 102). In New York, they co-wrote her first single, 'Everybody' (1982), which, together with 'Holiday,' the next year, launched her career and the wild popularity of Dance Music. They continued to work on projects together. Next up was Mark Kamins, the musically astute Danceteria deejay who re-produced and promoted the single, and got Seymour Stein to listen to it and sign her with Sire Records, a Warner subsidiary. (It seems entirely appropriate that the negotiation took place in Stein's hospital room, where he lay recovering from a heart attack: Arts & Entertainment, December 1993). Her first manager, Camille Barbone, jump-started Madonna's fledgling career and helped support her until she was a hit. By now the lines of people who have both contributed to and benefited from Madonna's career are too long to contemplate.

The tabloids charge Madonna with using people and moving on, from friends and early bandmates, to benefactors, to bigtime producers; lamentably, however, in her defence, among ambitiously successful people in a competitive and individualistic world, this is a common occurrence, and consistent with the motive forces of capitalism. More notable is the deep level of trust, loyalty, and easy affection she appears to build with those in her inner circle, and the longevity of her apparently respectful relationships with those closest to her, such as her publicist and her manager, who have helped her coordinate her multifaceted career since the mid-1980s.

Prior to the release in 1992 of the Penny Marshall film *A League of Their Own*, during the production of which they became friends, Rosie O'Donnell, who appears to adore Madonna without excusing her, tenderly scolded her on *The Arsenio Hall Show* (re-run 15 July 1994). O'Donnell busts Madonna by saying 'You're trying to come across as a cold bitch, but you're not,' and she goes on to convey what a sweet, considerate, kind person Madonna really is. Later in the show, Madonna's father makes a surprise appearance. The two of them look relaxed with each other, and mutually bemused. He says of his daughter that 'she's done a real good job' and he's 'proud and happy for her success.' (For his birthday, Madonna reports, she bought her father things he apparently really wanted, a John Deere mower and a chainsaw.) When Arsenio, who hadn't yet been in conflict with Madonna, said of her that she's the 'sweetest, kindest girl in the world,' her father agreed, saying that her meanness is pretense. (He did allow as to how he didn't like seeing her masturbate in *Truth or Dare*.)

In a single-minded, disciplined way, Madonna has continued over the years to add dimension to her career, even though having long ago achieved the highest rank of celebrity and wealth. I expect she has a vision for her multiple talents beyond demystifying sex and making an unfathomable amount of money. Thousands of people have auxilliary music-industry jobs in part because of Madonna's success. With her company, Maverick, she now has the resources to delegate most of her backstage work to other people. It appears, however, that she does need to be in control. The way for a CEO to hold onto autocratic power is to scrutinize every detail connected to the enterprise, to never delegate the most important decisions, and to recognize before anyone else what's important to a company's success. Madonna says of her job as the head of Maverick in the early 1990s: 'There's the bands I have to go see and the tapes I have to listen to, and there's the publishing deals I have to approve of, and there's the employees that I have to hire to run the company and the interviews that have to take place and the scripts I have to read for movies that I would like to act in. And there's the books I'd like to read that I would consider buying to make movies out of as a producer, and the list is endless.' (Orth, 1992: 301).

Madonna attributes her need to be in control to childhood losses, beginning with her mother's death when she was just five years old. She remembers of her mother's last days at home: 'I was so little and I put my arms around her and I could feel her body underneath me sobbing ... I think that made me grow up fast. I knew I could be either sad and weak and not in control, or I could just take control and say it's going to get better' (Worrell, 1985: 61). As she later explained herself, determinedly but with theatrical self-mockery, 'I will never be hurt again, I will be in charge of my life, in charge of my destiny. I will make things work. I will not feel this pain in my heart' (Orth, 1992: 306).

And so she works, and spurns vacations. For the *Sex* book she personally examined 20,000 photographs before making decisions on which ones to include. As a business colleague put it, 'She's willing to defer everything for this [ever-greater success]. For more covers of magazines. More just feeds on itself. It's like an addiction' (Orth, 1992: 301). Another colleague says of her hunger (for approval, money, love, power, security), 'Nothing will ever be enough. Never' (ibid.). Apart from collectivist aboriginal and some Eastern cultures, populations at large in these times of élite abundance and mass scarcity could be described as obsessively seeking approval, money, love, power, and/or security, and it's seldom enough. Moreover, given the directions her life has taken, it would seem that Madonna's drive comes from artistic compulsion.

'A young writer is said to have sent his poems to Rilke asking Rilke to tell him if he was really a poet; Rilke sent the poems back unread, telling the young writer that he would know himself that he was a poet when he thought that unless he wrote poetry he would die' (Reiman, 1990: 50). This is the kind of passion for creative work that Madonna conveys, and (as is true of any artist whose work is for the purpose of communication) an audience is essential to her performance. Clearly her business acumen has facilitated her performance, recording, video, film, and publishing opportunities. Critics may attack her with presumptuous, shallow, and unfair judgments, but, given the nature of the businesses she's in, she needs the critics as much as she needs the audiences, of which critics are a hypothetically detached extension.

Madonna's sure-footed ambition is matched by her discipline, which has included two and a half hours daily of strenuous physical work-outs (*Young and Modern*, 1993: 48). Early in her career, Madonna's image included alcohol and cigarettes (Marlboro Lights), but if she ever had a problem she apparently got healthy. Reportedly, except for performance purposes, she doesn't drink alcohol, smoke, or do other drugs (although she reports that, in the past, she experimented with numerous recreational drugs, including Ecstasy). She eats healthful food. She is not a party animal. She's been trained with the body-centred discipline of the dancer, and she said of her pre-maternal life that she lived like a monk.

The angularity of her perfectly conditioned body prompted Uli Edel, the director of her 1993 bondage film *Body of Evidence*, to compare her muscled arms to boxer Sugar Ray Leonard's; he asked her to stop working out during the filming, in a vain attempt to give her character softer curves (Cable Information Network, 22 January 1993). That same discipline extends to every aspect of her work, according to associates such as Donna Russo, a Warner Brothers executive who worked with Madonna in the 1980s: 'She's a perfectionist of the first order. And I admire that, because it's so hard to be that disciplined. It's like she's been in a Buddhist temple in her past life or something' (quoted in Gaar, 1992: 335).

Madonna never stops. Where, then, is she headed? She said frequently in interviews that she wanted to have a child, a regular family. With that as his cue, in 1989, seven years before the birth of Madonna's daughter, one writer projected the following: 'Flash forward ten years (to 1999) ... Your latest album, just released under the name Louise Ciccone, has just gone platinum, the public drawn to songs about flowers and mountains and being in love. You're happily married, with kids, and the Madonna and Child headlines have long since lost their tacky resonance. Sometimes you wake up and you can't stop smiling. Life's good. You're good. And most of all, you're you. Hey, maybe it was worth all that pain' (Mathur, 1989: 72). This idea of Madonna's mega-career as something to just hold her over until she gets a husband, children, and perfect satisfaction through domestic bliss might seem ludicrous in light of her life experience: her massively publicized 1985 marriage to and 1989 divorce from Sean Penn; her provocative fling with Warren Beatty; her lesbian-erotica photo layout for *Rolling Stone* (Meisel, 1991: 43–51); her teasing on *Late Night with David Letterman* with Sandra Bernhard, acting like lesbian girlfriends (NBC, 2 July 1988); her video 'Justify My Love' (1990), which, like others, was banned from MTV for nudity and polymorphous sex among males and females, brown, black, and white; her publicized dates with various pretty young men and women; her popularity with gays; her influence as one of the few white megastars to regularly show up on African-American radio charts; her *Sex* book. This Madonna did not add up to a candidate for wide-eyed domesticity in the countryside, with homemaking overshadowing a part-time music career.

Years later, in late 1995, Madonna herself was declaring in every interview her intention to become a mother as soon as possible, as soon as she finished filming *Evita*. She teased that she would like Sean Penn to be the father. She also said that, after the movie wrapped, she would 'put a couple of ads in the *New York Times* and the *Village Voice* and see who applies for this fatherhood gig' (Primetime, 1995). It turned out to be Carlos Leon, who in photographs is dark, athletic, gorgeous, geared towards show business, and employed as her personal trainer. She became pregnant while working on the film. Madonna as madonna with child was a startling thought. But, as Susan McClary put it, reflecting on Madonna's work: 'Madonna's art itself repeatedly deconstructs the traditional notion of the unified subject with finite ego boundaries ... Her pieces explore ... various ways of constituting identities that refuse stability, that remain fluid, that resist definition' (1990: 2). Her life as offered to and presented by the media is always on the edge of ambivalence and change. Now that she has a baby, Madonna *could* become a self-produced, magnificent home-body, stay-at-home-mom, president of the PTA, joining with other parents to protect her kids from the filth of popular culture. Indeed, in 1996, while riding horseback in a beautiful country setting, Madonna says 'I thought to myself, I could have this life if I wanted it. Children and a husband waiting to have lunch with me. And then I remembered I had about eight months of work ahead of me. A girl can dream, can't she?' (Madonna, 1996: 223).

In the early 1980s, Madonna was linked by the media with distinctive young men like deejay/producer John 'Jellybean' Benitez (very seriously), Prince (a musical partnership), model and video actor Tony Ward, and John F. Kennedy, Jr, whom she pursued. Following her divorce from Sean Penn, she continued to refer to Penn as the love of her life (Rapping, 1994: 55). She later dated Warren Beatty, towards whom she was likewise publicly generous after the break-up. As with Penn earlier, she conveyed that her attraction to Beatty hadn't ended with his mating with another beautiful woman, and fatherhood.

In her film *Truth or Dare*, she let Beatty expose her for caring only about life in front of the camera. In 1991 her escort to the Oscar awards ceremony was the sexually ambiguous king of artifice, Michael Jackson, then her main commercial competition. She was close to former rapper Vanilla Ice, who posed for her *Sex* book but later regretted it because he didn't want to be identified with 'all the other people in there, a bunch of freaks. I'm no freak' (Hatt and Dampier, 1995: 96). Also, in the early 1990s, Madonna was linked with flash basketball players – Charles Barkley and Dennis Rodman. Rodman, who dated Madonna for two months, later published a book which included a derogatory chapter on her, the lament of a rejected man: despite their intimacy, he seemed to not understand her boundaries. She has found extraordinary men to wear on her arm, but Paglia may be right that it would be hard for Madonna to find a public man as powerful as she is (1994: 237). Madonna herself says of power, a definition that came to her in a dream, 'Power is being told you are not loved and not being destroyed by it' (1996: 225).

Perhaps identifying with royalty, when the unhappy life of Princess Diana hit the headlines Madonna declared to the press, 'I invite her to come and live in my apartment' (*Maclean's*, 12 October 1992: 69), suggesting that she, of all people, would protect Diana from the media's prying eyes. It's awesome to imagine what the media would make of Madonna housemating with the Princess, whom Paglia describes as being Madonna's 'sole contemporary parallel as an international pop diva' (1994: 168). Given Madonna's wealth and her circulation in the social worlds of art and fashion, she does rub shoulders with the *glitteratti*, very wealthy, aristocratic people like designer Gianni Versace, who, according to *Vanity Fair* (January 1997: 89), is also friends with Princess Diana.

Career-wise, Madonna started with a bang. Her first album, *Madonna*, recorded in 1982 and released in 1983, eventually sold 100 million copies worldwide. By 1985 she was a star. The three Radio City Music Hall concerts which opened her first promotional tour sold out in about thirty-five minutes. At one point she had six singles in the Top Forty (Garratt, 1986: 12). Cruising fresh from the film *Desperately Seeking Susan*, and presenting herself as having unbounded self-confidence, Madonna said she didn't expect to limit her career to being a rock star: in twenty years (2005) she expected to be a great actress (Worrell, 1985: 63).

In her first decade as a megastar, Madonna shocked public sectors and compelled critics to pay attention to her, because she kept filling cultural space with images that combine the most sensitive nerve centres in the Western universe – Sex and Race. 'She seduces us by underscoring the intricate relationship between these cultural obsessions as they pertain to the inextricably connected preoccupation with Wealth and Power' (Waters, 1991: 55). As a young woman, with the tabloid hounds at her heels, she cruised New York, Los Angeles, and the Miami South Beach drag scenes: wherever transgressors were, there Madonna would be. As Maggie Smith said (playing *The Prime of Miss Jean Brodie*), 'If scandal is to your taste, I shall give you a feast.'

In the end, Madonna both exploits and transgresses conventional power imbalances, while multiplying her wealth within the framework of capitalist entertainments. She is objectified for profit but she is herself the author of her own objectification: 'The star is to be understood as unique within the realm of commodities; at once labor in process *and* the product of labor. Thus, although there will always be a fair amount of mystification, the star displays – as an inevitable part of the performance itself – the effort that goes into his or her own making' (Seigworth, 1993: 295). She is a global mass-market commodity and the creative head of the various corporations that are Madonna, and because she is a talented, monster superstar, she is not constrained by exigencies, fluctuations, and inequities of a political economy that grossly limits the lives of most working and unemployed people. Since her debut album in 1983, 'as the premier female recording artist on the planet, Madonna has generated sales of more than $1.2 billion' (to 1996: *Vanity Fair*, November 1996: 36). She self-commodifies for our amusement, but her heart is revealed. She mocks herself as surely as she mocks all of us, and for me that is her saving grace.

8
Role Model?

As a young woman, early in her career, Madonna spoke in awe of Hollywood legends Carole Lombard, Claudette Colbert, Judy Holliday, Marilyn Monroe. She loved them as glamorous, smart, screwball comedians who, in her words, 'give you a taste of real life, some poignance, and leave you feeling up at the end – none of that adolescent-fantasy bullshit' (Schruers, 1985: 30). Six years later, 1991, herself still a major supplier of adolescent fantasy, she was identifying with the 1930s actress Louise Brooks, because 'she was hyperactive, she didn't mince words, and she was a rebel.' (Brooks did the majority of her films in Europe, where nudity was not prohibited.) Madonna had also decided that, when she was no longer sufficiently beautiful to be a star, she would be a director (Fisher, 1991: 36, 39). In 1993, on the international 'Girlie Show' tour, she donned a tuxedo and an androgynous attitude for a take-off on Marlene Dietrich. All of Madonna's glamorous role models have been either already or nearly dead; she does not acknowledge competition among her contemporaries; and, since Cyndi Lauper in the mid-1980s, the critics have rarely compared her to anyone else, dead or alive.

As a performer Madonna signifies the times she lives in, a postmodern period in which everything can be taken apart, difference is celebrated, social hierarchies are under attack, and nothing is certain or predictable. Meanwhile, as always, many kids are growing up in a world that doesn't welcome them or make them feel needed. As Ann Kaplan observed in 1987, when Madonna was still new, many of her most avid fans were prepubescent girls: 'It is perhaps Madonna's success in articulating and parading the desire to be desired in an unabashed, aggressive, gutsy manner (as against the self-abnegating urge to lose oneself in the male that is evident in the classical Hollywood film) that attracts the hordes of 12-year-old fans who idolize her and crowd her concerts' (1987: 126). John Fiske agrees with the 'gutsy manner' characterization as the reason young girls were so smitten with Madonna: 'The teenage girl fan of Madonna who fantasizes her own empowerment can translate this fantasy into behavior, and can act in a more empowered way socially, thus winning more social territory for herself. When she meets others who share her fantasies and freedom there is the beginning of a sense of solidarity, of a shared resistance, that can support and encourage progressive action on the microsocial level.' (1989: 172).

Those same kids are now young women who still follow Madonna's career, and some did 'make some socially progressive uses of her texts' (Fiske, 1989: 190). Two reviewers (the first female, the second male), at different stages of her career, offer conflicting interpretations of Madonna's effects, which, taken together, signify the conundrum of trying to pinpoint Madonna's own point of view:

Madonna embodies and resolves contradictions that bombard young women: a whore who's still a virgin, a wise woman who's still a naive little girl, an innocent who can bite forbidden fruit and remain untainted. (Garratt, 1986: 13)

It's fine to say that this is all make believe, but to the thousands of teenage Madonna fans who are going to, one way or another, look at this book [*Sex*], those fantasies may seem real ... Madonna [should consider] teenage boys who think that because Madonna wants to be raped, it's okay to rape. (Andrews, 1992: A2)

Through the 1990s, Madonna has maintained her power to dominate the entertainment media. Her early fans are ageing with the former collector of 'boy toys,' and new fans come on board with each album or video release. Her fashion influence has crossed generations. Teenagers in the mid-1980s entered Madonna look-alike contests in suburban malls, and went on talk shows, wearing metal, plastic, and jewelled crosses as earrings and necklaces, clashing colours, corsets as outer-garments, white, raggedy lace tights, black tube skirts rolled down to expose belly button and underwear, high heels with anklets, and streaked, tangly hair tied up in rags, scarves, ribbons or pantyhose – looking, in Kaplan's words (1987: 126), like a 'cross between a bordello queen and a bag lady' (a comparison not intended to denigrate bordello queens, bag ladies, or even Madonna wannabes). Madonna, explaining her early wardrobe, says, 'The way I dressed in the beginning of my career was a reflection of me being incredibly poor. I just wore things I had left over from my training as a dancer: skirts and tights that I cut off below the knees. I would use the rest of the tights to tie my hair back. Then, suddenly, that became *the look*, which was funny because I was just making the best of my situation.' (Madonna, 1996a).

Clearly, however, she was using fashion creatively and with intent. The corset, for example, was introduced in the Victorian era as an actual and symbolic instrument of the constraint of women. When Madonna brought it into view, and wore it over other clothes, she popularized the corset (like the bra) as a symbol of liberation. (My friend Cris says, with pointed irony, 'Before Madonna, who *knew* we were supposed wear our underwear on the outside? *Who knew*??') By the early 1990s, the breast-enhancing bustier, popularized by Madonna, was a fashion commonplace among adolescent girls, young women, and women wanting to be young. Madonna's own original bustier made the CBC news when it was stolen from a display at Fredericks of Hollywood, during the looting that accompanied the uprising in South-Central Los Angeles in April–May 1992. (She replaced the stolen bustier with another from her historic collection.) She also, in the 1980s, exposed and sexualized the bared belly button, which by 1996 was status quo in mainstream youth fashion.

John Fiske observed of Madonna in 1989 that she both colluded with patriarchal meanings and offered resistance by projecting independent sexuality. This contradiction results in 'an anxious, unstable tension.' Fiske continues: 'She is excessive and obvious; she exceeds all the norms of the sexualized female body and exposes their obviousness along with her midriff. Her sexualization of her navel is a parody of patriarchy's eroticization of female body fragments – she is a patriarchal text shot through with skepticism' (1989: 124). Fiske's characterization reads as both literal description – we can imagine her belly button – and succinct analytical deconstruction, but the question of intention remains. Is this Madonna's intended meaning and purpose, to humorously protest the commercially viable sexist objectification and fragmentation of the female body? Or is this just the reading of intellectuals concerned with gendered representations? When she was a young artist, did her fans read her this way? Or would a fan just mimic her, and beautify (with fashion, or piercing) yet one more erogenous zone on her own body as a device to enhance her status as a sexy young woman? Whether or not they were cognizant of it, Madonna's early fans participated with her in the parody of the commercial fragmentation of the female body. The problem is that parody not recognized as parody unwittingly legitimizes that which is being parodied.

It is because preadolescent and adolescent girls have looked up to her as a mentor, and the public long ago conceded that she is a monumental cultural icon, that Madonna invites so much attention. Most seriously to critics, in terms of her influence on youth, she blatantly exploits the shock value of her sexualized images without critical comment. The *Vanity Fair* layout, where she poses as a seductive child in pigtails with bared breasts and buttocks, aroused even more outrage than the *Sex* book, as expressed in a public letter to Madonna from the president of MediaWatch, a Canadian organization which monitors female representations in the media: 'In ten pages of baby-powder poses, your insidious impersonations of innocence reached greater depths of depravity than I think even you imagined ... What about the child you mimic? ... She doesn't even have a fraction of the control over her life that you've earned ... What is there to protect her? What advice would you give to the prepubescent ten-year-old whose uncle sees

her as the ripe and seductive schoolgirl your pictorial portrays?'
(Graydon, 1992: 5).

In the interview accompanying the *Vanity Fair* photographs,
Madonna exposes stark insensitivity to the implications of her representations. Implying that sex is neutral at any age, void of power
relations, she says, 'I don't think that sex is bad ... I think the problem is that everybody's so uptight about it that they make it into
something bad when it isn't, and if people could talk about it freely,
we would have people practicing more safe sex, we wouldn't have
people sexually abusing each other.' (Orth, 1992: 212). It's easy to
agree with elements of the repression hypothesis, that if people
would just loosen their bodies, dissolve their guilt, and free up their
minds they would find a world of glorious sexuality awaiting them.
This is very different from representing children as knowing sexual
seducers. As response to the libertarian attitude, Henry Giroux
makes my point in his discussion of the power differentials
reflected in the texts of 'high and low' cultures: 'it is imperative that
the ... power relations in which different texts are produced be distinguished so that it becomes possible to understand how such
texts, in part, make a difference in terms of reproducing particular
meanings, social relations, and values ... (1993: 69).

Not all young people are enamoured of Madonna, as documented by Carl Taylor in a study of gangs in Detroit. A thirteen-
year-old girl defends Madonna against her friends' criticisms, but a
sixteen-year-old boy carries on, ' ... that bitch is fake to the max,
she's nothing but a ho ... look at her with all them faggot dancers,
she is that HO ... She the kinda bitch that tries to get all the fellas
and want her ass kiss all the time,' to which Madonna's young
defender responds, 'she is in charge. She got all them boys working for her, it's her show, she's the one.' The fray continues, with a
fourteen-year-old boy asserting that 'Madonna is a little white ho,
trying to dance with niggahs – the bitch is out of control. She ain't
blond, her titties is them plastic ones ... She like that little white
college girl at the Center. Bitch talking like she one of us.' A seventeen-year-old chimes in: 'Madonna is selling pussy ... if a black babe
did what she did everybody would be illing. Madonna kissing
another babe is freaky, white people like that ... she only want the

dancing homeboys, the fags, black fags dancing with her white blond ass out front ... just another white bitch' (Taylor, 1993: 155–7). This is rough condemnation, from young people coming up on the streets. If these attitudes are representative of street kids', Madonna's career may be more dependent on the white middle-class than one might think, which may be entirely suitable for a wealthy white woman entering middle age.

Women who rely on their sexuality as a strategy for gaining some autonomy most conspicuously include women who sell physical sex, who typically begin their street work as youth running away from abusive homes (cf. Lowman, 1987). Feminists commonly observe that Madonna's sexual themes (which she attributes to the constraints of the Church) suggest some unresolved issues. As restrained examples, Susan Cole's response to the *Vanity Fair* photos, and the *Sex* book, was to observe that 'Madonna's sexual ferocity [is] mixed with the desperation of a true survivor' (1993: 37). And bell hooks implores Madonna to explore memories of her 'childhood in a troubled family in a way that enables her to understand intimately the politics of exploitation, domination, and submission,' as a means of producing work 'that will be truly transgressive – acts of resistance that transform rather than simply seduce' (1992: 164).

When I have told female friends or students (ages eighteen to fifty-plus) that I am interested in Madonna, one of their first comments has frequently been: 'I think she was abused,' as a way of explaining her. Approximately half of all females will be abused in their lifetime, and women who pay attention to other women can usually recognize the symptoms. The tabloid media had a field-day when Madonna went to the police to report violence against herself in her marriage, but she kept her dignity and didn't cooperate with the media at any level. After the divorce, she continued to speak of Sean Penn as the love of her life. (She later amended this to say that her daughter was the love of her life.) In a 1995 photo, years later, she looks joyfully surprised to see him as they embrace – almost alone on a stage in New York, where Penn helped present her with the award honouring her as 'Most Fashionable Artist for 1995' (*Province*, 1995).

Whatever violence she may have experienced as a non-consensual victim, Madonna wouldn't be unique. If success is the best payback, she has it. Healing is another matter, but Madonna also has help with that, including her psychiatrist (a standard celebrity perk) and a spiritual faith ironically informed by Catholic symbology. Any experiences of victimization Madonna may have endured, and what she does or doesn't consciously make of it in her work, is her own – unless we buy into the view of Madonna as public commodity. Her official contract with the public is only to perform artistically, which may or may not include baring her soul or being a good role model.

It would help if Madonna and other celebrities would become as adamant and outspoken about violence against women and children in public pronouncements as they are about, for example, AIDS or the environment. But we can't expect that celebrities, who generally get paid lofty amounts only if they lift people's spirits, will volunteer as representatives for women in pain. Only Madonna can decide what she wants to sell to her public, and even if, like so many women, she has 'something to hide,' the question of whether she has a responsibility, as a role model, to validate other survivors by talking about the issues is moot, for all practical purposes. It would not be in her self-interest commercially. At the same time, she is highly visible and she is emulated, which imposes responsibility.

Madonna is hounded by the media and seems perpetually prepared for the camera, but she's also artful in her evasions. Never, when she's in the public eye, does she directly communicate whether she's making it all up and staging a scripted public appearance, or allowing a glimpse of her unrehearsed self. She rarely gives power to the interrogator. She does say the following: 'So many celebrities make some kind of public confession – "Oh, I was abused as a child" or "I have a drinking problem." I have no excuses and I have no apology. And that's very bewildering to people' (quoted in Heath, 1994: 132).

On 14 December 1994, MuchMusic Television ('Spotlight') replayed interviews with Madonna, who herself asked, then answered, the questions: 'Why are they afraid? So many people are afraid to have a point of view, to strike out on their own. In our society [non-conformity is] looked at as a weakness, something to be ashamed of.' These are *adult* judgments she laments. In fact, bold kids have been mightily inspired by her, as have renegades of all colours and ages in all kinds of places. It's the vulnerablity of her fan constituencies that is at issue here, not the conformist for whom Madonna is anathema.

Just as Madonna offends conformists, so does she offend those opposing sexism, ageism, racism, classism, and so on. In much of her work, Madonna makes the common liberal error of obscuring the complex dynamics of power relations – between white people and people of colour, affluent and low-income, men and women, straights and gays, old and young, and every combination thereof. She acts as if everyone has equal power in sexual discourse and practice, but neutrality is a means of denying the potential oppressiveness of power imbalances.

In the first half of the 1990s, in my view, Madonna's more controversial videos did not offer viable scripts for young women seeking sexual knowledge and freedoms, but Madonna is still a worthy role model as she moves from one persona to another. The role of Evita, and becoming a mother, radically changed her image, but her strengths have been constant. At every stage of her early career, she shines with passion for her work. She seeks out good teachers and producers. She keeps her antennae on alert. She trains. She maintains a strong body and good health. She uses her intelligence. She's disciplined and consistent in her focus. She's unafraid of her strengths. She can laugh at herself. And in all these ways she is someone to emulate.

Young people have sat in rapture at Madonna's behest, not because their elders thought she would influence them wisely, but because the opposite is true. She is correctly perceived as dangerous to the repressive, sexual ideologies of her morality critics, but there is overwhelmingly popular support for her deviancies. It is in the telling that she gets into trouble with moral authorities, giving voice to that which was hidden. But she does not signify an instrumentalist force who implants naïve young minds with demonic notions and, like the great Whore of Babylon, erodes their moral fibre and leads them to the gates of self-destruction and hell. In her effects, she is much more complicated than that, just as the audience members who applaud her are much more complicated than the mythical one-dimensional fan. To suggest that being moved by Madonna is a consequence of media propaganda and brainwashing is an insult to her fans, for whom her unrelenting message is to exercise their own choices and agency.

The fan empowered by her use of Madonna to change her relationships with boys may extend this empowerment into her relationships within the family, within the school, or within the workplace. It may be part of the new way in which she walks down the street or the shopping mall, demanding that people take notice of her; it may be part of the process of claiming places within the street for women, of breaking the gendered meanings of indoors and outdoors; it might be part of changing and reducing the male's voyeuristic rights and pleasures. (Fiske: 1989: 191)

I raise the question of whether Madonna is a strong role model for young people, and especially for girls, because, contra Fiske, she is so frequently criticized for setting a bad example. In the end, I conclude that the question of whether Madonna serves as a constructive role model, or whether she has that responsibility, is a false issue. The very idea of a role model is problematic in that it presumes consensual values, which is clearly a mistaken view of the world in which we're living, no matter where we find ourselves. It presumes that there is some clearly defined standard of maturity on which we could all agree and to which all young people should aspire. But, even taking cultural diversity into account, and the ways by which social, economic, and political inequities affect the construction of values, conflicts, and boundaries, the individual is always the final arbiter in choosing mentors. Coming to terms with this process often includes going through stages of idealization and, often, disillusionment. Those who, like Madonna, are sufficiently courageous to take major risks of rejection in order to follow their own star cannot be consistently expected to please everyone whose respect they may covet.

Madonna is a remarkable woman. We can marvel at her talents

or be in awe of her gutsiness as a woman with working-class sensibilities and appeal, who defies the gendered limits of femininity. At the same time we may deplore what could be perceived as the narcissism of her youth or her wild recklessness as a smart, sassy sex messenger. She's living her life and doing her work as she chooses, without asking permission, stretching to the outer limits of her own understanding. In this respect, if you ask me, she is the best role model in town.

9

Only Madonna Knows

The male-dominant press has consistently denigrated Madonna less for her 'sexual ferocity,' as Cole put it (1993), than for qualities more readily identified in terms of class or ethnicity. Raised in a large Italian family in ethnically mixed suburbs, she was attracted to the music of Motown from neighbouring Detroit, a white girl attracted to the black community and street life, identifying with socially designated Others. Disciplined and soon earning her own way, she revelled in defiance, and working-class white girls and black gay boys were among the first to say 'Yes!' Regarding class identity, in the theatre advertising flyer for *Evita*, Madonna is quoted as saying emphatically that she comes from 'a working class background, definitely' (Famous Players, 1996: 11).

Madonna, like pop culture generally, has been geared to working- and middle-class youth. Predictably, she offended the sensibilities of adults invested in sheltered lives, whose religion imposes anti-sex moral judgments, or whose class position imposes constricting social proprieties. Her flamboyance, coarse language, provocative wardrobe, and in-your-face attitude did not endear her to people with 'refined taste' or conservative attitudes. Her reputation as a bad girl has had less to do with sex, in the end, than with her ethnic, wrong-side-of-the-tracks personality, though they can't be readily separated.

This problem surfaced when she took ownership of a historic, luxury Los Angeles estate (once owned by gangster Bugsy Siegel), in a conservative, elegant, wealthy canyon setting, and proceeded to paint the mansion, which is virtually a castle, in red and yellow stripes. Her neighbours were horrified: 'It looks like something out of Barnum & Bailey' (Sullivan, 1993). They were not placated when Madonna's representatives tried to reassure them that the colours would fade to pastels, and that the castle would eventually resemble a rustic, Italian villa. She finally sold it, but only because as a new mother it would no longer serve her needs.

One of Foucault's persistent admonitions is 'know "yourself" by transgressing your limits; practice liberty' (Simons, 1995: 125). At the conclusion of a lengthy interview for *Rolling Stone*, Carrie Fisher suggested to Madonna: 'You like to test your parameters by exceeding them,' to which Madonna responded, 'That's it, absolutely. You got it' (1991: 120). Not only did young Madonna seem not to worry about what the neighbours would think, but she seemed to take pleasure when her choices offended them. Such unbounded arrogance, ingenuousness, or naïvety, as a means of exceeding boundaries, has been something both frightening and marvellous to behold.

Madonna's intelligence doesn't always come across in live or transcribed print interviews, which are generally conducted by powerful, male celebrity TV journalists and writers who meet up with her in London or wherever she happens to be. She sometimes comes across as self-conscious, uninspired, and flat. Her videos and live performances, by contrast, reveal an uncommon conceptual and artful imagination. As Paglia says, 'in music and dance, Madonna does her deepest thinking' (1994: 369). Her career overall is evidence of exceptional ability to creatively maximize her resources. To follow her career as she's shaped it, she does things that look incredibly uncreative and tacky, but her most low-brow moments, when she seems to go for the cheapest possible laugh, are often strategic coups.

For example, on 31 March 1994 she acted out on the CBS *Late Show with David Letterman*. Letterman's 'humorous' introduction of her as having 'slept with some of the biggest names in the entertainment industry' prompted Madonna's own opening question: 'Why are you so obsessed with my sex life?' (Mailer, 1994: 42). It was downhill from there, with Madonna alluding to her undergarment's odorific possibilities for Letterman, using the (bleeped) F-word over and over, like a racy mantra, and asserting other body-fluid references. I wondered, along with a whole lot of other people, if, through her isolation from and power over the masses, Madonna was suffering from some regressive malady that was rendering her stupid and out of control. Her biblical foresisters – Jezebel, Delilah, Bathsheba, and Salome, great, dignified Whores all, but dangerous – would have been embarrassed for her. It was a strange way to use her magnificent power. I was disappointed, because on her behalf I'd snobbishly persuaded sceptical middle-aged friends to watch the show, with the prediction that, with Letterman's free rein, Madonna would reveal her genius.

Madonna's 'display' may have been planned for subversive, strategic purposes, such as ratings, the sensational publicity her shenanigans inevitably generate, and the obvious free-speech issues she keeps raising. Although she was no Lenny Bruce, she wasn't far from the spirit of Larry Flynt, *Hustler* publisher, who is quoted as saying, 'Tastelessness is a necessary tool in challenging preconceived notions in an uptight world where people are afraid to discuss their attitudes, prejudices and misconceptions' (Kipnis, 1992: 376). In an interview with *Details* magazine, Madonna 'swears she didn't' plan the débâcle (Heath, 1994: 185), but according to Madonna in her *Esquire* interview with Norman Mailer (1994), Letterman and Madonna had agreed in advance to trade insults, in keeping with their mutually irreverent public characters.

The Book of Revelation tells us that the great Whore of Babylon, that most wicked of cities, is the Mother of Harlots. Nickie Roberts reminds us that Babylonian temple whores included singers, musicians, and dancers (1993: 7), and this was honourable. The ancient Greek courtesans, the *hetaeras*, were honoured as healers. Many hundred years later, in England, 'actress' was synonymous with 'whore' (ibid.: 146). The connection between female entertainers, whore status (for better or worse), and the force of Church mythology and moral sanctions against prostitutes is by now a very old relationship. An important apocalyptic symbolism infuses Madonna's references to the church, in juxtaposition with her clear rejection of the Church's potent representations of women's place on this earth.

In her representational blendings of sex and religion, the sacred and the profane, Madonna dissolves the binarism of the whore/madonna dichotomy. She harks back to the honourable days, when the prostitute was held up as a sacred being in the court. If the whore is sacred, and the mother is sacred, all women are sacred. The duality shatters: women are women are women. But of course they are not. Particularities such as colour and class are as basic as sex/gender in their effect on social positioning. Not all whores are sacred, nor all mothers, but neither are all of them profane. Veronica Vera, a New York prostitute performer, speaks of crossing lines that close up as they are crossed, including the 'line between madonnas and whores.' She speaks of herself as a 'shady madonna – a woman is not just a madonna or a whore. She is both of these at once and all points in between.' Annie Sprinkle (1991), another noted New York prostitute performer, hosts salons at her home which are 'a refuge for erotic, philosophical and spiritual learning ... Here women learn how to recognize themselves as both sluts and goddesses, and to unite these archetypes' (Bell, 1994: 155, 188–9).

In the early days of her career, Madonna had lively company in redefining the terms of the Whore in contemporary culture. Shannon Bell writes about performance art as a site of resistance, where working girls, as well as dykes, fags, and other Others, can 'reclaim and remap their own identities, to deconstruct the masculinist, feminist, and heterosexual inscriptions on their bodies.' And she writes of the 'conscious crossing and recrossing of the line between the sacred and profane until one slides and dissolves into the other' (1994: 17, 142). Women who prostitute have been organizing since the early 1970s to reclaim their respectable identity and to assert their human rights (Pheterson, 1989, Faith, 1993b), through organizations such as COYOTE (Call Off Your Old Tired Ethics, San Francisco), PUSSI (Prostitutes United for Social and Sexual Integration, England), PLAN (Prostitution Laws Are Nonsense, England), POWER (Prostitutes and Other Women for Equal Rights, Vancouver), and PONY (Prostitutes of New York).

They gather for the International Committee for Prostitutes' Rights, and they are decidedly feminist, even though many agree that prostitution itself is not a feminist practice, but rather a way to make a living.

Through Madonna's revision of women's right to set the terms of sexual engagement, she has toppled the symbolism and reconstructed it in her own image. And having done so, she is changing her tune. On 21 September 1994, it was announced by the press that Madonna was giving up on sex as a lure, and again she reiterated that she's 'not a lesbian' (*Vancouver Sun*, 1994). Lesbians yawned, but comics got some new mileage from it, as did right-wing TV journalist Rush Limbaugh, for whom it was victorious proof that 'mainstream culture is winning' (Fox Network, 23 September 1994).

Meanwhile, with musical shifts giving more weight to her gift for lyrical songwriting, Madonna released *Bedtime Stories* (1994), a collection of ballads with hooks which went straight up the charts, although worldwide sales for this collection were lower than for her dance albums. In the 'Secret' video, Madonna presents happy, sexy, independent women taking us through city streets to a fabulous beat and meeting up with neighbourhood kids, gorgeous guys licking their lips, trannies, prostitutes, biracial lovers, folks playing pool – and as double spectators, through windows, getting glimpses of regular folks in regular home situations. Madonna appears in a project apartment family scene wearing lingerie, this time singing 'Until I loved myself, I wasn't loving anybody else.' The video image of Madonna's character's familial ease with her African-American husband or lover, and his or their son, coincided with a lengthy interview in *Spin* magazine, conducted by Bob Guccione (who, not incidentally, is the publisher of the feminist-maligned *Penthouse* magazine). Here she speaks to the gender complications she's experienced (given that men are commonly threatened by her), in particular within close relationships with African-American men:

I always thought that I appealed to the black and/or gay comunities because they're minority groups and they are prejudged based on things that they have no control over ... [The equality within relationships that she anticipated didn't materialize.] And I came to the realization that a strong female is frightening to everybody, because all societies are male-dominated – black societies, poor people, rich people, any racial group, they're all dominated by men. A strong female is going to threaten every-body across the board.

... Even really successful, intelligent men are so fucking scared of me, and buy into the hype. I think a lot go, 'no, I can't be linked with this per-son, she may overshadow what I do.' (Guccione, 1996: 44–5)

Madonna would be more convincing as a feminist if she would stop seeking approval from and comparing herself to men (as in her oft-expressed attitude, 'Why should they get away with raunch if I can't?') and just be more woman-identified, with all the choices that implies. Prostitution in ancient Rome was 'linked to worship of the goddess Venus, who was regarded as the whores' protector,' and it was the repentant whore Mary Magdalene, the antithesis of the Madonna (aka Mary, the Virgin Mother), 'who played such a central role in the drama of Christ's life' (Roberts, 1993: 45, 57). Mary Magdalene, some 300 years later, was anointed the patron saint of whores in Paris (ibid., 77), and was the inspiration for Houses of Magdalene that originated in Spain and sprang up across Europe, providing shelter to retired prostitutes (Faith, 1993b: 73). Madonna's in an excellent position to be an ally to women who need allies.

It may or may not be encouraging, that is, in women's favour, to read in the Guccione interview that Madonna *loves* Alanis Moris-sette's record; 'I know I'm supposed to say that, 'cause she's on my label, but thank God for people like that' (1996: 45). She's thank-ing God for a woman whose song to her estranged boyfriend brashly, unapologetically uses the F-word, and asks whether his new girlfriend goes down on him in the theatre. When I listen to Morissette and her lesser-known contemporaries, I realize how hard we've been on Madonna. I also realize how hard Madonna has had to work so that artists like Morissette can move right into the mainstream.

In a very different tone from Morissette's, Madonna, too, sings on the subject of losing a man in a 1995 hit single. Inserted in her hit ballads-compilation album *Something to Remember*, 'You'll See' is a poignant, haunting, sorrowful, brave, strong, and perhaps auto-biographical song, and it was an instant hit. To my amazement, in the course of just one February '96 day of errands, I heard the song being played on tape or radio in the drugstore, supermarket, cor-ner store, unisex hair salon, and, ironically somehow, in the wait-ing-room of the ear doctor's office. In this song she vows to handle the break-up with her lover all by herself – 'I know I'll stay alive, all on my own. I don't need anyone ... I'll stand on my own this time' – and to come through all the better for it ('you'll see'). The song is a strong declaration of independence by a vulnerable woman who is nevertheless determined to take care of herself, and would be consoling to anyone between or fed up with relationships. Con-tradictorily, the publicity photo for the new release shows Madonna on a bed, with hefty décolletage arising from her slinky, silver, jewelled slip-dress, her hair falling loosely over her eye, wear-ing a come-hither look. The album, with four new songs (includ-ing her cover of a Marvin Gaye hit, 'I Want You,' of which the subtext is 'I want you to want me'), was nominated for a Grammy as the best pop album of 1995, 'losing' to Joni Mitchell's *Turbulent Indigo*. (As a sweet end-note, when Madonna was young she espe-cially loved Mitchell's *Court and Spark* album.)

Madonna presents so many contradictory facets of her being that she is unknowable to the spectator as someone apart from her work. Whether dismissed as a shallow, commercial ho, celebrated as a heroic Amazon *artiste*, or dissected as an object of serious art and music criticism, she's calling the shots for her career. No one can predict what she'll do next. On both intuitive and calculated levels, Madonna, and only Madonna, seems to know what she's doing.

An interesting footnote to twentieth-century pop history occurred in the autumn of 1995 in connection with Madonna's one-time escort, John F. Kennedy, Jr – whose father and uncle Rob-ert, as president and attorney general of the United States, respec-tively, were both rumoured to have had an affair with Marilyn Monroe, Madonna's one-time role model and send-up. John, Jr, an attorney, became a journalist with the publication of the first issue of his new, glossy, political lifestyle magazine, *George*. The magazine is named for his nation's first president – as parodied in a provocatively adapted period costume for the cover photo modelled by his nation's first lady of image, Cindy Crawford. Kennedy's first invited contributor to the 'If I Were President' column was Madonna. And what would she do if she were President of the United States? Nothing. She would reject the position:

I like the idea of being an inspiration to the downtrodden, of educating the masses. I like the idea of fighting for equal rights for women and gays and all minorities. I like the idea of embracing other countries and other cultures and promoting world peace. Fighting the good fight, as it were. But I think I'd rather do it as an artist. Because artists are allowed to make mistakes and artists are allowed to have unconventional ideas and artists are allowed to be overweight and dress badly and have an opinion. Artists are allowed to have a past. In short, artists are allowed to be human. And presidents are not. So the question is, how can someone be a good leader if he or she isn't allowed to be human? ... I'd rather eat glass. (Madonna, 1995: 280)

She did concede that, if she *were* the president, 'in some parallel universe where there wasn't any pain or prejudice, where the National Enquirer did not exist and women were allowed to empower themselves without being labeled heretical and perverse,' for starters she would pay schoolteachers 'more than movie stars or basketball players'; she would send the grand patrons of late-twentieth-century U.S. censorship (Rush Limbaugh, Bob Dole, and Jesse Helms) to hard-labour camps; she would deport Howard Stern and welcome Roman Polanski back into the country; and, as her *coup de grâce*, 'The entire armed forces would come out of the closet.' I'd vote for her (despite her apparent affection for Polanski, convicted in his forties for having 'sexual intercourse' with a thirteen-year-old girl).

On 2 January 1996, CBS news reported that Madonna would be required to testify as a witness on her own behalf in open court on a stalking case. In the usual heavy-handed way that courts treat victims and witnesses (a form of harassment, affecting both female and male, which discourages prosecutions), the Los Angeles Superior Court judge threatened to jail her and impose a fine of $5 million if she didn't show up on 3 January. In May 1995 her bodyguard shot at the stalker as he came over the wall of her mansion in Los Angeles. This same stalker had also broken into her home in Miami. Victims'-rights groups saw it as an important opportunity for her to take a stand against those who violate and terrorize women. Madonna anticipated the court experience as a direct opportunity for the stalker to get her attention and energy, to give him what he was after all along. As a good citizen who, unlike most others, could have come up with $5 million, Madonna did appear in court, but while testifying stoically she did not glance in the stalker's direction: the silent treatment, a woman's occasionally successful weapon, effectively demonstrated by one of the formerly busiest mouths and brassiest attitudes in show business.

On 22 March 1996, only ten months following the over-the-wall incident, the man was convicted on five counts of stalking (Madonna), assault (against the bodyguard), and threatening (both); he was sentenced to ten years in prison. A lot of people who work to prevent violence against women, including stalking, would be thrilled if such relatively swift and sure 'justice' were commonplace – notwithstanding the consistent evidence that prisons, and other punitive responses by the state, exacerbate rather than abate obsessions and violences. Madonna is temporarily safe from this particular stalker, but this wasn't her first. In the late 1980s, she was haunted by a woman stalker, Darlene (Andersen, 1991: 275), and there could have been others. She is still and always vulnerable to every pathological fan lurking on the horizon of her celebrity, in this time of cultural barbarism folding back on itself.

In 1992, Andrew Lloyd Webber, producer of the revival of his stage version of *Evita*, spurned Madonna's publicly expressed interest in the Broadway part on the grounds that, at thirty-four, she was too old to play Argentinian Evita Perón at thirty-three. He later said, confusingly, that what he meant was: 'by the time anybody gets around to making the movie, she'll be too old' (Zoglin, 1997:

42). Moreover, in his view, Madonna's appeal to mainstream audiences had been hurt by the S/M in her *Sex* book and her *Body of Evidence* feature film. Over many years, interest in the film part of Evita had been attributed to women who would seem to have little in common: Charo, Barbra Streisand, Pia Zadora, and Meryl Streep. In 1996, Michelle Pfeiffer's unavailability (Griffin, 1995: 82) led to Madonna's ambition being realized when she appeared (going on age thirty-eight) in the film version of *Evita*, directed by Alan Parker, with co-stars Antonio Banderas (Ché, the Everyman narrator) and Jonathan Pryce (Juan Perón).

Madonna's infatuation with the Spanish actor is fetchingly replayed in her 1991 film *Truth or Dare*; she coyly eyes Banderas at a party, but the spectator is led to believe that she is rebuffed because he was then an honourable married man. (In 1997 he still is, but now with a new Hollywood wife, Melanie Griffith.) In late 1996 interviews, Madonna suggested that the crush had subsided long before her documentary was filmed. Nevertheless, the press made hay with the expectation that romantic sparks would fly between the two of them on the *Evita* set. In her diary, the night before Banderas's arrival in Buenos Aires to begin filming, Madonna writes humourously, 'The press is trying to make a big deal about my competing with his girlfriend [Griffith], which is ludicrous because everyone knows I would never date a man who wears cowboy boots,' (Madonna, 1996b: 187).

Alan Parker described in a CNN interview (14 January 1997) how Madonna was victorious after over seven years of negotiations and changes in the film's personnel. He says that Madonna was an easy (second) choice for the role, that she sent him a 'beautifully written, impassioned hand-written letter,' promising him that she 'would sing and dance her heart out' for him. It was a role she knew she was born to play; her letter persuaded him, and her performance convinced him. In November 1996, in *Vanity Fair*, Madonna said of that letter: 'I did not write this letter of my own free will. It was as if some other force drove my hand across the page.' Thus begins 'Madonna's Private Diaries,' wherein Madonna takes the reader on a journey from the beginning of her research in Argentina to the completion of the film and second stage of her pregnancy (Madonna, 1996b). This is a remarkable account for its engaging narrative style and her candour.

She writes in her entry of 20 January 1996, in response to Argentinians telling her to go home, 'I'm sure they'd come over for tea if I invited them. None of this discourages me.' But on 25 January she writes, 'I've got to stop reading the papers. I am portrayed as either a stupid cunt who doesn't deserve to play Santa Evita or a spoiled American movie star who has no interest in the truth.' In fact, Madonna engaged in serious research, and met with scholars, officials, and many people who were acquainted with Eva Perón, including aristocracy with whom she shared a knowledgeable appreciation for art, architecture, and period furnishings. She searched through the archives for perspectives on Evita, and on the side had discussions with the library director about Latin authors and European cinema. She searched for Eva Perón through the sounds and sights of the city.

In a discussion with the chief of police and his lieutenant, who reassured her she didn't have to worry about death threats, the lieutenant 'said the most amazing thing – that people were angry with Evita in her day for the same reason they are angry with me today. That we are women with success and power.' She is insulted that Argentinian president Menem would meet with Claudia Schiffer, the model, and the Rolling Stones rock band, and not meet with her. She protests. Arrangements are made. She is flown by helicopter to a secret rendezvous on a secluded estate. 'President Menem was very charming. I was surprised at how much I liked him ... when I caught him staring, his eyes stayed with mine' (Madonna, 1996b: 223). They talked about metaphysics. This was, of course, the same president who had said that Madonna should stay away, joining the sentiment that she would bring shame to the memory of Evita, and who, until the eleventh hour, refused to give the film crew permission to use the balcony of the Casa Rosada, where Evita had lived with Perón.

While making the film in Argentina, with the whole world watching via television, and constant attention upon her from both throngs of fans and unfriendly critics who ridiculed her, Madonna suffered the pressures of portraying a character who had such importance to an entire nation, even while winning them over. Anticipating a 6 February 1996 press conference with the conservative Argentinian press, Madonna noted, 'They're going to ask me stupid questions. They are going to be rude, reactionary, and ignorant' (1996b: 188). As it turned out, it was a good session, except for 'a few cranky questions from a few women who looked like they didn't have enough love in their lives.' On a day when Madonna was exhausted, 'I want to cry for all the sadness in the world, but mostly my own. Dear God, what have I gotten myself into? What is happening to me?' (ibid.: 223). She writes of the alienation and loneliness of her isolation and cultural displacement; she refers to the hotel room as her prison. On the sets she contends with heat exhaustion, insects, and marathon filming, all the while in the early stage of pregnancy.

'Evita' Peron was a girl from rural poverty who successfully sold herself in the city, became a successful radio actor, and married Juan Perón, who became the president in 1945. Among the masses, she took on saintly proportions for her work with the poor, but she was disdained by the Church, the State, and the rich. Before making her acquaintance, President Carlos Menem declared Madonna 'unsuitable' for the part of Evita and predicted that 'the masses would not tolerate her presence' (*Kingston Whig-Standard*, 1996). *People* magazine quoted Madonna regarding her appropriateness for the role: 'People see Eva Perón as either a saint or the incarnation of Satan. I can definitely identify with her' (Cerio, Healy, and Yoo, 1996: 48). Argentinians in significant numbers did protest the casting, and demonstrated against Madonna and the film crew. *People* reports that about fifty walls were spray-painted with the slogan 'Viva Evita! Fuera Madonna!' (Long Live Evita; Get Out, Madonna). Madonna was able to use the experience in her performance. When Evita had gone to France, in the late 1940s, she had had the same experience, with crowds chanting 'Whore, go home!'

Both irritating and cheering her, Madonna's fans demonstrated in her honour, marching to her hotel, chanting for her, playing her song 'Like a Prayer.' From the balcony, Madonna 'waved and blew kisses and almost started to cry.' After considerable negotiation, President Menem finally consented to letting the crew film Madonna on the balcony of the Casa Rosada, before thousands of extras looking up at her with 'hungry eyes.' This was the same spot where Evita had stood before the masses, and Madonna said, 'I felt her enter my body like a heat missile ... she is haunting me. She is pushing me to feel things. When you want something bad enough the whole earth conspires to help you get it' (Madonna, 1996b: 226). Evita died in 1952, at age thirty-three, six years before Madonna's birth. When Madonna as Eva Perón looks out on the massive crowds filling the street, and with deep emotion sings Tim Rice's lines 'I love you and hope you love me ... the actress hasn't learned the lines you'd like to hear ...' it's as if Evita *is* living in Madonna's soul.

Quietly and strategically, Madonna quickly won over popular opinion in Argentina. Young girls wrote her name on their bodies. The bishop 'said he would not be averse to blessing Madonna because, after all, Christ himself had not turned his back on the prostitute' (Escobar, 1996: C1). Having moved into character, in public appearances and interviews she impressed the spectator with her earnestly charming Evita-like mannerisms and demeanour (ibid.: C7). In her diary she wrote humbly, before leaving Argentina, 'I do feel like I have earned a modicum of respect here. Like anything important in life it must be earned' (Madonna, 1996b: 226).

Having conquered Argentina, Madonna and the *Evita* film company moved on to Hungary, where they were subsequently banned by the bishop from filming in a particular Budapest cathedral. Her sacrilegious use of the cross in her music performance offended the officials of a Church just regaining its political foothold (Fox Network News, 28 March 1996). She writes:

The bishop will not let me in his church. I am a bad girl. A fallen woman. A sinner.

If I gave him an autographed picture he would probably change his mind. The bishop can kiss my ass. I'm not groveling for one more person in the name of this movie. There is no more skin left on my knees. I will never apologize for my behavior. Neither would Evita. (Madonna, 1996b: 227)

She's cold and uncomfortable in Hungary, and worries about the effects on her baby of the strenuous dancing and other physical demands of the filmmaking. But she appreciates the manners of the people. No one crowds her; even adoring fans give her respectful space.

Stars of Madonna's commercial magnitude bring with them not only their crafts and their brilliance; as well, they bring the ideological baggage of the cultures that bred and that support them on the market. They are confronted with the often impossible challenge of staying true to their own vision while appealing to widely diverse audiences, usually of a particular generation, but across the boundaries of power relations which divide people within real, lived social worlds.

Self-selected audiences see themselves, their values, attitudes, and feelings reflected back to themselves from the stage, but it may not be the artist they see, but rather their own projection of what they expect, fear, or want to see or hear. What the artist says and what the listener receives may be very different messages, although the spectator–performer interaction affects both; in effect, the audience also performs, with the artist and with one another as audience. As discussed by Tania Modleski, the audience consists of 'actual social subjects who by virtue of their complex histories and multiple cultural affiliations (educational, religious, vocational, political, etc.) always, it is argued, exceed the subject implied by the text' (1991: 36). Audiences are not simply duped by the magic from the stage; they are investing it with their own multiple meanings. Madonna isn't a witch who compels vacuous babes and hunks to take off their clothes. In their myriad varieties, her fans have agency and are daily making choices as entertainment consumers that, given ideological extremes among those choices, confound orthodox neo-marxist notions of false consciousness or the contemporary idea of internalized oppression as a static condition. And even if Madonna's fans were robots, she would confound even them with her quick identity shifts. If Madonna's performance is the 'text,' and the audience is the 'reader,' John Fiske says it precisely: 'For a text to be popular, it must "utter" what its readers wish to say ...', according to their differences as individuals and in their social locations (1989: 146).

In a discussion of French scholar Jacques Derrida's work on the difficulty of defining generic Woman, philosopher Drucilla Cornell writes in a way that well describes the difficulty of figuring out who Madonna might be from the representations she presented as a young woman bursting onto public-media and popular consciousness. Cornell is writing about the search for the universal Woman, through endless fictional representations. Her discussion explains clearly why no woman can be Everywoman; no woman can embody the knowable Truth of Woman: 'It is only through ... metaphors, representations, and fictions that we attempt to reach Woman. We cannot separate the Truth of Woman from the fictions in which she is represented and through which she portrays herself. In this sense, she becomes veiled ... the fictions in which we confront Her always carry within the possibility of multiple interpretations' (Cornell, 1993: 88).

Madonna's hard-core audiences have moved easily with her from one persona to another, and Madonna has moved easily from one technical medium to another. Popular culture is a corporate-controlled set of industries (which could decentralize in this era of new, home-based technologies). Popular music is constructed from late-twentieth-century technology, sophisticated marketing techniques, and billions of dollars exchanged every year as tools of persuasian. Waiting to judge it are the gatekeepers of morality. They have failed in their efforts to silence Madonna, because, in the detached financial world of advanced, corporate capitalism, profit motive, in tandem with free speech protections, generally supersedes morality or censorship issues. Madonna's power does not protect her from the tabloid syndrome, whereby, as observed by her former husband, Sean Penn, readers of gossip magazines are 'all lookin' to guide your life ... because they don't have their own, I guess' (CNN, 19 January 1996). She has generally handled the tabloids with dignity, and it is telling that no scandals of conse-

quence have surfaced concerning her personal life. It appears
from the banal level of the unrelenting gossip about her that few
people are as well equipped as Madonna to thrive in the fish-bowl,
rumour-mongering climate of celebrity. There's nothing to tell.
It's all been told and it wasn't shocking. Her life has not been scandalous. She saves her artful controversy for the stage.

Although Madonna's way of combatting sexual inhibition and
repressive institutions has been to present herself as raunchy and
smart-alecky in her act, in interviews she often comes across as vulnerable or defensive. She doesn't relinquish her power, but she
lets the viewer see a creative person trying to stay centred while the
bawdy Madonna myths multiply around her, fuelled by her own
imagination and filled with inevitable distortions. A key source of
contradictory Madonna messages has been her body of sexy video
work. Having announced in 1994 that she was moving away from
uninhibited sex as her dominant message, in 1996 she is challenging the efficacy of video as her dominant medium: 'the whole
visual element ultimately stumps the growth of [a musical] artist, I
think ... People used to really concentrate on the songs, and either
identified with them or not, but now when you hear a song on the
radio, you don't just hear the song, you think about the video,
about the artist ... all these distractions that have nothing to do
with the music' (Guccione, 1996: 45).

What appear to be Madonna's contradictions are aspects of her
multidimensionality, a self-identified working-class girl who is
unimaginably wealthy, receives global adulation, and mingles with
aristocrats. Her street talk contrasts with her educated tastes in art.
Her sacrilege contrasts with her abiding loyalty to her Catholic
identity. She is vulgar and she is refined. She breaks down stereotypes and she conforms to them. Her incongruity is part of her
attraction. She knows it as only she can. It's intentional. She's an
eternal dialectic: for every resolution of her character, she returns
with yet another new character begging for its opposite. It is interesting that Madonna, as the utterly elegant Evita, with scarcely a
residual trace of her former trashy selves, and the younger Courtney Love as the unrepentantly trashy Althea, wife of Larry Flynt the
porn king, were in competition for 1996 movie awards for roles
which, in both cases, critics agreed they were 'born to play.'

Performers who break the mould are tantalizing if only because 'it's new and different' (as Dana Carvey's 'Church Lady' would say, with pursed lips). But Madonna's music and presentations of self are not new so much as a reconstruction of familiar ingredients, in recalled or new, and often strange and outrageous, blendings. As a young woman beginning her career before the masses, she danced to the beat of the cultural and sexual pulses of contemporary youth. As she enters her serious post-*Evita* stage, she would seem to be letting go of frivolity and chronic sexual display. The girls who wanted to capture boy toys, like Madonna did, and the boys who wanted girls to treat them like boy toys, like Madonna did, are also growing up, and in the new millennium their kids will be recycling trends started by Madonna in the 'last century.'

Whatever she decides to do next, and only Madonna can imagine what that might be, it is a fair bet that it will be interesting. As of 1996, before her daughter's birth, Madonna had no plans to settle down. 'It's certainly more important to take a stand on something and offend people, than to be careful all of your life and have everyone approve of what you do. Or, as my psychiatrist likes to say, better to live one year as a tiger than 100 as a sheep' (quoted in Guccione, 1996: 94).

Postscript

It was everywhere on the news: Lourdes Maria Ciccone Leon was born by cesarean at the Good Samaritan Hospital in Los Angeles at 4:01 p.m., 21 October 1996, 6 pounds, 9 ounces, thick black hair. It's reported by every media outlet that the new mother, Madonna, and father, Carlos Leon, are ecstatic. (She was attended, ironically, by respected pediatrician Paul Fleiss, whose infamous daughter Heidi successfully led a corps of call-girls through Hollywood society.) Her partner, Carlos, and her sister Melanie were with her through the twelve preceding hours as she laboured towards 'the greatest miracle of my life.' When she and the baby went home, the tabloid press hid in neighbours' trees with zoom lenses pointed at her windows. They give her no rest with her baby. But this was not a sensational story so much as a transforming one. Becoming a mother, so personal an event, raised Madonna's femininity status in the public eye. She is, indeed, in one interview after another, more appealingly feminine than at any time in her, by 1997, fourteen years of fame. She gave her baby the name of the site in southwest France where, in 1858 (one century before Madonna Ciccone's birth), young Bernadette had eighteen visions of the Virgin Mary, the Madonna, and later became a nun. ('Lourdes' is pronounced with one syllable in French; Madonna's daughter's name has two, Lourd-es.) (In her *Sex* book, Madonna invents a character named Lourdes, a young, beautiful, dark-haired sales girl who offers generous sex to a customer in the dressing-room.)

The film *Evita* opened in New York and Los Angeles on Christmas Day 1996, and opened in other selected cities on 10 January. The reviews were mixed, but audiences swarmed to it. In just four days the film, in limited release, had earned $11 million (CNN, 10 January, 1997). Not a conventional musical; no spoken narrative or dialogue, which is not to everyone's liking; not an opera – it is a new art form, a visual and musical enchantment, a spectacular production. Madonna has eight-five stunning costume changes, and Evita fashions and coiffures are instantly paraded down Paris runways. Her voice is very clear, strong, rich with emotion, and pleasing, with beautiful phrasing. The casting is perfect and she plays off Jonathan Pryce and Antonio Banderas with the self-assurance of a seasoned actress. As is true of her co-stars, she is altogether convincing. Madonna and Evita fuse in an entirely believable character, particularly given that Madonna's appearance is so eerily like the photos of Perón. (To achieve the affect she was fitted with dark brown contact lenses over her brilliant blue eyes, and a mouthpiece to cover the sexy gap between her front teeth.) Everyone involved in the film speaks in very positive, respectful terms about working together. In the notes to the CD soundtrack of the film, Madonna gives 'special thanks to Joan Lader for helping me find my voice, to David Caddick [co-producer, conductor] for his patience and guidance and to Caresse Henry-Norman [personal assistant] for her strength.' Everyone is talking about Antonio Banderas's musical charm. Madonna is praised by all her film colleagues for her discipline, reliability, stamina, passion, focus, cooperation, and professionalism in every way. The choreography is brilliant, the lighting is brilliant, it is a brilliantly directed film. The film has revived interest in Evita: I've heard tell of at least six new books in press (in early 1997) about the life of Eva Perón.

Pre-Christmas '96, Madonna was everywhere on the news. There are items about making the film, and about her baby. When the baby is two months old, they travel to premières in Spain and in Italy (where, due to new motherhood, perhaps, she kept powerful people waiting an hour and a half for her arrival, and some aristocrats walked out). In October 1996, she was on the cover of *People*, looking gentle, soft, wistful, and utterly natural ('Mama Madonna!'). In

October she is also on the cover of *Vogue*, in Evita mode ('Madonna's Moment – as Evita, mother, and fashion force.') In November she showed up on the cover of *Vanity Fair*, looking like royalty in her wide-brimmed, feathered hat, and black fur stole. The inside stories of both *Vogue* and *Vanity Fair* featured an exquisite collection of photos, by Steven Meisel and Mario Testino, respectively, of Madonna in Evita high fashion, each pose more breathtaking than the last. Her facial expressions change from one photo to the next, and from even a subtle change she can produce a different woman. In January 1997 the *US* magazine special issue 'Biggest Stories of '96' featured Madonna on the cover, 'Viva La Diva! Madonna, Evita & Child.' *Time* magazine (20 January, 1997), with another Evita cover story, concedes that we, the public at large, can't 'avert [our] eyes from Madonna for too long' (Zoglin, 1997: 40). The press has never been so attentive, respectful, and kind towards her, despite obstinate Madonna-trashers.

Initial audience responses to *Evita* have been favourable to enthusiastic, although critics' reviews are mixed. (Siskel and Ebert gave it two thumbs up.) The absence of dialogue was frustrating for some, but the film is a major artistic achievement, and other Broadway musical successes are in now in line for Hollywood productions. Madonna was awarded the Golden Globe as Best Actress in a Comedy or Musical. Antonio Banderas was nominated for Best Actor. The film also received nominations for Best Picture, Best Song ('You Must Love Me,' which received the award), and Best Director.

Suddenly there was no sign of Madonna's former bawdy self. She appeared on talk shows, seeming to waver between the deep emotions of new motherhood and utter serenity. She and Oprah Winfrey seemed to have been sympatico, ribbing each other about when or whether they would get married, seeming to agree they'd rather not. Arousing tender sentiment, Madonna brought tears to everyone's eyes when she talked about how the first time she felt her baby kick was on Mother's Day, and described seeing the light of recognition in her daughter's eyes: 'when I look into my daughter's eyes I feel I'm being healed.' She appears vulnerable but elegant. The press comments on the changes in her appearance – a healthy, calm, womanly countenance, a 'maternal glow.' She's much looser when she appears with her pal Rosie O'Donnell, TV's hottest star in 1996–7. Enjoying her silly, bratty joke, Madonna plays off Rosie's reign as 'Queen of Nice' (an honour bestowed on her by *Time* magazine) by speculating on which of the many other talk-show hosts might actually *hate* the nice Rosie O'Donnell. And she amuses Lauren Holly, the second guest, by asking her whether her husband, Jim Carrey, cracks jokes in bed. Rosie and Madonna banter with each other as to who's the best mother (each according the honour to the other), and they sing together about the changes in Madonna's life, ending the song with Madonna singing happily,

> Goodbye, Blond Ambition
> This girl doesn't have the time to strike a pose
> Throw-up's on my clothes
> My old bras have all been put away
> Milk truck is the only role I'm pla-a-a-ying

They stand together as a terrific long-time friendship between two brilliant, quirky, motherless girls from big Catholic families who ended up at the forefront of the entertainment industry.

In November 1996, Madonna discusses her early career choices in her 'Private Diaries': 'I often say I have no regrets, but I suppose in the end I do. If I had known that I would be so universally misunderstood, maybe I wouldn't have been so rebellious and outspoken … I wonder if I could ever have been the kind of sweet, submissive, feminine girl that the entire world idealizes' (Madonna, 1996b: 157). Madonna continues, speaking now of Eva Perón: 'She wanted to be remembered for her goodness. The desire of someone who has lived her life completely misunderstood.' My wish would be for Madonna to go on being rebellious and outspoken without fear of censure or misunderstanding, but knowing it's inevitable for anyone who takes risks. For her to be otherwise would be our loss. After all, tigers are an endangered species.

Selected Works of Madonna

by Frances Wasserlein

I was visiting with Karlene one afternoon, early in 1996, when she told me she'd finished drafting her book about Madonna. As we talked about the book, and what might happen to it, I commented that I thought there was probably a lot of information about Madonna on the Internet. Then, foolishly, as it turns out, I opined that it would be next to no trouble to locate this information. Karlene said she was trying to get an appendix together, and I agreed to try to do it. She suggested I consider whether I was being perhaps a little too cavalier about the complexity of such a task. I should have listened to her and withdrawn my offer. But I'm glad I stuck with it.

As you have, no doubt, already figured out, Karlene knows a great deal about Madonna and about the volume of work Madonna has produced and been associated with. What neither of us knew was that Madonna's fans, an interestingly international lot, have put literally billions of bytes on web sites all over the world. Anyone looking for information about Madonna will face what I did: an overwhelming rush of facts, photographs, lists, comments, dreams, fantasies, and downright weirdness, on web sites from Singapore to Denmark to Canada to the United States, on sites at universities, on sites beautifully designed and others which are, at best, 'under construction.'

I have gathered the information we agreed would be most useful to the readers of this book. And at the end of this appendix, I've provided a little more information about what you might find if you go to the Internet. But, watch out, the surf's very high on Madonna – and the waves are getting bigger and bigger and closer together. And then there are the sneaker waves ... but you'll see what I mean.

THEATRE

Material in this section is from Adam Sexton, ed., Desperately Seeking Madonna: In Search of the Meaning of the World's Most Famous Woman *(New York: Delta Books, 1993).*

1987 *Goose and Tom-Tom* (by David Rabe). Lincoln Center Theater workshop
1988 *Speed-the-Plow* (by David Mamet). Produced by the Lincoln Center Theater at the Royale Theater

VIDEOGRAPHY

Material in this section is from Bill Vipond [vipers@wchat.on.ca] Friday, 14 June 1996; http://www-scf.usc.edu/~caulfield/ <Keith Caulfield>; *Adam Sexton, ed.*, Desperately Seeking Madonna: In Search of the Meaning of the World's Most Famous Woman *(New York: Delta Books, 1993); Patricia Romanowski and Holly George-Warren, eds.*, The New Rolling Stone Encyclopedia of Rock & Roll *(New York: Fireside, 1983, 1995).*

Music Videos

This list does not include clip compilations, or versions of videos released outside the United States. See Internet Resources for locations of extensive, overwhelmingly detailed lists.

1982 'Everybody' Directed by Ed Steinberg. From the album *Madonna.*
1983 'Burning Up' Directed by Steve Barron. From the album *Madonna.*
1984 'Lucky Star #1' Directed by Arthur Pierson. From the album *Madonna.*
     'Lucky Star #2' (Extended Version) Directed by Arthur Pierson. From the album *Madonna.*
     'Like A Virgin #1' Directed by Mary Lambert. From the album *Like a Virgin.*
     'Borderline' Directed by Mary Lambert. From the album *Madonna.*
     'Holiday #1' [Low-budget, not released.] Unknown director. From the album *Madonna.*

1985 'Dress You Up #1' Directed by Danny Kleinman. From the album *Like a Virgin.*

'Dress You Up #2' [Extended with introduction and different angels.] Directed by Danny Kleinman. From the album *Like a Virgin.*

'Crazy For You #1' ['Crazy for You' and 'Gambler' were made with footage from *Vision Quest.*] Directed by Harold Becker. From the album *'Vision Quest' – Original Motion Picture Soundtrack.*

'Gambler' ['Crazy for You' and 'Gambler' were made with footage from *Vision Quest.*] Directed by Harold Becker. From the album *'Vision Quest' – Original Motion Picture Soundtrack.*

'Material Girl' Directed by Mary Lambert. From the album *Like a Virgin.*

'Into the Groove' [Made with film clips from *Desperately Seeking Susan.*] Directed by Susan Seidelman. From the album *You Can Dance.*

1986 'Live to Tell' Directed by James Foley. From the album *True Blue.*

'Papa Don't Preach' Directed by James Foley. From the album *True Blue.*

'True Blue' (European Version) Directed by James Foley. From the album *True Blue.*

'Open Your Heart' Directed by Jean Baptiste Mondino. From the album *True Blue.*

1987 'Who's That Girl?' Directed by James Foley. From the album *'Who's That Girl?' Original Motion Picture Soundtrack.*

'La Isla Bonita' Directed by Mary Lambert. From the album *True Blue.*

1989 'Express Yourself #1' Directed by David Fincher. From the album *Like a Prayer.*

'Oh Father' Directed by David Fincher. From the album *Like a Prayer.*

'Cherish' Directed by Herb Ritts. From the album *Like a Prayer.*

'Like a Prayer' Directed by Mary Lambert. From the album *Like a Prayer.*

'Dear Jessie' [Released outside the United States. Animated, with pink elephants; Madonna does not appear.] Unknown director. From the album *Like a Prayer.*

1990 'Vogue' Directed by David Fincher. From the album *I'm Breathless – Music from and Inspired by the Motion Picture 'Dick Tracy'*.
'Justify My Love' Directed by Jean Baptiste Mondino. From the album *The Immaculate Collection*.

1991 'Holiday #2' [Made with film clips from *Truth or Dare*.] Directed by Alek Keshishian. From the album *Like a Virgin*.
'Like a Virgin #2' [Made with film clips from *Truth or Dare*.] Directed by Alek Keshishian. From the album *Madonna*.

1992 'This Used to Be My Playground' Directed by Alek Keshishian. From the album *Barcelona Gold*.
'Deeper and Deeper' Directed by Bobby Woods. From the album *Erotica*.
'Erotica' Directed by Fabien Baron. From the album *Erotica*.

1993 'Bad Girl' Directed by David Fincher. From the album *Erotica*.
'Rain' Directed by Mark Romanek. From the album *Erotica*.
'Fever' Directed by Stephan Sednaoui. From the album *Erotica*.

1994 'I'll Remember' Directed by Alek Keshishian. From the album *'With Honors' – Original Motion Picture Soundtrack*.
'Secret' Directed by Melodie McDaniel. From the album *Bedtime Stories*.
'Take a Bow' Directed by Michael Haussman. From the album *Bedtime Stories*.

1995 'I Want You' Directed by Earle Sebastian. From the album *Inner City Blues – The Music of Marvin Gaye*.
'Human Nature' Directed by Jean Baptiste Mondino. From the album *Bedtime Stories*.
'Bedtime Story' Directed by Mark Romanek. From the album *Bedtime Stories*.
'You'll See' Directed by Michael Haussman. From the album *Something to Remember*.

1996 'Love Don't Live Here Anymore' Directed by Jean Baptiste Mondino. From the album *Something To Remember*.
'You Must Love Me' Directed by Alan Parker. From the album *'Evita' – The Complete Motion Picture Soundtrack*.
'Don't Cry for Me Argentina' [Made with film clips from *Evita*.] Directed by Alan Parker. From the album *'Evita' – The Complete Motion Picture Soundtrack*.

Commercially Available Videos

Material in this section is from Variety's *Video Directory Plus, 1996. CD.*

[unknown]	'Dick Tracy [PG]' Distributor: WGBH Boston.
[unknown]	'Like a Virgin' Distributor: Videotakes.
[unknown]	'Madonna' Distributor: WEA.
1980	'A Certain Sacrifice' Distributor: Ingram.
1985	'Desperately Seeking Susan' Distributor: HBO Video.
1986	'Shanghai Surprise' Distributor: Family Home. 'Shanghai Surprise' Distributor: Live Home Video.
1987	'Who's That Girl?' Distributor: Warner Home.
November 1987	'Live: The Virgin Tour' Distributor: WEA.
1988	'Ciao Italia: Madonna Live from Italy' Distributor: WEA.
1989	'Bloodhounds of Broadway' Distributor: Columbia.
1990	'Dick Tracy' Distributor: Facets. 'Justify My Love' Distributor: WEA.
November 1990	'The Immaculate Collection' Distributor: Warner Home.
1991	'National Enquirer: The Untold Story of Madonna' Distributor: Good Times. 'Truth or Dare' Distributor: Live Home Video.
February 1991	'Dick Tracy' Distributor: Image Entertainment.
August 1991	'Women in Rock' Distributor: Atlantic Video.
1992	'A Certain Sacrifice' Distributor: Worldvision.
1993	'A League of Their Own' Distributor: Columbia Tristar 'Madonna Exposed' Distributor: Good Times.
April 1994	'The Girlie Show – Live' Distributor: WEA.
February 1995	'A League of Their Own' Distributor: Columbia Tristar.
October 1995	'Stop with the Kicking' Distributor: New Line Cinema.

TOURS

Material in this section is from Bill Vipond [vipers@chat.on.ca], Friday, 14 June 1996.

1985 The Virgin Tour
1987 Who's That Girl? World Tour
1990 Blond Ambition World Tour
1993 The Girlie Show World Tour

FILMOGRAPHY

*Material in this section is from The Internet Movie Database Ltd [at http://
us.imdb.com/Movies], 1990–1996; http://das-www.harvard.edu/users/students/
Zheng_Wang/Madonna/*

1985 *Vision Quest* (USA)
        Director: Harold Becker
        Producers: Warner – Adam Fields (executive), Peter Guber, Jon
        Peters, Stan Weston (executive)
        Madonna's role: [Special appearance]
1985 *Desperately Seeking Susan* (USA)
        Director: Susan Seidelman
        Producers: Orion Pictures Corp. (distributor) Michael Peyser
        (executive), Sarah Pillsbury, Midge Sanford – Sexton–HBO
        Madonna's role: Susan
1985 *A Certain Sacrifice* (USA)
        Director: Stephen Jon Lewicki
        Producers: Sexton–Commtron (1980)
        Madonna's role: Bruna
1986 *Shanghai Surprise* (UK)
        Director: Jim Goddard
        Producers: HandMade Films – Robin Douet (co-producer) George
        Harrison (executive), John Kohn, Denis O'Brien (executive), Sara
        Romilly (associate)
        Madonna's role: Gloria Tatlock

1987 *Who's That Girl?* (USA)
    Director: James Foley
    Producers: Guber-Peters Company/Warner Brothers, Roger Birn-
    baum (executive), Peter Guber (executive), Rosilyn Heller, Jon
    Peters (executive), Bernard Williams
    Madonna's role: Nikki Finn

1989 *Bloodhounds of Broadway* (USA)
    Director: Howard Brookner
    Producers: RCA/Columbia
    Madonna's role: Hortense Hathaway

1990 *Dick Tracy* (USA)
    Director: Warren Beatty
    Producers: Silver Screen Partners IV/Touchstone Pictures, Warren
    Beatty, Jon Landau (co-producer), Art Linson (executive), Floyd
    Mutrux (executive), Barrie M. Osborne (executive), Jim Van Wyck
    (associate)
    Madonna's role: Breathless Mahoney

1991 *Truth or Dare* [*aka: In Bed with Madonna*] (USA)
    Director: Alek Keshishian
    Producer: Madonna (executive)
    Madonna's role: Herself

1992 *Shadows and Fog* (USA)
    Director: Woody Allen
    Producers: Orion Pictures Corp. (distributor), Robert Greenhut,
    Charles H. Joffe (executive), Jack Rollins (executive)
    Madonna's role: Marie

1992 *A League of Their Own* (USA)
    Director: Penny Marshall
    Producers: Columbia Pictures – Elliot Abbott, Ronnie D. Clemmer
    (co-producer), Robert Greenhut, Joseph Hartwick (co-producer),
    Amy Lemisch (associate), Penny Marshall (executive), Bill Pace (co-
    producer)
    Madonna's role: Mae Mordabito

1993 *Snake Eyes* [*aka: Dangerous Game*] (USA)
    Director: Abel Ferrara
    Producers: Maverick Picture Company, Mary Kane, Ron Rotholz
    (executive)
    Madonna's role: Sarah Jennings

1993   *Body of Evidence* (Germany, USA)
    Director: Ulrich Edel
    Producers: Dino De Laurentiis, Stephen Deutsch (executive),
    Bernd Eichinger (co-producer), Melinda Jason (executive), Her-
    man Weigel (co-producer)
    Madonna's role: Rebecca Carlson
1995   *Four Rooms* (USA)
    Director: Allison Anders (segment 'The Missing Ingredient')
    Producers: Miramax Films – Lawrence Bender, Paul Hellerman (co-
    producer), Scott Lambert (co-producer), Alexander Rockwell
    (executive), Quentin Tarantino (executive), Heidi Vogel (co-
    producer)
    Madonna's role: Elspeth (segment 'The Missing Ingredient')
1995   *Blue in the Face* (USA)
    Directors: Paul Auster, Wayne Wang
    Producers: Miramax Films (distributor)/Blue in the Face. Greg
    Johnson, Harvey Keitel, Peter Newman, Diana Phillips, Bob Wein-
    stein, Harvey Weinstein
    Madonna's role: Singing Telegram
1996   *Girl 6*
    Director: Spike Lee
    Producers: 20th Century Fox Film (distributor)/Fox Searchlight
    Pictures
    Madonna's role: Herself (cameo)
1997   *Evita* (USA)
    Director: Alan Parker
    Producers: Warner Brothers, Robert Stigwood, Andrew G. Vajna
    Madonna's role: Eva Perón

DISCOGRAPHY

Material in this section is from http://www.cs.uit.no:80.Music/View/madonna
[The Department of Computer Science and University of Tromsø, Nor-
way]; *http://www.cs.rpi.edu/~kenny/madonna_lyrics/HomePage.html* [Kenny
Zalewski], *kennyz@cs.rpi.edu, kennyz@ifsintl.com; http://www-scf.usc.edu/
~caulfiel/<Keith Caulfield>*; Patricia Romanowski and Holly George-Warren,
eds., The New Rolling Stone Encyclopedia of Rock & Roll *(New York: Fire-*

side, 1983, 1995); Phil Hardy and Dave Laing, with Stephen Barnard and Don Perretta, Encyclopedia of Rock *(New York: Schirmer, 1988); Adam Sexton, ed.,* Desperately Seeking Madonna: In Search of the Meaning of the World's Most Famous Woman *(New York: Delta Books, 1993).*

1982   12″ Single
Song: 'Everybody' written by Madonna and Steve Bray.
Produced by Mark Kamins on Sire label.

1982/3 12″ Single
Song: 'Burning Up,' written by Madonna, and 'Physical Attraction,' written by Reggie Lucas.

1983   *Madonna*
Songs: 'Lucky Star' written by Madonna; 'Borderline' written by Reggie Lucas; 'Burning Up' written by Madonna; 'I Know It' written by Madonna; 'Holiday' written by Curtis Hudson and Lisa Stevens; 'Think of Me' written by Madonna; 'Physical Attraction' written by Reggie Lucas; 'Everybody' written by Madonna and Steve Bray.
Produced by Reggie Lucas, John 'Jellybean' Benitez, and Mark Kamins on Sire Label.
Hit singles: 'Holiday,' 'Borderline,' 'Lucky Star.'

1984   *Like a Virgin*
Songs: 'Material Girl' written by Peter Brown and Robert Rans, 'Angel' written by Madonna and Steve Bray; 'Like a Virgin' written by Billy Steinberg and Tom Kelly; 'Over and Over' written by Madonna and Steve Bray; 'Love Don't Live Here Anymore' written by Miles Gregory; 'Dress You Up' written by Peggy Stanziale and Andrea LaRusso; 'Shoo-Bee-Doo' written by Madonna; 'Pretender' written by Madonna and Steve Bray; 'Stay' written by Madonna and Steve Bray.
Produced by Nile Rodgers on Sire label.
Hit singles: 'Like a Virgin,' 'Material Girl,' 'Angel,' 'Dress You Up.'

1984   *Vision Quest [soundtrack]*
Songs: 'Gambler' written by Madonna; 'Crazy for You' written by
Madonna.
Produced by 'Jellybean' Benitez on Geffen label.
Hit single: 'Crazy for You.'

1986   *True Blue*
Songs: 'Papa Don't Preach' written by Brian Elliot, additional lyr-
ics by Madonna; 'Open Your Heart' written by Madonna, Gard-
ner Cole, and Peter Rafelson; 'White Heat' written by Madonna
and Pat Leonard; 'Live to Tell' written by Madonna and Pat
Leonard; 'Where's the Party' written by Madonna, Stephen Bray,
and Pat Leonard; 'True Blue' written by Madonna and Stephen
Bray; 'La Isla Bonita' written by Madonna, Pat Leonard, and
Bruce Gaitsch; 'Jimmy Jimmy' written by Madonna and Stephen
Bray; 'Lover Makes the World Go Round' written by Madonna
and Pat Leonard.
Produced by Madonna, Patrick Leonard, and Stephen Bray on
Sire label.
Hit singles: 'Live to Tell,' 'Papa Don't Preach,' 'True Blue,'
'Open Your Heart,' 'La Isla Bonita.'

1987   *You Can Dance [club DJ remix of hits]*
Songs: 'Spotlight' written by Madonna and Stephen Bray; 'Holi-
day' written by Curtis Hudson and Lisa Stevens; 'Everybody' writ-
ten by Madonna and Stephen Bray; 'Physical Attraction' written
by Reggie Lucas; 'Over and Over' written by Madonna and
Stephen Bray; 'Into the Groove' written by Madonna and
Stephen Bray; 'Where's the Party' written by Madonna, Stephen
Bray, and Patrick Leonard; 'Holiday' (Dub Version) written by
Curtis Hudson and Lisa Stevens; 'Into the Groove' (Dub Version)
written by Madonna and Stephen Bray; 'Where's the Party' (Dub
Version) written by Madonna, Stephen Bray, and Patrick
Leonard.
Produced by Madonna, Stephen Bray, 'Jellybean' Benitez, Mark
Kamins, Reggie Lucas, Nile Rodgers, and Patrick Leonard on Sire
label.

1987   *Who's That Girl? [soundtrack]*
Songs: 'Who's That Girl?' written by Madonna; 'Causing a Commotion' written by Madonna; 'The Look of Love' written by
Madonna; '24 Hours' written by Duncan Faure; 'Step by Step'
written by Club Nouveau; 'Turn It Up' written by Michael Davidson; 'Best Thing Ever' written by Scritti Politti; 'Can't Stop' written by Madonna; 'El Coco Loco' (So So Bad) written by Coati
Mundi. On Sire label.
Hit singles: 'Who's That Girl?,' 'Causing a Commotion.'

1989   *Like a Prayer*
Songs: 'Like a Prayer' written by Madonna and Patrick Leonard;
'Express Yourself' written by Madonna and Stephen Bray; 'Love
Song' written by Madonna and Prince; 'Till Death Do Us Part'
written by Madonna and Patrick Leonard; 'Promise to Try' writ-
ten by Madonna and Patrick Leonard; 'Cherish' written by
Madonna and Patrick Leonard; 'Dear Jessie' written by Madonna
and Patrick Leonard; 'Oh Father' written by Madonna and
Patrick Leonard; 'Keep It Together' written by Stephen Bray;
'Spanish Eyes' written by Madonna and Patrick Leonard; 'Act of
Contrition' [The prayer]. On Sire label.
Hit singles: 'Like a Prayer,' Express Yourself,' 'Cherish,' 'Oh
Father,' 'Keep It Together.'

1990   *The Immaculate Collection*
Songs: 'Holiday,' 'Lucky Star,' 'Borderline,' 'Like a Virgin,'
'Material Girl,' 'Crazy for You,' 'Into the Groove,' 'Live to Tell,'
'Papa Don't Preach,' 'Open Your Heart,' 'La Isla Bonita,' 'Like a
Prayer,' 'Express Yourself,' 'Cherish,' 'Vogue,' [See original
releases for songwriters.] 'Justify My Love' written by Lenny Krav-
itz, additional lyrics by Madonna; 'Rescue Me' written by
Madonna and Shep Pettibone. On Sire label.
Hit singles: 'Justify My Love,' 'Rescue Me.'

1991   *I'm Breathless: Songs from and inspired by the film 'Dick Tracy'*
Songs: 'He's a Man' written by Madonna and Patrick Leonard;
'Sooner or Later' written by Stephen Sondheim; 'Hanky Panky'

written by Madonna and Patrick Leonard; 'I'm Going Bananas' written by Michael Kernan and Andy Paley; 'Cry Baby' written by Madonna and Patrick Leonard; 'Something to Remember' written by Madonna and Patrick Leonard; 'Back in Business' written by Madonna and Patrick Leonard; 'More' written by Stephen Sondheim; 'What Can You Lose' written by Stephen Sondheim; 'Now I'm Following You' (Part I) written by Andy Paley, Jeff Lass, Ned Claflin, and Jonathan Paley; 'Now I'm Following You' (Part II) written by Andy Paley, Jeff Lass, Ned Claflin, and Jonathan Paley; 'Vogue' written by Madonna and Shep Pettibone. On Sire label. Hit singles: 'Vogue,' 'Hanky Panky.'

1992   *Erotica*
Songs: 'Erotica' written by M. Ciccone and S. Pettibone; 'Fever' written by J. Davenport and E. Cooley; 'Bye Bye Baby' written by M. Ciccone and S. Pettibone; 'Deeper and Deeper' written by M. Ciccone, S. Pettibone, and T. Shimkin; 'Where Life Begins' written by M. Ciccone and A. Betts; 'Bad Girl' written by M. Ciccone and S. Pettibone; 'Waiting' written by M. Ciccone and A. Betts; 'Thief of Hearts' written by M. Ciccone and S. Pettibone; 'Words' written by M. Ciccone and S. Pettibone; 'Rain' written by M. Ciccone and Shep Pettibone; 'Why's It So Hard' written by M. Ciccone and S. Pettibone; 'In This Life' written by M. Ciccone and S. Pettibone; 'Did You Do It?' written by M. Ciccone and A. Betts; 'Secret Garden' written by M. Ciccone and A. Betts.
On Maverick/Sire label.
Hit singles: 'Deeper and Deeper,' 'Bad Girl,' 'Rain,' 'Erotica.'

1995   *Bedtime Stories*
Songs: 'Survival' written by Madonna and Dallas Austin; 'Secret' written by Madonna and Dallas Austin; 'I'd Rather Be Your Lover' written by Madonna, Dave Hall, Isley Brothers, and C. Jasper; 'Don't Stop' written by Madonna, Dallas Austin, and Colin Wolfe; 'Inside of Me' written by Madonna, Dave Hall, and Hooper; 'Human Nature' written by Madonna, Dave Hall, S. McKenzie, K. McKenzie, and M. Deering; 'Forbidden Love' written by Babyface and Madonna; 'Love Tried to Welcome Me' writ-

ten by Madonna and Dave Hall; 'Sanctuary' written by Madonna,
Dallas Austin, Anne Preven, Scott Cutler, and Herbie Hancock;
'Bedtime Story' written by Nellee Hooper, Bjork, and Marius
DeVries; 'Take a Bow' written by Babyface and Madonna.
On Maverick/Sire label.
Hit singles: 'Secret,' 'Take a Bow,' 'Bedtime Story,' 'Human
Nature.'

1995   *Something to Remember*
Songs: 'I Want You' written by Leon Ware and T-Boy Ross;
'I'll Remember' [Theme from 'With Honors'] written by Patrick
Leonard, M. Ciccone, and Richard Page; 'Take a Bow' written by
Madonna and Babyface; 'You'll See' written by Madonna and
David Foster; 'Crazy for You' written by Madonna; 'This Used to
Be My Playground' written by Madonna and Shep Pettibone;
'Live to Tell' written by Madonna and Patrick Leonard; 'Love
Don't Live Here Anymore' written by Miles Gregory; 'Something
to Remember' written by Madonna and Patrick Leonard; 'Forbid-
den Love' written by Babyface and Madonna; 'One More
Chance' written by Madonna and David Foster; 'Rain' written by
Madonna and Shep Pettibone; 'Oh Father' written by Madonna
and Patrick Leonard; 'I Want You' (orchestral) written by Leon
Ware and T-Boy Ross.
On Maverick/Sire label.
Hit singles: 'You'll See,' 'Love Don't Live Here Anymore.'

1996   *'Evita' – The Complete Motion Picture Soundtrack*
Songs: 'Complete soundtrack' written by Andrew Lloyd Webber
and Tim Rice.
Produced by Nigel Wright, Alan Parker, Andrew Lloyd Webber,
David Caddick on Warner label.
Hit single: 'You Must Love Me.'

SONGS PERFORMED BY MADONNA
ON OTHER RECORDINGS

1990   *Justify My Love (maxi-single)*
       Song: 'Justify My Love' (The Beast Within Mix) remixed by
       Lenny Kravitz and Madonna, lyrics taken from the Bible

1992   *Red Hot + Dance*
       Song: 'Supernatural' (Original Arms House Mix). written by
       Madonna and Patrick Leonard.

1194   *Secret* (UK import maxi-single)
       Song: 'Let Down Your Guard' (Rough Mix Edit) written by
       Madonna and Dallas Austin

1995   *You'll See* (maxi-single)
       Song: 'Veras (You'll See)' written by Madonna and David Foster –
       Spanish lyrics: Paz Martinez; 'Goodbye to Innocence' written by
       Madonna and Shep Pettibone.

STRAY TRACKS

1984   Song: 'Ain't No Big Deal'; on *Revenge of the Killer B's* (various art-
       ists) on Warner Brothers label.

1987   Song: 'The Look of Love & Can't Stop'; on *Who's That Girl?* (vari-
       ous artists) on Sire label.

1987   Song: 'Santa Baby' written by J. Javits and P. Springer; on *A Very
       Special Christmas* (various artists) on A & M label.

[n.d.]   Song: 'Supernatural'; 'Cherish' B side

I have spent quite a bit of time on the World Wide Web (WWW) while gathering information about Madonna and her work, locating, downloading, reading, laughing, wondering, being amazed and confused, being frustrated, crashing my computer at 1:00 a.m. trying to download a huge file. Because things are changing so quickly on the WWW, Karlene and I decided that it would be most useful to tell you about the kinds of things you can find out there, rather than providing you with a list of sites you might visit that would be out of date, or woefully incomplete, by the time this book is published.

I *will* tell you this: if you don't have a favourite search engine, I'd suggest you try the ones which I have listed below. The search engine is a remarkable, if fallible, tool. I think it might be possible to find every single mention of the word 'Madonna' present on every single WWW site, and those would include every mention of, for example, sixteenth-century Italian paintings, sites about alleged appearances of 'Mary, Mother of God' (also known as the Madonna) in locations ranging from Michigan to the former Yugoslavia, as well as those sites with mention of Madonna Ciccone. On the day I looked at this file for what I hope is the last time (24 January 1997), I found 63,378 hits (mentions of the word 'Madonna') on about 40,000 sites on AltaVista® alone.

The search engines which produce the best results for me are the following:*

www.metacrawler.com	I always start with this one on a new topic because it engages other search engines and gives you a wide sampling of 'hits.'
www.altavista.digital.com	This site seems to hit a good range of arts and culture sites, along with personal pages and commercial sites.
www.yahoo.com	This is presented as a 'cool' engine, and it provides one of the most straightforward ways for the uninitiated to get around in its list of results. Arranges 'hits' by categories.

---

*There are many other search engines, and you may find them more satisfactory than the ones I've mentioned. The point here is not a contest about whose are better, but to suggest a place to begin for the new surfer.

www.lycos.com   This is my favourite search engine. The vari-
                       ety seems the widest, and the way the results
                       are presented has consistently given me the
                       most satisfying material.

On the WWW sites built and maintained by Madonna's fans, you will find endless versions of lists of Madonna's hit recordings, singles and albums, with chart positions around the world carefully recorded and updated, along with comments about the agreements or disagreements among those fans whose pages contain the information. Members of this 'community' all seem to 'know' one another. In addition you can find the corporate WWW sites, record labels and the like, who are in the Madonna business, including of course, Madonna herself.

If you've been afraid to venture out into the surf of the WWW, perhaps your interest in Madonna is the perfect board to ride, even if you don't feel like you can stand up for long, if I may push the metaphor. I've always found that my curiosity about something is the best impetus to learning new skills that will help satisfy that curiosity. I do admit that, at the beginning of my adventures, I was a little bit hesitant about setting out into the WWW. I sometimes felt like I might just be overwhelmed by some found bit of information, or find out something I didn't want to know. Whether my computer crashes, dumping me out with dispatch to the C:>, or I come to the end of my energy to surf, I have, despite my apprehension, learned something satisfying almost every time. And in the course of looking for Madonna, I learned that one of the overwhelming things about the WWW is that there is so much on it. When I began to surf, there were some 33 million web pages; now there are millions more, and the number is increasing moment by moment.

Because my intellectual training is in the discipline of history, and because, despite my best efforts to cleanse myself of what I believe to be conservative tendencies about method, the vestiges of methodology courses still haunt me, and I do wonder about the authenticity of the information that's out there. There aren't ways to verify the kind of infor-mation people put up on their sites, for example, sites listing people's personal recording collections. It's clear that there are many Madonna fans who seek possession of every recording she's released, from all over the world. Some of the lists give record labels; some note the producers of the various cuts; some include dates, order numbers, and comments about whether there are notes. There are lists of hit singles, and the names of the recordings on which they were originally released. All of these are maintained by fans. There's a site maintained by a fan resident in Europe with an enormous database of recordings, with information about what must be nearly all of the releases in every country (there are more than 1,400 items on the list). On the WWW site for Madonna's label, a place where one could reasonably expect to find out about every-thing she's ever recorded, there is no such list. What is on the label sites are the recordings on which this year's advertising budget is being spent. Marketing. Marketing. Marketing.

The various WWW recording-sales establishments have backlists of recordings by Madonna and others. But these are there for the purpose of getting your disposable income transferred to the bank account of the seller, not for the hungry-eyed researcher.

Nowhere have I been able to locate a list which includes the names of the players and technical people on Madonna's recordings. I think this is remarkable, on the one hand, and entirely consistent with the Madonna business, on the other. The Madonna business is about marketing Madonna, not about building the reputation of back-up singers/vocalists, session musicians, and producers. Their reputations are built in the stu-dios, and by their agents and representatives. Their reputations are suffi-ciently well known to the people who hire them, or to those who are seeking people to work on Madonna's next venture. There isn't, appar-ently, a purpose in a fan collecting that information. Otherwise, I'm certain it would have been done by now, because almost everything else has been.

Madonna's fans have made certain, and will continue to do so, that they and everyone else knows everything about Madonna that she wants them to know. There aren't really any surprises in what you'll find (well, except perhaps the fantasy/dream sites), beyond the sheer volume of the information, and the tenacity with which the fans search out and present that information.

I'm not a fan. But I am interested in how it is that capital exploits human sexuality to produce, manipulate, and maintain desire in 'fans' for products and information, and, of course, to produce profit. I'm grateful to Karlene for her work on Madonna, and for her patience with this very small contribution of mine to her work. I've had an opportunity to mull over these curiosities about the Madonna business in relation to such embodied and disembodied desires as I've gone about other tasks in my own busy life. I hope the material I've selected from the vast amount available aids you, too, in your consideration of the value and effect of Madonna's work.

References

Aaron, Charles. (1996). 'Singles: The Top 20 of '95.' *Spin*, January, 88.

Abley, Mark. (1992). 'Sixteen Ways to Think of Madonna's Book.' *Montreal Gazette*, 24 October, J4.

Andersen, Christopher. (1991). *Madonna Unauthorized*. New York: Island.

Andrews, Marke. (1992). 'Mistake you for a hooker? Don't flatter yourself.' *Vancouver Sun*, 23 October, A2.

Bakshi, Renu. (1989). 'Pepsi & Virgins.' *The Peak*. Simon Fraser University. 16 March, 14.

Bego, Mark. (1985). *Madonna!* New York: Pinnacle.

– (1992). *Madonna: Blond Ambition*. New York: Harmony.

Bell, Shannon. (1994). *Reading, Writing & Rewriting the Prostitute Body*. Bloomington: Indiana University Press.

Bernauer, James W., and Michael Mahon. (1994). 'The Ethics of Michel Foucault.' In *The Cambridge Companion to Foucault*, ed. G. Gutting, 141–58. Cambridge: Cambridge University Press.

Bertilsson, Margareta. (1991). 'Love's Labour Lost? A Sociological View.' In *The Body: Social Process and Cultural Theory*, ed. M. Featherstone, M. Hepworth, and B.S. Turner, 297–324. London: Sage.

Bogle, Donald. (1980). *Brown Sugar: Eighty Years of America's Black Female Superstars*. New York: Plenum.

Bordo, Susan. (1993). '"Material Girl": The Effacements of Postmodern Culture.' In *The Madonna Connection*, ed. C. Schwichtenberg, 265–90. Oxford: Westview.

Boston Women's Health Collective. (1970). *Our Bodies Our Selves*. Boston: Health Collective and New England Free Press.

Bourdieu, Pierre. (1984). *Distinction: A Social Critique of the Judgement of Taste*. Trans. R. Nice. Cambridge, MA: Harvard University Press.

Braidotti, Rosi. (1991). *Patterns of Dissonance: A Study of Women in Contemporary Philosophy*. Trans. Elizabeth Guild. New York: Routledge.

Brant, Beth. (1994). *Writing as Witness: Essay and Talk*. Toronto: Women's Press.

Bright, Susie. (1993). 'A Pornographic Girl.' In *Madonnarama: Essays on Sex and Popular Culture*, ed. L. Frank and P. Smith, 81–6. San Francisco: Cleis.

Butler, Judith. (1990). *Gender Trouble: Feminism and the Subversion of Identity*. London: Routledge & Kegan Paul.

– (1993). *Bodies That Matter: On the Discursive Limits of 'Sex.'* New York: Routledge.

Califia, Pat. (1980). *Sapphistry: The Book of Lesbian Sexuality*. New York: Naiad.

– (1981). 'Feminism and Sadomasochism.' *Heresies* (Sex Issue) 12: 30–4.

Carpenter, Teresa. (1992). 'Riding Herd on Madonna.' *Vancouver Sun* ('Saturday Review'), 24 October, D5.

Cerio, Gregory, Laura Sanderson Healy, and Paula Yoo. (1996). 'Don't Yell at Me, Argentina.' *People*, 26 February, 48–50.

Champagne, John. (1993). 'Sabat Madonna.' In *Madonnarama: Essays on Sex and Popular Culture*, ed. L. Frank and P. Smith, 111–38. San Francisco: Cleis.

Chesney-Lind, Meda, and Randall G. Shelden. (1992). *Girls: Delinquency and Juvenile Justice*. Belmont: Brooke/Cole.

Cole, Susan G. (1993). 'Cole's Notes: Making Sense of Madonna.' *Herizons* (Spring): 37.

Collins, Jim. (1989). *Uncommon Cultures: Popular Culture and Post-Modernism*. New York: Routledge.

Cornell, Drucilla (1991). *Beyond Accommodation: Ethical Feminism, Deconstruction and the Law*. New York: Routledge.

– (1993). *Transformations: Recollective Imagination and Sexual Difference*. New York: Routledge.

Coward, Rosalind. (1985). *Female Desires: How They Are Sought, Bought and Packaged*. New York: Grove Weidenfeld.

Crimp, Douglas, and Michael Warner. (1993). 'No Sex in Sex.' In *Madonnarama: Essays on Sex and Popular Culture*, ed. L. Frank and P. Smith, 93–110. San Francisco: Cleis.

Cuddihy, John Murray. (1987). *The Ordeal of Civility: Freud, Marx, Lévi-Strauss, and the Jewish Struggle with Modernity*. Boston: Beacon.

Dafoe, Chris. (1993). Interview, CBC Television Newsworld, 2 January.

Danuta Walters, Susana. (1995). *Material Girls: Making Sense of Feminist Cultural Theory*. Berkeley: University of California Press.

Davidson, Arnold. (1994). 'Ethics as Ascetics: Foucault, the History of Ethics, and Ancient Thought.' In *The Cambridge Campanion to Foucault*, ed. G. Gutting, 115–40. Cambridge: Cambridge University Press.

de Lauretis, Teresa. (1994). *The Practice of Love: Lesbian Sexuality and Perverse Desire*. Indianapolis: Indiana University Press.

Deutschmann, Linda B. (1994). *Deviance and Social Control*. Scarborough, ON: Nelson Canada.

Devaney, John. (1992). 'Madonna & Marilyn: What Today's Winner Learned from Yesterday's Loser.' *Memories: The Magazine of Then and Now*, January, 24–9.

Devor, Holly. (1989). *Gender Blending: Confronting the Limits of Duality*. Bloomington: Indiana University Press.

Dijkstra, Bram. (1986). *Idols of Perversity: Fantasies of Feminine Evil in Fin-de-Siecle Culture*. Oxford: Oxford University Press.

Dimen, Muriel. (1984). 'Politically Correct? Politically Incorrect.' In *Pleasure and Danger: Exploring Female Sexuality*, ed. C.S. Vance, 138–48. London: Routledge & Kegan Paul.

Dollimore, Jonathan. (1991). *Sexual Dissidence: Augustine to Wilde; Freud to Foucault*. Oxford: Oxford University Press.

Dwyer, Victor. (1992). 'Woman Warrior: An Author Makes a Frontal Assault on Feminism.' *Maclean's*, 16 November, 77.

Easton, Susan M. (1994). *The Problem of Pornography: Regulation and the Right to Free Speech*. London: Routledge.

Eribon, Didier. (1991). *Michel Foucault*. Cambridge, MA: Harvard University Press.

Escobar, Gabriel. (1996). 'Argentina cries for Evita as played by Madonna.' *Vancouver Sun*, 9 February, C1, 7.

Faith, Karlene. (1976). *Inside/Outside*. Los Angeles: Peace Press.

– (1993a). 'Gendered Imaginations: Female Crime and Prison Movies.' In R.R.E. Kania, ed., *The Justice Professional* (Special Issue: Media, Crime and Criminal Justice) 8/1: 53–69.

– (1993b). *Unruly Women: The Politics of Confinement and Resistance.* Vancouver: Press Gang.

– (1994). 'Resistance: Lessons from Foucault and Feminism.' In *Power/Gender: Social Relations in Theory and Practice,* ed. L. Radtke and H.N. Stam, 36–66. London: Sage.

Faith, Karlene, ed., with Written Word Collective. (1975). *Women's Music.* Santa Cruz: University of California Press.

Fisher, Carrie. (1991). 'True Confessions.' *Rolling Stone,* 13 June, 35–40, 120.

Fiske, John. (1987). 'British Cultural Studies and Television.' In *Channels of Discourse,* ed. R.C. Allen, 254–90. Chapel Hill: University of North Carolina Press.

– (1989). *Understanding Popular Culture.* London: Routledge.

Flynn, Thomas. (1994). 'Foucault's Mapping of History.' In *The Cambridge Campanion to Foucault,* ed. G. Gutting, 28–46. Cambridge: Cambridge University Press.

Foucault, Michel. (1977). *Discipline and Punish: The Birth of the Prison.* Trans. A. Sheridan. New York: Pantheon.

– (1978). *The History of Sexuality.* Vol. 1: *An Introduction.* New York: Random House.

– (1980). *Power/Knowledge: Selected Interviews and Other Writings, 1972–1977.* Ed. Colin Gordon. Brighton: Harvester.

– (1985). *The History of Sexuality.* Vol. 2: *The Use of Pleasure.* New York: Random House.

– (1986). *The History of Sexuality.* Vol. 3: *The Care of the Self.* New York: Random House.

– (1988). *Politics, Philosophy, Culture: Interviews and Other Writings, 1977–1984.* Ed. Lawrence D. Kritzman. New York: Routledge.

– (1989). *Foucault Live (Interviews, 1966–84).* Ed. Sylvère Lotringer. New York: Semiotext(e).

France, David. (1992). 'Was It Good for You, Too?' *Esquire.* September, 103–4.

Frank, Lisa, and Paul Smith. (1993). 'Introduction: How to Use Your New Madonna.' In *Madonnarama: Essays on Sex and Popular Culture,* ed. L. Frank and P. Smith, 7–19. San Francisco: Cleis.

Friday, Nancy. (1973). *My Secret Garden.* New York: Doubleday.

Fried, Stephen. (1992). 'The New Sexperts.' *Vanity Fair.* December, 132–44.

Frith, Simon. (1988). *Music for Pleasure.* New York: Routledge.

Frug, Mary Joe. (1992). *Postmodern Legal Feminism.* New York: Routledge.

Fuller, Janine, and Stuart Blackley. (1995). *Restricted Entry: Censorship on Trial.* Vancouver: Press Gang.

Fuss, Diana. (1995). *Identification Papers.* New York: Routledge.

Gaar, Gillian G. (1992). *She's a Rebel: The History of Women in Rock & Roll.* Seattle: Seal.

Gamman, Lorraine, and Margaret Marshment, eds. (1989). *The Female Gaze: Women as Viewers of Popular Culture.* Seattle: Real Comet.

Garratt, Sheryl. (1986). 'How I Learned to Stop Worrying and Love Madonna ...' *Women's Review* 5: 12–13.

George, Boy. (1995). 'Northwest Afternoon,' ABC-TV (Channel 10), 10 October.

George, Leonard. (1995). *Crimes of Perception: An Encyclopedia of Heresies and Heretics.* New York: Paragon.

Gilmore, Mikal. (1987). 'The Madonna Mystique.' *Rolling Stone,* 10 September, 36–88.

Giroux, Henry A. (1993). *Border Crossings: Cultural Workers and the Politics of Education.* New York: Routledge.

– (1994). *Disturbing Pleasures: Learning Popular Culture.* New York: Routledge.

Goldsby, Jackie. (1993). 'Queen for 307 Days: Looking B(l)ack at Vanessa Williams and the Sex Wars.' In *Sisters, Sexperts, Queers: Beyond the Lesbian Nation,* ed. A. Stein, 110–28. New York: Plume.

Gowing, Laura. (1994). 'Language, Power and the Law: Women's Slander Litigation in Early Modern London.' In *Women, Crime and the Courts in Early Modern England,* ed. Jenny Kermode and Garthine Walker, 26–47. Chapel Hill: University of North Carolina Press.

Graydon, Shari. (1992). 'Open Letter to Madonna.' *Viewpoints,* October, 5.

Greenberg, David F. (1988). *The Construction of Homosexuality.* Chicago: University of Chicago Press.

Griffin, Kevin. (1992a). 'Madonna's *Sex* book arrives to brisk sales.' *Vancouver Sun,* 23 October, B7.

– (1992b). 'Madonna's steamy book expected to be hot seller.' *Vancouver Sun,* 20 October, A3.

Griffin, Nancy. (1995). 'One on One – Pfeiffer.' *Premiere Special: Women in Hollywood,* December.

Grossberg, Lawrence, Cary Nelson, and Paula Treichler, eds. (1992). *Cultural Studies*. New York: Routledge.

Guccione, Bob, Jr. (1996). 'Live to Tell.' *Spin*, 41–7, 94–5.

Hall, Stuart. (1996). *Stuart Hall: Critical Dialogues in Cultural Studies*. Ed. D. Morley and K.-H. Chen. London: Routledge.

Harland, Richard. (1987). *Superstructuralism: The Philosophy of Structuralism and Post-Structuralism*. London: Methuen.

Hatt, Doug, and Cindy Dampier. (1995). 'Vanilla Chills.' *People*, 13 November, 95–6.

Heath, Chris. (1994). 'The Madonna Complex.' *Details*. December, 130–9; 184–6.

Henderson, Lisa. (1993). 'Justify Our Love: Madonna and the Politics of Queer Sex.' In *The Madonna Connection*, ed. C. Schwichtenberg, 107–28. Oxford: Westview.

Holden, Stephen. (1992). 'Selling Sex and (Oh, Yes) a Record.' *New York Times*, 18 October, H28.

hooks, bell. (1992). *Black Looks: Race and Representation*. Toronto: Between the Lines.

– (1994). *Outlaw Culture: Resisting Representations*. New York: Routledge.

James, David. (1991). *Madonna: Her Complete Story*. Chicago: Publications International.

Kaplan, E. Ann. (1987). *Rocking around the Clock: Music Television, Postmodernism, and Consumer Culture*. New York: Methuen.

– (1988). 'Introduction.' In *Postmodernism and Its Discontents*, ed. E. Ann Kaplan, 1–6. London: Verso.

King, Norman. (1991). *Madonna: The Book*. New York: Morrow.

Kinsman, Gary. (1987). *The Regulation of Desire*. Montreal: Black Rose.

Kipnis, Laura. (1992). '(Male) Desire and (Female) Disgust: Reading *Hustler*.' In *Cultural Studies*, ed. L. Grossberg, C. Nelson, and P. Treichler, 373–91. New York: Routledge.

Kitzinger, Celia. (1994). 'Problematizing Pleasure: Radical Feminist Deconstructions of Sexuality and Power.' In *Power/Gender: Social Relations in Theory and Practice*, ed. H. Lorraine Radtke and Henderikus J. Stam, 194–209. London: Sage.

Krafft-Ebing, Richard von. (1965; original 1886). *Psychopathia Sexualis*. Trans. Franklin S. Klaf. New York: Bell.

Krassner, Paul. (1996). 'An Interview with Terry Southern.' Reprinted in *The Realist*, Spring, 1–2, 6–8.

Lacombe, Dany. (1994). *Blue Politics: Pornography and the Law in the Age of Feminism.* Toronto: University of Toronto Press.

LePage, Mark. (1992). 'After six steamy tunes Madonna spoils everything by getting heavy.' *Montreal Gazette*, 31 October, E1.

– (1993). 'Immaterial Girl?' *Montreal Gazette*, 16 October, E1, E4.

Lewis, Lisa A. (1990). *Gender Politics and MTV: Voicing the Differences.* Philadelphia: Temple University Press.

Linden, Robin Ruth, ed., with Darlene E. Pagano, Diana E.H. Russell, and Susan Leigh Starr. (1982). *Against Sadomasochism: A Radical Feminist Analysis.* East Palo Alto: Frog in the Well.

Lombroso, Cesare, and William Ferrero (1899; original 1895). *The Female Offender.* New York: Appleton.

Lorde, Audre. (1987). Interview with Susan Leigh Starr. In *Against Sadomasochism: A Radical Feminist Analysis*, ed. Robin Ruth Linden, with Darlene R. Pagano, Diana E.H. Russell, and Susan Leigh Starr, 66–71. East Palo Alto: Frog in the Well.

Lynch, Bernard J. (1995). 'A Land Beyond Tears.' In *Lesbian and Gay Visions of Ireland: Towards the Twenty-first Century*, ed. Íde O'Carroll and Eoin Collins, 212–20. London: Cassell.

MacCannell, Dean, and Juliet Flower MacCannell. (1993). 'Violence, Power and Pleasure: A Revisionist Reading of Foucault from the Victim Perspective.' In *Up Against Foucault: Explorations of Some Tensions between Foucault and Feminism*, ed. C. Ramazanoğlu, 203–38. London: Routledge.

Macey, David. (1994). *The Lives of Michel Foucault.* London: Vintage.

Madonna. (1992). *Sex.* New York: Warner Books.

– (1995). 'If I Were President.' *George: Not Just Politics as Usual* (Inaugural Issue), October/November, 280.

– (1996a). 'In the Closet with Madonna.' *Vogue*, October, 306.

– (1996b). 'Madonna's Private Diaries.' *Vanity Fair*, November, 174–88, 223–32.

Mailer, Norman. (1994). 'Norman Mailer on Madonna: Like a Lady. *Esquire: The Magazine for Men*, August, 41–56.

Masters, W., and V. Johnson. (1970). *Human Sexual Inadequacy.* Boston: Little, Brown.

Mathur, Paul. (1989). 'Wishing on a Star' *Spin*, 5 April, 70–2.

McCann, Graham. (1991). 'Biographical Boundaries: Sociology and Marilyn Monroe.' In *The Body: Social Process and Cultural Theory*, ed. M. Featherstone, M. Hepworth, and B.S. Turner, 325–38. London: Sage.

McClary, Susan. (1990). 'Living to Tell: Madonna's Resurrection of the Fleshly.' *Genders*, 7 (Spring): 1–21.

– (1991). *Feminine Endings: Music, Gender and Sexuality*. Minneapolis: University of Minnesota Press.

McLeod, Dan. (1993). 'Madonna Remains Direct and Unflinching.' *The Georgia Straight*, 15–22 January, 13.

Miller, James. (1993). *The Passion of Michel Foucault*. New York: Simon & Schuster.

Modleski, Tania. (1991). *Feminism without Women: Culture and Criticism in a 'Postfeminist' Age*. New York: Routledge.

MuchMusic. (1996). Interview replay. 'Spotlight' (Madonna). 22 February.

Nakayama, Thomas K., and Lisa N. Penaloza (1993). 'Madonna T/Races: Music Videos Through the Prism of Color.' In *The Madonna Connection*, ed. C. Schwichtenberg, 39–55. Oxford: Westview.

Orth, Maureen. (1992). 'Madonna in Wonderland.' *Vanity Fair*. Photos by Steven Meisel. October, 212–306.

Paglia, Camille. (1992). *Sex, Art, and American Culture*. New York: Vintage.

– (1994). *Vamps & Tramps*. New York: Vintage.

Patton, Cindy. (1993). 'Embodying Subaltern Memory: Kinesthesia and the Problematics of Gender and Race.' In *The Madonna Connection*, ed. C. Schwichtenberg, 81–105. Oxford: Westview.

Pavletich, Aida. (1980). *Rock-A-Bye, Baby*. Garden City, NY: Doubleday.

Pels, Dick, and Aya Crébas. (1991). '*Carmen* – Or the Invention of a New Feminine Myth.' In *The Body: Social Process and Cultural Theory*, ed. M. Featherstone, M. Hepworth and B.S. Turner, 339–70. London: Sage.

Pheterson, Gail, (1989). *A Vindication of the Rights of Whores*. Seattle: Seal.

Pirrie Adams, Kathleen. (1991). 'Bad Sisters: Punk Culture and Feminism.' *Fuse* 14 (5 & 6): 22–7.

Primetime. (1995). ABC Television, 13 December.

Probyn, Elspeth. (1992). 'Technologizing the Self: A Future Anterior for Cultural Studies.' In *Cultural Studies*, ed. L. Grossberg, C. Nelson, and P. Treichler, 501–11. New York: Routledge.

Rapping, Elayne. (1994). *Media-tions: Forays into the Culture and Gender Wars*. Boston: South End.

Reiman, Jeffrey. (1990). *Justice and Modern Moral Philosophy*. New Haven: Yale University Press.

Rice, Susan Tracy, and Robert Haven Schauffler. (1927). *Mothers' Day: Its History, Origin, Celebration, Spirit and Significance as Related in Prose and Verse*. New York: Dodd, Mead.

Rich, Adrienne. (1983). 'Compulsory Heterosexuality and Lesbian Existence.' In *Powers of Desire: The Politics of Sexuality*, ed. A. Snitow, C. Stansell, and S. Thompson, 177–205. New York: Monthly Review.

Roberts, Nickie. (1993). *Whores in History: Prostitution in Western Society*. London: HarperCollins.

Rosenzweig, Ilene. (1994). *The I Hate Madonna Handbook*. New York: St Martin's.

Rubin, Gayle. (1984). 'Thinking Sex: Notes for a Radical Theory of the Politics of Sexuality.' In *Pleasure and Danger: Exploring Female Sexuality*, ed. C.S. Vance, 267–319. Boston: Routledge & Kegan Paul.

Russell, Diana E.H. ed. (1993). *Making Violence Sexy: Feminist Views on Pornography*. New York: Teachers College Press.

Russo, Vito. (1987). *The Celluloid Closet: Homosexuality in the Movies*. New York: Harper & Row.

Salamon, Julie. (1996). 'Madonna's Moment.' *Vogue*, October, 300–13, 378–9.

Schruers, Fred. (1985). 'Lucky Stars.' *Rolling Stone*, 9 May, 27–32.

Schwichtenberg, Cathy, ed. (1993). *The Madonna Connection: Representational Politics, Subcultural Identities and Cultural Theory*. Oxford: Westview.

Schulze, Laurie, Anne Barton White, and Jane D. Brown. (1993). '"A Sacred Monster in Her Prime": Audience Construction of Madonna as Low-Other.' In *The Madonna Connection*, ed. C. Schwichtenberg, 15–37. Oxford: Westview.

Scott, Ronald B. (1993). 'Images of Race and Religion in Madonna's Video "Like a Prayer": Prayer and Praise.' In *The Madonna Connection*, ed. C. Schwichtenberg, 57–77. Oxford: Westview.

Seigworth, Greg. (1993). 'The Distance Between Me and You: Madonna and Celestial Navigation (or You Can Be My Lucky Star)' In *The Madonna Connection*, ed. C. Schwichtenberg, 291–318. Oxford: Westview.

Sexton, Adam, ed. (1993). *Desperately Seeking Madonna: In Search of the Meaning of the World's Most Famous Woman*. New York: Delta.

Simons, Jon. (1995). *Foucault and the Political*. London: Routledge.

Skow, John. (1985). 'Madonna Rocks the Land.' *Time*, 27 May, 56–9.

Smith, Wes. (1989). *The Pied Pipers of Rock-'n'-Roll: Radio Deejays of the 50's and 60's*. Marietta GA: Longstreet.

Sprinkle, Annie. (1991). *Post Porn Modernist*. Amsterdam: Torch.

Stacey, Jackie. (1989). 'Desperately Seeking Difference.' In *The Female Gaze*, ed. L. Gamman and M. Marshment, 112–29. Real Comet.

Starr, Victoria. (1994). *k.d. lang: All You Get Is Me*. Toronto: Random House.

Stein, Arlene, ed. (1993). *Sisters, Sexperts, Queers: Beyond the Lesbian Nation*. New York: Plume.

Sullivan, Meg. (1993). 'Madonna's garish colors upset neighbors.' *Montreal Gazette*, 3 July, F1.

Taylor, Carl S. (1993). *Girls, Gangs, Women and Drugs*. East Lansing: Michigan State University Press.

Tetzlaff, David. (1993). 'Metatextual Girl: Patriarchy Postmodernism Power Money Madonna.' In *The Madonna Connection*, ed. C. Schwichtenberg, 239–63 Oxford: Westview.

Thompson, Douglas. (1991). *Like a Virgin: Madonna Revealed*. London: Birch Lane.

Toobin, Jeffrey. (1994). 'X-Rated.' *The New Yorker*, 3 October, 70–8.

Turner, Kay. (1993). *I Dream of Madonna: Women's Dreams of the Goddess of Pop*. New York: HarperCollins.

Udovitch, Mim. (1997). 'Madonna.' *US* magazine, January, 54–6, 98.

Valverde, Mariana. (1985). *Sex, Power and Pleasure*. Toronto: Women's Press.

Vines, Gail. (1993). *Raging Hormones: Do They Rule Our Lives?* Berkeley: University of California Press.

Wallace, Bruce. (1993). 'CTV Poll. Fantasies: Surf, Sand and Sex.' *Macleans*,' 4 January, 30.

Waters, Jack. (1991). 'Madonna: Having It Both Ways.' *Fuse* 14 (5 & 6): 55–7.

Weber, Max. (1946, original in 1915). 'The Social Psychology of the World Religions.' In *From Max Weber: Essays in Sociology*, ed. and trans. H.H. Gerth and C. Wright Mills, 267–301. New York: Oxford University Press.

Weeks, Jeffrey. (1991). *Against Nature: Essays on History, Sexuality and Identity*. London: Rivers Oram.

Whisman, Vera. (1993). 'Identity Crises: Who Is a Lesbian, Anyway?' In *Sisters, Sexperts, Queers: Beyond the Lesbian Nation*, ed. A. Stein, 47–60. New York: Plume.

Willis, Ellen. (1983). 'Feminism, Moralism, and Pornography.' In *Powers of Desire: The Politics of Sexuality*, ed. A. Snitow, C. Stansell, and S. Thompson, 460–7. New York: Monthly Review.

Worrell, Denise. (1985). 'Now: Madonna on Madonna.' *Time*, 27 May, 60–4.

Wylie, Philip. (1955). *A Generation of Vipers*. New York: Rinehart.

Wyman, Max. (1993). 'Learning to raise the cultural standard.' *Vancouver Sun*, 7 May, D3.

Zoglin, Richard. (1997). 'Mad for Evita.' *Time*, 20 January, 40–3.

Zollo, Paul, and Kevin Odegard. (1989). 'Madonna: The Songtalk Interview.' *SongTalk: The Songwriter's Newspaper* 2 (11): 7–9.

Uncredited Articles

Advocate. (1992). 'World News.' Issue 618: 32.

Famous Players. (December 1996). 'Holiday Movies.' 11.

Kingston Whig-Standard. (1996). 'Madonna as Evita sparks controversy.' 22 January, 14.

Maclean's. (1992). Untitled. 12 October, 69.

Montreal Gazette. (1992a). 'Madonna 101: Basket-weaving of the 90s in U.S. universities.' 19 September, E4.

– (1992b). 'British MP seeks to have Madonna's book *Sex* banned.' 17 October, E2.

– (1992c). 'Madonna hotline sizzles as true blue fans lend material support to embattled star,' 31 October, E7.

Newsweek. (1992). 'Talking with Madonna: The Unbridled Truth.' 2 November, 102–3.

People. (1992). 'Naked Ambition,' 2 November, 56–7.

Premiere. (1995). 'Autographed 8 × 10 Photos,' August, 102.

Vancouver Province. (1995). 'Mix of music and fashion,' 5 December, A20.

Vancouver Sun (1992a). 'Is it art? Or porn? Controversy looms over Madonna's explicit book on sex,' 10 September, A3.

– (1992b). 'Editorial: Madonna not much help.' 19 October, A2.

– (1992c). 'No ban but *Sex* faces India seizure.' 3 November, C3.

– (1993a). Untitled, 10 July, B1.

– (1993b). 'Madonna given Kohl shoulder,' 28 September, C6.

– (1993c). 'MuchMusic censors preview Madonna,' 30 November, C6.
– (1994a). 'Madonna on nudity,' 5 February, B3.
– (1994b). 'Material Girl to change her material,' 21 September, D4.
Young and Modern. (1993). '20 Questions with Madonna,' January, 46–9.

Index